THE PROCEEDINGS OF THE 7th INTERNATIONAL HUMANITIES CONFERENCE

ALL & EVERYTHING 2002

Nathan Batalion
Keith Buzzell
Ana Fragomeni
Seymour Ginsburg
Bert Sharp
Paul Beekman Taylor
Nicholas Tereshchenko

Published by All & Everything Conferences
2011

Second Edition Published 2011
Published by All & Everything Conferences on behalf of the Planning Committee
© Copyright 2011 by Seymour B. Ginsburg and Ian C. MacFarlane

First Edition Privately Published 2002
Published by the Conveners of the International Humanities Conference: All and Everything 2002
© 2002 Seymour B. Ginsburg, Dr. H. J. Sharp, and Marlena O'Hagan-Buzzell

The contents of this publication may not be reproduced or copied in whole or part in any book, magazine, periodical, pamphlet, circular, information storage or data retrieval system, or in any other form without the written permission of the Planning Committee.

Any profit from the sale of these Proceedings will be devoted to the funds for the organization of future Conferences of a similar nature.

Published by All & Everything Conferences

Website: www.aandeconference.org
Email: info@aandeconference.org

Second Edition Print

ISBN-10: 1-905578-22-9
ISBN-13: 978-1-905578-22-1

Also Published as
Second Edition eBook
ISBN-10: 1-905578-23-7
ISBN-13: 978-1-905578-23-8

Table of Contents

Foreword 4
Conference Program 5
Advisory Board 10
Speakers 12
Introduction 15
Gurdjieff's Meetings and Non-Meetings with Remarkable and Unremarkable Men and Women 1935-1949 20
Gurdjieff's Meetings and Non-Meetings with Remarkable and Unremarkable Men and Women 1935-1949 - Questions & Answers 35
Triads and Laws 38
Triads and Laws - Questions & Answers 51
Seminar 1 - Chapters 8, 9 & 10 of Beelzebub's Tales to His Grandson 54
Gurdjieff's Enneagramatic View 77
Gurdjieff's Enneagramatic View - Questions & Answers 87
The Kahunas and Gurdjieff's Three Brain Beings 95
The Kahunas and Gurdjieff's Three Brain Beings - Questions & Answers 102
An Accursed Mirage 113
An Accursed Mirage - Questions & Answers 121
Seminar 2 - Chapters 11, 12 & 13 of Beelzebub's Tales to His Grandson 130
Remembering Gurdjieff 138
Remembering Gurdjieff - Questions & Answers 141
The High Commission and Other Sacred Individuals: What Do They Represent? 144
   How to "Read" Beelzebub's Tales, with Particular Reference to the "High Commission", other "Sacred Individuals" and Beelzebub's "Saturnian" Connection 146
   How to "Read" Beelzebub's Tales - Questions & Answers 152
   The High Commission and Other Sacred Individuals - What Do They Represent? 154
   The High Commission and Other Sacred Individuals, What Do They Represent? 160
   Discussion about how the procedures for the email discussion groups worked 168
   The High Commission and Other Sacred Individuals: What Do They Represent? - Questions & Answers 170
Seminar 3 - Chapter 44 Beelzebub's Tales to His Grandson 175
Seminar 4 - Where Do We Go From Here? 185
Appendix 1 - Report on an Experiment 202
Appendix 2 - List of Attendees 204
Index 205

Foreword

The International Humanities Conference - All & Everything convened in Bognor Regis, England in March 2002.

This year as the conference took shape we found ourselves in a very different situation. The events of September 11th clearly influenced some of the decisions that were made in planning the conference. Briefly, the question of whether we should have the conference this year at all arose. Would people fly? Indeed they did fly.

Among the conferees there were more than a few new faces, as well as, friends from past conferences who rejoined us again this year. The multi cultural dimension of the conference continues to deepen our ever growing appreciation of the different perspectives we share. These valued differences serve collectively and individually to broaden our horizons in the pursuit of a unique and common aim in 'fathoming the gist' of *Beelzebub's Tales to His Grandson*.

We continue to view the conference as a 'work in progress', an experimental process. For the last two years several conferees have participated in an email discussion group over the course of months. This year three very provocative papers were presented as a result. Another was an experiment with 'attention exercises' in which we asked Toddy Smyth, a former student of Anne Lou Staveley, to lead an 'attention exercise' class during the lunch break Toddy's impressions, 'Report on an experiment', can be found in appendix I. A third was the admission of a paper from someone unknown to us which was read by a member of the reading panel. While the paper was quite interesting we found during the Q&A session, that this experiment highlighted the difficulty of engaging a perspective in the absence of the writer who put forth the perspective. The afternoon Seminars, in which we discuss, question, disagree, and exchange impressions with respect to *All and Everything*, have become increasingly more active with broad participation.

The Q&A periods and afternoon seminars are recorded, and it is the responsibility of the presenter or facilitator to transcribe the tapes for the Proceedings. The reader is advised to bare in mind the diversity of people and language. We are from Greece, Switzerland, Brazil, Canada, Holland, England, Norway, and the States. For this reason the task of transcribing can be challenging (not to mention that there may be more than one person talking at a time!).

Marlena O'Hagan Buzzell

Conference Program

THE INTERNATIONAL HUMANITIES CONFERENCE

All &Everything

2002

A Gathering of the Companions of the Book

March 13-March 17, 2002

The Royal Norfolk Hotel

Bognor Regis

England

<u>*Organizing Committee Members*</u>

USA

Seymour B. Ginsburg, Harry Bennett, Patricia Bennett, Marlena Buzzell, Conti Canseco Meehan

Europe

Frank Brzeski, H.J. Sharp,

South America

Ana Fragomeni

All &Everything 2002 Program

Day 1. Wednesday March 13th.

15.00 - 17.00 Meeting of the Organizing Committee.

20.30 - 21.30 Informal Getting to Know You Session. Chair: Marlena Buzzell.

Day 2. Thursday March 14th.

08.00 - 09.00 Sitting.

09.00 - 09.30 Introduction : Sy Ginsburg.

Greetings, messages, announcements, copying, recording and ordering facilities. List of addresses for future contact and exchanges.

History and Genesis of the Conference: Bert Sharp.

Session 1.

09.30 - 11.00 **Gurdjieff's Later Material Question.** *Prof. Paul Beekman Taylor.*

11.00 - 11.30 Morning Coffee.

Session 2.

11.30 - 12.45 **Triads and Laws.** *Ana Fragomeni.*

12.45 - 14.30 Lunch Break.

01.30 - 02.15 Attention Exercises [optional]. Led by Toddy Smyth.

Conference Programme

Seminar 1.

14.30 - 15.30 Chapters 8, 9 & 10 of **Beelzebub's Tales to his Grandson.**

Facilitator: Keith Buzzell.

15.30 - 16.00 Afternoon Tea.

Seminar 2.

16.00 - 17.00 Continuation of Seminar 1.

Session 3.

20.00 - 21.00 **Gurdjieff's enneagramatic view - how and why it supercedes modern physics' and chemistry's understanding of the nature of the world we live in.** *Nathan Batalion.*

read by Keith Buzzell.

Day 3. Friday March 15th.

08.00 - 09.00 Sitting.

Session 4.

09.30 - 10.45 **The Kahunas and Gurdjieff's Three Brained Beings.** *Bert Sharp*

10.45 - 11.15 Morning Coffee.

Session 5.

11.15 - 12.30 **An Accursed Mirage.** *Keith Buzzell.*

12.30 - 14.30 Lunch Break.

01.30 - 02.15 Attention Exercises. [optional] led by Toddy Smyth.

Seminar 3.

14.30 - 15.30 Chapters 11, 12 & 13 of Beelzebub''s Tales to his Grandson.

Facilitator: John Scullion.

All & Everything Conference 2002

15.30 - 16.00 After noon Tea.

Seminar 4.

16.00 - 17.00 Continuation of Seminar 3.

Session 6.

20.00 - 21.00 Recollections of Gurdjieff. Prof. Paul Beekman Taylor

Day 4. Saturday March 16th.

08.00 - 09.00 Sitting

Session 7.

09.30 - 10.45 Three Papers: from the Theme, "The High Commission and other Sacred Individuals, What do they Represent?"

Introduction: The origin and purpose of the email discussion group. Sy Ginsburg

1. *How to "Read" Beelzebub''s Tales with Particular Reference to the "High Commission", other "Sacred Individuals" and Beelzebub''s "Saturnian Connection"* Nicolas Tereshchenko. Read by Sy Ginsberg

2. *The High Commission and other Sacred Individuals - What do they represent?* Ana Fragomeni.

3. *The High Commission and other Sacred Individuals - What do they represent?* Sy Ginsburg.

10.45 - 11.15 Morning Coffee.

Session 8.

11.15 - 12.30 Open discussion on the questions raised in Session 7.

12.30 - 14.30 Lunch Break.

Seminar 5.

14.30 - 15.30 Chapter 44 of Beelzebub's Tales. Man''s Understanding of Justice.

Facilitator: Nick Bryce.

15.30 - 16.00 Afternoon Tea.

Seminar 6.

16.00 - 17.00 Continuation of Seminar 6. Facilitator:

19.30 Conference Banquet.

Day 5. Sunday March 17th.

08.00 - 09.00 Sitting

Session 9.

09.00 - 10.00 Open Forum. Where do we go from here? Facilitator: John Scullion

10.30 - 11.00 Morning Coffee.

Session 10.

Continuation of Open Forum

Advisory Board

PROFESSOR MASASHI ASAI holds the chair of English Literature and Cultural Studies at Kyoto Tachibana Women's University and has made a significant contribution to studies of D. H. Lawrence (who visited the Prieuré in February 1924). As an undergraduate in Kyoto, he contacted a working group (which he now leads) instituted by Gurdjieffians from California. His unprecedented contributions to the dissemination of Gurdjieff's ideas in Japan include the translation *of Beelzebub's Tales to His Grandson, Life is Real Only Then, When "I am", In Search of the Miraculous* and James Moore's, *Gurdjieff, The Anatomy of a Myth*.

J. WALTER DRISCOLL is an independent scholar focused on Gurdjieff studies since the 1960's. He met and corresponded with Wilhelm Nyland and his groups in Warwick, NJ and Seattle from 1970 until Nyland's death in 1975. Following postgraduate training in 1978, he embarked on his major work *Gurdjieff an Annotated Bibliography* (Garland Publishing, 1985) in collaboration with The Gurdjieff Foundation of California. He is now engaged on a second edition for which he solicits material and is associate editor of the "Gurdjieff Homepage" at www.gurdjieff.org. He assisted George Baker with *Gurdjieff in America: An Overview* (American Alternative Religions, 1995).

WIM VAN DULLEMEN is a Dutch musician and musicologist who have placed his gifts at the service of the Work. Shortly after completing his studies under the composer W. Wijdeveld and becoming a professional concert pianist he had a crucial meeting (in 1968) with J. G. Bennett. For 13 years he was the Class pianist for the eminent French Movements teacher Solange Claustres. He has propagated the Gurdjieff/de Hartmann musical 'oeuvre' in 'workshops', articles, courses, lectures, and concerts - sometimes independently and sometimes in collaboration with Mme Claustres and the French pianist Alain Kremski.

DR. MASSIMO INTROVIGNE is managing director of CESNUR, the Centre for Studies on New Religions in Torino, Italy. CESNUR's library hosts one of the most significant collections of Fourth Way Books in Southern Europe. He teaches at Queen of The Apostles University in Rome and is the author of twenty books in the field of sociology of religion and contemporary esotericism. He has lectured often and sympathetically on Fourth Way-related subjects.

PROFESSOR WALLACE MARTIN teaches modern literature and critical theory at the University of Toledo. His writings include *'The New Age' Under Orage*.

DR. H J. SHARP took a first degree is Physiology and an M. Sc. in Metallurgy by private study while working in industry. He later earned his Ph.D. in Material Science. Subsequently, he has become involved in psychological transformation of himself and others, a much more difficult endeavour. In this he has been helped by many including Ronald and Murial Oldham and Lewis

Advisory Board

Creed, when he was able to visit the Dicker, John Castanios Flores, who led a large Work group in Mexico and came to Littlehampton to end his days, and by Nicholas Tereshchenko and Sy Ginsburg. There have been many others speaking through the written page and in other ways and perhaps most of all, in a special way, his dear wife and daughter.

PROFESSOR PAUL BEEKMAN TAYLOR (who for the past 30 years held the chair of Medieval English languages and literature at the University of Geneva) grew up at the Prieuré and was thus from earliest childhood immersed in a Gurdjieffian milieu. Later adopted by Jean Toomer, he lived in New York City and Doylestown, Pennsylvania, and after the war sustained contact with Gurdjieff in New York and Paris. He has published ten books and over a hundred articles. Published in 1998, *Shadows of Heaven: Toomer and Gurdjieff* (Samuel Weiser, Inc.) draws on his and his mother's experiences with both men. His most recent book *is Gurdjieff and Orage: Brothers in Elysium.* (Samuel Weiser, Inc. 2001).

PROFESSOR JON WOODSON is a Professor of English on the faculty of Howard University in Washington, D.C. He is the author of *To Make a New Race: Gurdjieff, Toomer, and the Harlem Renaissance* (University of Mississippi Press, 1999). Since commencing work on his doctoral dissertation on the poet Melvin B. Tolson in 1973, he has researched and published in the area of Fourth Way concepts as they have been employed in modern literature.

Speakers

Nathan B. Batalion

Nathan B. Batalion (BA-Religion; MA-Asian Studies; MBA-Accounting) was Assistant Professor of Accounting and Finance at Hartwick College following a 25-year career as a CPA and Wall Street entrepreneur. He is currently a Ph.D. student and assistant instructor in philosophy at Binghamton University. His Ph.D. thesis project, *Another Way of Seeing*, outlines a vision of nature based on his unique aphasic experiences. Besides academic publications, he is author *of 50 Harmful Effects of Genetically Modified Foods* and a long-time holistic health activist. Professor Batalion further studied acupuncture/oriental medicine at Pacific Institute of Oriental Medicine and envisioned/funded the Gerson Wellness Center at Sedona, an alternative cancer treatment center.

Professor Batalion was a student of the late Willem Nyland at the Chardavoyne Group in Warwick, New York.

Keith A. Buzzell, D.O.

Dr. Buzzell is a 1960 graduate of the Philadelphia College of Osteopathic Medicine. He met Irmis Popoff (N.Y. Foundation) in 1971 and formed groups under her supervision into the 1980s. Buzzell met Annie Lou Staveley, founder of the Two Rivers Farm in Oregon, in 1988 and maintained a Work relationship with her up to her death. He continues group Work in Bridgton, ME.

Ana Fragomeni

Graduating with a degree in architecture in 1962 from ANF - The University of Brazil, Rio de Janeiro, Ana pursued post-graduate studies in Computer Science. She worked as Planning and Organizing Coordinator for the finance ministry and further developed her administrative skills at IAAP Paris in 1978.

Since her youth she has been continuously interested in 'all and everything', exploring several paths of self development, esoteric studies and symbology until, in 1982, the books of Mouravieff and Ouspensky led her to the Fourth Way. She joined Durval Teixeira's group (Uberlandia, MG) and participated in the Work which was led in Brazil under the general direction of Natalie de Salzmann.

In 1990 she retired from public service and, with three children grown, she devoted herself to the study and propagation of Gurdjieff's teaching. She opened a small publishing house (Editora

Gilgamesh) and maintained the web-site 4C-Gurdjieff Brazil at www.4C.com.br. Having been introduced to the A&E Conferences by Nicholas Tereshchenko, Ana attended the 2000 conference, giving an informal presentation on the enneagramatic structure on the life and writings of Gurdjieff.

She is the author of the *Dicionario Enciclopedico de Informatica* (Informatics Encyclopaedic Dictionary - English and Portuguese), published in 1986 by Ed. Campus, Sao Paulo. In addition to her primary interest which encompasses Work and the Enneagram, she has now embarked upon a historical and cultural research and study of art, music and sacred architecture.

Seymour B. (Sy) Ginsburg, J.D.

Sy Ginsburg was born in Chicago in 1934 and currently resides in Florida. He was introduced to the Gurdjieff Work by Sri Madhava Ashish, an eminent theosophical scholar and Hindu monk, who became his mentor over a 19 year period. Ginsburg was a member of the Gurdjieff Society of Florida and later a co-founder of the Gurdjieff Institute of Florida. Currently, he is a Director of The Theosophical Society in Miami & South Florida and facilitator of the Gurdjieff Study Group at The Theosophical Society.

H. J. Sharp, Ph.D.

Dr. Sharp took a first degree in Physiology, and an M.Sc, in Metallurgy by private study while working in industry. He later earned his Ph.D in Material Science. Subsequently he has become involved in psychological transformation of himself and others, a much more difficult endeavor. In this he has been helped by many, including Ronald and Murial Oldham and Lewis Creed, when he was able to visit the Dicker, John Castanios Flores, who led a large Work group in Mexico and came to Littlehampton to end his days, and Nicolas Tereshchenko and Sy Ginsburg. There have been many others speaking through the written page and in other ways and perhaps most of all, in a special way, his dear wife and daughter.

Professor Paul Beekman Taylor

For the past 30 years Professor Taylor held the chair of Medieval English languages and literature at the University of Geneva. He grew up at the Prieuré and was thus form earliest childhood immersed in a Gurdjieffian milieu. Later adopted by Jean Toomer, he lived in New York City and Doylestown, Pennsylvania, and after the war sustained contact with Gurdjieff in New York and Paris. He has published ten books and over a hundred articles. Published in 1998, *Shadows of Heaven: Toomer and Gurdjieff* (Samuel Weiser, Inc.) draws on his and his mother's experiences with both men. His most recent book is *Gurdjieff and Orage; Brothers in Elysium* (Samuel Weiser, Inc. 2001).

All & Everything Conference 2002

Nick Tereshchenko

Nicolas Tereshchenko was born in Odessa (then in Russia, now in Ukraine), which his parents left in 1920 to go to Serbia, where he had his primary schooling. In 1926 the family moved to Paris, France, where he completed his secondary education, and in 1935 went to live in England, his father having become a lecturer at Balliol College, Oxford. Nick completed his University studies in London in 1941, volunteered for a war commission in the Indian Medical Service, served in India and Assam and was demobilized in 1946. Married in 1942, divorced by mutual consent in 1963, he now has four children, five grand-children and four great-grand-children. He has been interested in all the branches of "occultism" (in the widest sense of this word) from a very early age, and since 1952 has been admitted as an initiated member into several fraternal organizations. He began to study the Tarot in 1956 and to write about it, and other subjects, in 1973. In 1958 he met George Ivanovich Gurdjieff's Teaching through reading P. D. Ouspensky's *In Search of the Miraculous* and since then has studied the Fourth Way and followed the Work assiduously, being fortunate to attend a group in Paris presided by Madame Jeanne de Salzmann from 1981 until her death in 1990. He now lives in South Australia, where he continues his studies and research on several Esoteric subjects, including Freemasonry, the Golden Dawn and the Rosicrucians. But mostly he is studying Mister *Gurdjieff's Beelzebub's Tales to His Grandson*, now published in the original Russian, and working with Mister Gurdjieff's practical Work techniques.

He has written, and had several articles published in English and French on the Work, as well as a book on *Mister Gurdjieff and the Fourth Way*, still unpublished in English, but published as two volumes in French as *Gurdjieff Et La Quatrieme Voie* and *Le Message De Gurdjieff*.

Introduction

Sy Ginsburg

Good morning everyone. Welcome to All and Everything 2002. On behalf of the planning committee, I would like to join with Marlena Buzzell who welcomed those of you who were here last evening to this seventh International Humanities Conference, All and Everything 2002. My name is Sy Ginsburg and I am one of the planning committee.

A small Gurdjieffian story:

There were four Gurdjieffians discussing and pondering what the significance was of a particular passage in *Beelzebub's Tales*. Three of them thought it meant one thing, but the fourth felt that it meant something entirely different. After much discussing and arguing, the fourth Gurdjieffian, despondent that he could not convince the others, looked up at the sky and said, "Mr. Gurdjieff, please give us a sign to prove that I am right." With that, a dark cloud floated over them and a bolt of lightning crashed down.

The fourth Gurdjieffian then turned to the others and said, "You see, I am right." But the first Gurdjieffian said, "That doesn't mean anything, it's just ordinary nature and it will be a rainy day."

So, they continued to discuss and argue and ponder, but none of them would change their positions. The fourth Gurdjieffian who felt very strongly in opposition to the other three was disgusted. He looked up at the sky again and he said, "Mr. Gurdjieff, please send another sign to prove that I am right." With that, two dark clouds came over them and two bolts of lightning crashed down onto the ground.

The fourth Gurdjieffian looked at the other three and he said, "You see, I am right." But the second Gurdjieffian said, "That doesn't mean anything. We are just having a big storm."

So, the four of them continued to discuss and to argue and to ponder what this passage meant. But none of them would change their positions. Three felt one way and one felt the other way. The fourth Gurdjieffian just shook his head. He looked up at the sky again and he called out, "Mr. Gurdjieff please send a message to convince these fools that I am right." With that, the whole sky darkened and a great voice boomed out. And the voice said, "He is right."

All & Everything Conference 2002

The fourth Gurdjieffian turned around, looking at the others and he said, "Now, you see that I am right." But the third Gurdjieffian said, "What does this mean that you are right, what does this mean. After all, it is still three to two."

Well, there is a principle here somewhere so I will leave you to ponder that.

My purpose this morning is to make some announcements before we actually begin the conference program. We usually start by reading the greetings that have been sent to the conference of which there are several.

(Letters of greeting are read.)

Now, I would like to call your attention to a few matters in the program.

This year there is a new category of papers. This has arisen because the reading panel very much liked two papers that were submitted, but because of illness and other circumstances the authors of neither can be here. Consequently, we are going this year to read these papers in the authors' absence. One is written by Nathan Batalion and will be read by Keith Buzzell. The other is written by Nicolas Tereshchenko and I will read that one.

One of the problems presented by such papers is that the readers, not having authored these papers, may not adequately be able to deal with questions you might have. So, if you have any questions about these papers that the readers cannot adequately deal with, you can email either of these authors and address your questions to them. These papers will be placed on the table at the rear of the room after they are read, along with the email address of each author. You can make a copy of the paper if you like, and then email your questions.

The other matter to which I would like to call your attention, is that there will be a slightly different format for the Saturday morning presentations. Normally, each morning is devoted to the presentation of two papers with an adequate question and answer session following each. For this conference, Saturday morning is given over to a subject that is entitled, "The High Commission and Other Sacred Individuals: What Do They Represent?"

This question arose from an email discussion group, the history of which will be explained on Saturday morning. There were several people who participated during the course of the past year in this email discussion group, and the result of it was the writing of three different papers on the subject, each one expressing a somewhat different view from the others. We will present all three papers Saturday morning. Then after the coffee break, there will be a forum that will allow you to express your views on this question. Between now and then you might want to look at *Beelzebub's Tales to His Grandson*, in order to help you formulate your view as to this question: The High Commission and Other Sacred Individuals, What Do They Represent?

Introduction

There is a Conference Information List on the rear table to which you are invited to inscribe your name, address, telephone, fax and email address. There is a place on the List for you to indicate if you would like to participate in a similar type of email discussion group during the ensuing year. Those who so indicate will be contacted during the year for the purpose of assigning you to a discussion group in which you are interested. Please sign this list as soon as possible. When it is complete we will have it copied, and a copy distributed to each one of you, so that you can readily communicate during the year.

I would like to remind everyone to please speak slowly and clearly when you are asking questions of the presenters or otherwise participating in a discussion. These sessions are being recorded for the purpose of preparing and publishing the Proceedings as we have done each year, and we would like these Proceedings to reflect the comments as accurately as possibly.

Finally, there is one more greeting that I saved until the end of these announcements. It is actually from one of the participants here, Anne Clark. It is entitled:

A Prayer for 9-11

That - We will Tune our Voices into our Hearts and Sing our Song of Love.
That - Our song will Honor Ourselves, Heal Ourselves, Energize Ourselves,
One - As - One to One Another.
That - Our tone will Awaken New Beginnings
Sounding a Lullaby from Deep Within the Mother's Love for One as All –

> With Love and may this spring issue a new peace and awareness.
> See you at "All & Everything 2002"

Now, Bert Sharp is going to talk about the history of the All and Everything Conferences.

Dr. H. J. (Bert) Sharp

Good morning everybody. It is nice to be here with you. I will try to keep it as short as I can.

This conference started because about a year before the first one, I was subscribing to the journal *GNOSIS*, which was published in America. It is no longer published, but it was dealing with esoteric matters. I wrote the editor a letter. In the letter I more or less said that I was puzzled because here we had C. G. Jung who was considered by some people to be a spiritual teacher rather than a psychiatrist, and here we have him training Maurice Nicoll as his replacement for England if not for the continent. After several years of being trained by Jung, Maurice Nicoll gets switched over and is trained by Gurdjieff. Then he was given permission to teach and he taught for the rest of his life. I said in the letter that it seemed strange to me that this switch happened. Was there some higher authority that was organizing this? Was this the way the Masters of Wisdom worked, preparing people for their task in life?

The letter was published and as result, Sy Ginsburg wrote to me and said that he wanted to come and see me, and Nicolas Tereshchenko wrote in the same vein. I had read some of Nicolas's material, so I was overjoyed to make contact with him that way. Then Russell Smith produced his erudite book, *Cosmic Secrets*, which became a talking point in groups such as this. So that was another reason for people to want to meet together.

The net result was that through correspondence with Sy, he was asking me if I could find a hotel to accommodate a small group of people to come and have a discussion on these sorts of matters. It soon became apparent that there wasn't a hotel big enough in Littlehampton, so I found this one, and we've been coming here ever since. That's how the conference started.

The first conference had about fifty people and the next one about forty. Since then the numbers have gravitated to between twenty-five and thirty, and I am very surprised that we have reached conference number seven.

There are three things that I would like to mention.

The first is that there was a paper that I presented that was read for me by Harry Bennett at A&E 2000 with the title, "When All Else Fails, Read the Instructions." It didn't seem to arouse any comments. It arose because Gurdjieff says in the last book he wrote before he died, *Life Is Real Only Then, When 'I Am'*, at page six and seven of the Prologue, that he realized no one could understand anything he had previously written, except perhaps for a few of those he had personally taught and even they understood very little. He then goes on in the Prologue to recount the three times he was shot. This is all to me essentially in the Hermetic Code being an exposition of the three stages of initiation.

I am then prompted to comment on the joke that was just told to us about the Gurdjieff group and the lightning flashes. Not many people know that as a result of high speed modern photography, we now know that when there is a big thundercloud overhead and there is an enormous flash of lightning from the cloud to earth, that is, in fact, preceded by a very faint flash from the earth to the cloud which creates an ionized pathway down which the main discharge can take place.

This seems to me to be a pattern in the way in which we have to do the work. It isn't that higher mind contacts us. We have to first do the work on ourselves so that we create a very faint pathway between our consciousness and higher mind. That pathway then is used by higher mind to inject whatever needs to be injected into us. So, the work has to start with the individual to prepare oneself for that which is to come.

I would also like to call our attention to a letter from Apollonius of Tyana which is quoted by Beryl Pogson in the introduction to her book, *In the East My Pleasure Lies*, as being an interpretation of Shakespeare's plays when using the Hermetic Code to interpret them. She says in this that the letter is what the work is all about.

It says, Beryl Pogson quoting in the introduction to her book, "Here is the core of the teaching in a letter from Apollonius giving the Pythagorean point of view. 'There is no death of anyone, but only an appearance, even as there is no birth of any save only in seeming. The change from being to becoming seems to be birth, and the change from becoming to being seems to be death. But in reality no one is ever born nor does one ever die. It is simply a being visible and then invisible, the former through the density of matter and the latter because of the subtlety of being. Being is forever the same, its only change being motion and rest. For being has this necessary peculiarity, that its change is brought about by nothing external to itself, but whole becomes parts and parts become whole in the oneness of the All. And if it be asked, what is this that sometimes is seen and sometimes is not seen, now in the same, now in the different, it might be answered: it is the way of everything in the world below, that when it is filled out with matter, it is visible owing to the resistance of its density but is invisible owing to its subtlety when it is rid of matter though matter still surround it in that immensity of space which hems it in but knows no birth and death'."

Beryl Pogson then says, "Don't you see, that that is the core of the teaching and this answers the questions that people ask."

Apollonius then goes on, 'But why has this false notion remained so long without refutation? Some think that what has happened through them they have themselves brought about. They are ignorant that the individual is brought to birth through parents, not by parents, just as a thing produced through the earth is not produced from it. The change that comes to the individual is nothing that is caused by his visible surroundings, but rather a change in the one thing which is in every individual.'

I think that takes a little bit of digesting, but to me it is very significant.

I would like to make a comment on the discussion which we have of the many levels of meaning of the *Tales*, which up until the last conference, I think, has been the principle objective of these meetings here. Now, of course, we have been adding the seminars on the *Tales* as well.

We should note the arrival of the third brain by evolution, the new intellectual mind: "intellect." One advantage has been the development of language enabling us to have audio communication and written communication bridging generations. It is a tremendous advance, but there has been a big price to pay. Since we now largely think in words, we have become limited to "knowing about" and no longer "know." 'The *Tales* are to help us to "know" not to "know about." So we need to try to go beyond the words. That is the message I would like to leave with you this morning.

Gurdjieff's Meetings and Non-Meetings with Remarkable and Unremarkable Men and Women 1935-1949

Professor Paul Beekman Taylor

In the course of a long evening session on 8 April 1924 in Juliet Rublee's apartment in Midtown Manhattan, Gurdjieff formally established a New York Branch of the Institute for the Harmonious Development of Man. Then, well after midnight refreshments, Gurdjieff responded at length to Dr. Louis Berman's question concerning the finances of the Institute. A. R. Orage transcribed Gurdjieff's reply, filtered through two translators, and checked his report the next afternoon for accuracy against the transcription made by Gurdjieff's secretary, Boris Feropintov. At Gurdjieff's urging, Orage later added the account to the end of his translation of Gurdjieff's Second Series, *Meetings with Remarkable Men*, which was completed in 1927. "The Material Question," the title Gurdjieff authorized, is a history of Gurdjieff's money-making projects from his early youth until his New York trip. Whatever the factual accuracy of his story, no one who knew Gurdjieff doubted one iota Gurdjieff's skill in answering the "dollar question." At any rate the "Material Question" coda to *Meetings* marks a radical shift from a search for remarkable men who would transmit esoteric lore to a search for remarkable men and women who would provide him with funds necessary to transmit that lore and its attendant pedagogical psychology to others. It was an auspicious sign when, at the conclusion of his exposé, a certain Mr. H. (Samuel Hoffenstein?) handed over a cheque and a pledge for further money, and Lady L. (Lilian Rothermere?) pledged half of her savings.

Ten years later, in the late winter of 1934-1935, Gurdjieff found himself at the end of his financial tether. He had lost the Prieuré eighteen months earlier because of outstanding debts. Now, he had two possibilities for the Institute on his mind. One was to repurchase the Prieuré or another suitable property in France. The other was to relocate the Institute in "America" (the name he used for the United States). After the defection of Orage in mid-1931, Gurdjieff had assumed that he had gained full control over Orage's former New York group, and that group had been, since 1924, the major financial support for Gurdjieff's operations. It is true that the group remained committed to Gurdjieff even after Orage left to resume his publishing career in London, and one reason, if not the crucial reason for this was Orage's own insistence that the "work" be carried on in his absence with his full moral support. Though happily ensconced in England with a new family and new career, Orage continued to be the moral glue that held the New York group intact in purpose, but his former pupils, either short of money or motivation, no longer made summer pilgrimages to the Prieuré.

Gurdjieff's Meetings and Non-Meetings

The work carried on by the New York group, however, had changed radically during the last year of Orage's presence. He had dedicated a great deal of energy in the late winter and spring of 1931 on two other projects besides discussing Gurdjieff's book and directing movement classes. One of these was instruction in writing for journal and book publication. The second was a project dear to his interests even before he had come into contact with Gurdjieff's ideas: Social Credit. Orage had entered Gurdjieff's world in 1922 in order to discover, among other things, a way to formulate and sell to an English audience the principles of Social Credit. He had lectured on Social Credit to New York's New School for Social Research with some success, and he found an audience for his economic theories among his group members. They, in turn, integrated Social Credit into their own program of study in the years following his departure.

Gurdjieff, for whom accidents have no significant consequence for the harmoniously developed person, seemed caught in an unfortunate spiral of accident in 1934 and 1935. Earlier in his Western operations, he had profited from the energies of a number of faithful "deputy stewards," or "remarkable men" to assist him in his work,[1] such as Ouspensky, Orage and Toomer. All of these were now absent from the scene, so that Gurdjieff; in November 1934 - a date to which he refers as an axial moment throughout *Life is real only then, when I am* - found himself with neither an executive staff nor a body of representatives for his teaching. The loss of the Prieuré was merely the first debilitating event in a bunched sequence. In May of 1934 Gurdjieff was in the United States to redress his losses. First, he contacted Toomer, whom he had foreseen since the late twenties as a successor to Orage as general director of the work in the United States, and suggested that they meet in Chicago, where Gurdjieff could profit from the occasion to visit the World's Fair. When Gurdjieff arrived in Chicago in June 1934, Toomer was not there, but was in New Mexico waiting for Marjorie Content's divorce proceedings in Reno to be completed. In New York in September, Jean and Marjorie were married, and Toomer politely notified Gurdjieff that, with his daughter and new wife, he would invest his current energies elsewhere and could not re-assume his former duties for Gurdjieff. Nonetheless, he closed his letter by saying: "At the same time I now, as always, want to do all I can to help spread the ideas that mean so much to me, that I believe the greatest ideas that contemporary man will be privileged to come in contact with."[2]

With Toomer indisposed, Gurdjieff found himself without a coordinator of the Chicago group, at that time the second most important Gurdjieff group in the United States in both numbers and financial contributions. Olga Ivanovna might have filled the gap temporarily, and in June Gurdjieff visited Olgivanna and Frank Lloyd Wright nearby in Spring Green, Wisconsin. In mid-February 1925 Orage and Toomer had talked with Olgivanna about locating the American Branch of the Institute in the United States, and early in the following winter he contacted Olgivanna again, but she was heavy with child and not disposed to consider the question. Now, a decade

---

[1] In his parabolic "autobiography," Gurdjieff recounted his adventures with a number of mentors that he classified as "remarkable men." After setting in place his Institute in Avon, near Fontainebleau, in 1922, he was the mentor himself to a number of remarkable men.
[2] Beineke Manuscript Library, Yale University, Toomer papers, Box 3, Folder 96.

later, Gurdjieff He hoped he might convince Wright to host the Institute,[3] but Wright and his wife had embarked on an ambitious school project of their after formally established the Taliesin Fellowship in 1932. Using the model of the Institute at Prieuré, they had converted Taliesin East in Spring Green, Wisconsin, and Taliesin West in the desert northeast of Scottsdale, Arizona, into architectural workshops involving projects encompassing all aspects of physical and intellectual labors. Wright's architectural students there, as Gurdjieff's pupils at the Prieuré, developed a heightened sense of self-reliance. They performed all the manual labor from digging wells to tailoring stone, from building to cooking, weaving and painting. And, of course, in a theatre they designed and built themselves, reminiscent of Gurdjieff's Study House, they watched films and performed music and dances. Gurdjieff and Wright got along well in Spring Green, but there was no question in the Architect's mind, or in his wife's, of converting their enterprise in Gurdjieff's direction. After Gurdjieff left, Wright announced publicly that Gurdjieff's ideas were the most important in the world.[4]

With both Toomer and Wright unavailable for his project, Gurdjieff returned to New York. Without sufficient funds to rent an apartment he moved in with Fred Leighton and turned once again to the members of the New York group for support, but by a third and most devastating "accident" six weeks later suddenly altered his relations. In the early morning of November 6th, 1934, after delivering a brilliant exposé of the Social Credit System on BBC radio in London, Orage died. The impact of this event on the New York group was swift and deep. Without Orage's moral support, few felt a desire to commit themselves conscientiously to Gurdjieff's present course. Furthermore, the aftermath of the October 1929 Stock Market crash diminished donations to the cause, and Franklin Roosevelt's various New Deal policies being put into effect squeezed tighter private spending. In short, money was not readily available for the kind of enterprise Gurdjieff might have envisioned for his Institute.

Gurdjieff occupied himself that autumn and winter writing his "Third Series," *Life is real only then, when I am*, a book in which he records the impact of Orage's death on him. Whether or not Gurdjieff realized the alienating effect that Orage's disappearance had upon the New York group as a whole, he acted, according to his own testimony can be taken as accurate, as if he felt alienated from the group. In short, he appeared to others as one exiled from his own work. He appeared restless and distracted to those about him in New York. Though he was eager to complete what would be his last period of writing, the shape of the third series was still unformed. He was systematically reshaping his text to focus on the events surrounding his breakup with Orage, and his own fascination with the question of aging. He took a brief pause in his work to take another trip to Taliesin East in February 1935 where he probed Wright's will to collaborate once more. Gurdjieff made the curious proposition to him that the architect prepare pupils for work with Gurdjieff in France, whereupon Wright replied that an exchange might better work the other way. Olgivanna intervened with obvious sympathy for Gurdjieff, but the master had no school left in France for pupils.

---

[3] Brendan Gill, *Many Masks* (NY: Da Capo, 1998), pp. 226-27.
[4] Madison Wisconsin *Capitol Times*, 12 September, 1934.

Toomer, Orage, and Wright were now out of the foreground of Gurdjieff's vista so he shifted his sights to search for ancillary persons and places. First he scanned the possibility of Taos, New Mexico and Mabel Dodge Luhan, who had offered her ranch through Jean Toomer's offices nine years earlier in 1926. What Gurdjieff did not know probably, was that Mabel had already decided in late November of 1934, in reaction to Toomer's marriage and Orage's death, to clear the accounts of her financial, if not moral relations, with the Gurdjieff work.[5] She took the occasion to ask Toomer to return the $14,000 she had "loaned" Gurdjieff as "seed money" in 1926, as well as the $1000 she had advanced Toomer as an investment in his career. Toomer replied apologetically from New York that Gurdjieff had applied her money to the maintenance of the Institute.

Though Mabel was not responsive to Gurdjieff's entreaty, forwarded through former Orage pupils, that she renew her pledge of her Taos home, she and other former friends of Orage in New Mexico were open to other avenues of aid for the continuation of a teaching in which they still fundamentally believed. It would have had little effect in New Mexico to evoke Gurdjieff's need, but Orage's name still drew attention, particularly among those who were "converted" to the Social Credit scheme, including one senator and the governor of New Mexico. Whether or not Gurdjieff understood or cared much for Orage's economic principles, the legacy of Orage's economic theory drew the attention of some New Mexicans to Gurdjieff's predicament. The name that was forwarded to Gurdjieff's was United States Senator Bronson M. Cutting who, in the summer of 1928 had had several long discussions with Orage in Santa Fe. Now, in the early spring of 1935, he was made aware of Gurdjieff's needs through close friends and political supporters in Santa Fe and Taos, including Mabel Luhan, Alice Henderson Corbin, Mary Austen, Martha Mann and Elizabeth (Betty) and Meredith Sage Hare. All of these, former friends and acquaintances of Orage, appealed to the senator on Gurdjieff's behalf but to what end?

Cutting is a pivotal figure in twentieth-century American politics. Born June 23 1888 on Long Island, he attended Groton and then Harvard in 1906. Restlessness and bronchial maladies disturbed his studies, and in 1909, having completed only a single year of his degree course, he left for California to regain his health. A year later he went to Santa Fe, "to die," as he told a fellow traveller. Instead of dying, thanks to the bright sun and dry clear air of the Sangre de Cristo Mountains, his health returned. In 1912, the year New Mexico was granted statehood, he bought a number of newspapers, including the *Santa Fe New Mexican,* and when war was declared he served as an officer in the American Army. After returning to New Mexico, he was asked by local politicians to organize American Legion posts for veterans in the fledgling state. Energetic and committed to public causes, Cutting became involved in New Mexico politics rapidly, and in 1927 he was appointed by the governor to fill out the senatorial term of Andrieus A. Jones who had died during his term of office. In July of 1928 Cutting entertained Orage and Jessie in Santa Fe, and,

---

[5] In the meantime, Mabel had proposed leasing her property as a "Dude Ranch," though that scheme fell through in 1929. Mabel's husband, the Taos Tiowa Tony Luhan, disliked Gurdjieff but had great admiration for Orage, whose meetings he regularly attended with his wife when they were in New York

despite the brevity of the Orages' visit, he was thoroughly converted to Orage's economics. During his first elected term of office (1928-1934) he made a solid reputation for himself supporting freedom of the press, veterans' bonuses, and economic reform.

A few days after Orage's death, Cutting, running as a liberal Republican, was elected to a six-year term in the Senate. On 11 November 1934, Mabel Dodge Luhan hosted a celebration dinner for him. In the months that followed he heard from Mabel and her cohorts about Gurdjieff's hopes to re-open the Institute. On May 6 1935, six months to the day after Orage's death, Cutting set out for Washington, carrying with him, it is thought, an offer to Gurdjieff for the work, either of a New Mexico location for a future Institute or of a pledge for financial support. Neither seems likely considering the time and circumstances in Cutting's career.[6] Nonetheless, it is reported that Paul E. Anderson, acting as Gurdjieff's secretary, "succeeded in arousing such keen interest on the part of Senator Bronson Cutting of New Mexico that he asked him to meet Gurdjieff with a view to buying back the Prieuré and leasing it to a resuscitated Institute."[7]

Cutting was on his way to Washington to answer charges of electoral illegalities made by Dennis Chavez, his democratic rival in the recent senatorial election that Cutting had won by some thirteen hundred votes.[8] His correspondence with his mother in Washington D. C., to whom he wrote weekly letters, mentions that he would also speak in Washington about the Independent Offices Appropriation Bill promised pensions to disabled veterans. Whatever his intentions were concerning Gurdjieff, he agreed to meet him. Cutting was attracted habitually to extraordinary people and he had heard much of Gurdjieff since Orage visited Santa Fe in 1928. It is unlikely that Cutting was prepared to advance money for Gurdjieff to repurchase the Prieuré or to acquire another property. In the first place, Cutting had little money to spare since his own investments had suffered terribly in the early days of the Depression. Secondly, he was not interested in Gurdjieff's teaching. He might have been willing, however, to offer Gurdjieff political support. Gurdjieff had been staying with Fred Leighton in New York during the winter, and Leighton, Jean Toomer's best friend, was in contact with Betty Meredith Hare, who had acted as intermediary between Orage and Cutting during the first half of 1934.[9] Leighton who transmitted to Betty Hare Gurdjieff's hopes, and she, in turn, conveyed them to Cutting. In effect, speaking on Gurdjieff's

---

[6] Gurdjieff had turned down Mabel Luhan's 1926 offer of her ranch for good reasons. Logistics required him to operate near a major urban center. Hellerau was close to Berlin, Fontainebleau close to Paris, Wright's Spring Green near Madison and Chicago, and Toomer's Doylestown close to New York and Philadelphia.

[7] John G. Bennett, *Gurdjieff: Making a New World* (London: Turnstone, 1973), p. 182. Following Bennett, Moore, p. 155, says Anderson brought news that an eminent politician was expressing serious interest in backing Gurdjieff financially, and Webb, p. 430 mentions Cutting's trip to see Gurdjieff, but does not state the specific reason

[8] After Cutting's death, Chavez was appointed to Cutting's Senate seat, and remained in that office until the 1940s.

[9] See letter from Orage to Cutting 8 January 1934 (Cutting Correspondence, Library of Congress, Box 11).

behalf, the group of women who had proved decisive in Cutting's election had petitioned the Senator to use his influence to have Congress pass an act granting Gurdjieff American citizenship. So Nick Putnam, who was said to be "like a son" to Gurdjieff,[10] and Philip Lasell, Gurdjieff pupil since 1927, agreed to accompany him to Washington as sponsors. Both had names of importance in American history. Putnam was descended from the Revolutionary War hero General Israel Putnam. His father was Lieutenant Israel Putnam who was killed in the 1918 Ardennes offensive in the dying days of the First World War Lasell descended from a colonial Huguenot family. His father was a wealthy New England manufacturer of textile machinery who owned numerous properties in Whitinsville in the Blackstone Valley of Massachusetts.[11]

Gurdjieff, with Putnam, Philip Lasell and Paul Anderson, acting as Gurdjieff's secretary, arrived in Washington from New York City in late April and waited ten days for the senator, but Cutting never arrived. In the air on his flight from Albuquerque on the evening of 6 May, Cutting left his seat near the rear of the plane to move forward to vacant seats side by side where he could nap. He was asleep when the pilot attempted an emergency landing near Macon, Missouri. A wing of the plane brushed the ground and the plane crashed. Cutting would probably have survived, as others did, had he remained in the rear with his seatbelt fastened. Instead, thrown about the fuselage by the crash, he suffered severe lacerations of the head. He was identified at the crash scene by the contents of his pockets, including a check for a telephone bill bearing his mother's name, Mrs. W. Bayard Cutting of New York City. He was carrying almost $600 in cash.[12]

Within a fortnight after Cutting's tragic disappearance - the last "accident" in a woeful series - Gurdjieff disappeared from the United States. Nothing certain is known of his whereabouts until the late summer of 1935 when he appeared in Germany briefly with, of all things, a German passport.[13] On 19 October, he resumed teaching on a modest level in the Grand Hotel, next door to Cafe de la Paix near the Opera.[14] It is supposed by some that he had returned to the Soviet Union

---

[10] Bennett, p. 182. "After the death of Orage his hopes of re-establishing the Institute rested entirely upon the U.S.A."

[11] Nick had told me that he had once been Gurdjieff's "sponsor," but I did not know at the time what this office meant. Lida Gurdjieff Wright confirmed this in a July, 2000 conversation, and her sister Luba Gurdjieff Everitt had told me earlier that in the early twenties Franklin Delano Roosevelt had promised Gurdjieff, for services rendered, to help him in the future in any way possible. Lasell, my father-in-law twenty years later, often mentioned that Gurdjieff was an American citizen, but though I did not believe him, I wondered why he would say this. A sketch book of his in my possession refers to the Washington trip.

[12] *New York Times* front page, 7 May 1935.

[13] Beth McCorkle, *The Gurdjieff Years 1929-1949: Recollections of Louise March* (Walworth: New York The Work Study Association, 1990), p. 67.

[14] Kathryn Hulme, *Undiscovered Country: A Spiritual Adventure* (Boston: Little Brown, 1966), p. 75. Most of the meetings of the "Rope" took place on the Left Bank in the Hôtel Napoléon Bonaparte where Solita Solano and Hulme were living.

as far as Central Asia.[15] In Washington, he might have thought what he had been heard uttering shortly before his death: "Begin in Russia, finish in Russia."[16] Even before the crash that killed Cutting, Gurdjieff had hedged his options by having Paul Anderson inquire about visa possibilities at the Russian Embassy in Washington. Apparently, the Soviet authorities gave Gurdjieff permission to return on the condition that he not teach. If this restriction were not a sufficient determent, the political climate in early 1935 was not favorable. Kirov had been assassinated in December 1934, and the full weight of Stalin's ethnic, linguistic and political purges was crushing the morale of the people, particularly in southern European and central Asian central Soviet republics.

At the time of Cutting's death and Gurdjieff's undoubted disappointment, the spirit of Orage was working behind scenes in the interests of both. Franklin Delano Roosevelt, the Democrat President of the United States, a friend of Cutting's from childhood, though unhappy with Cutting's refusal to shift political parties for the 1934 elections, had appointed Henry Agard Wallace as Secretary of Agriculture in 1933. Wallace, later Vice-President of the United States and candidate for the Presidency in 1948 on the Socialist platform, had listened appreciatively to Orage in the spring of 1931 in New York and had met Gurdjieff in the same period. Wallace had been on good terms with Senator Cutting, and lent support to his ideas on Social Credit. In early 1934 Wallace had appointed to his staff "Dr." Nikolai Konstantinovich Rerikh, Rerick, or, more commonly in the United States, Roerich (1874-1947), a White Russian painter-designer-mystic who had arrived in New York in 1920.

Roerich was born in St. Petersburg in 1874, and entered the Academy of Art there in 1893. His interest in Theosophy brought him into contact with Ouspensky, and his wife Helena was the first translator of the whole text of Blavatsky's *Secret Doctrine* into Russian at the end of the century. Roerich was active in the world of music and dance. He worked with Stravinsky and Diaghilev in 1913 as designer of the decor and costumes for *Le Sacre du Printemps*. It is likely that Thomas de Hartmann knew him there, considering that they moved in the same artistic circles. In 1920 the Roerichs moved to New York by way of London. Nikolai's travels about the United States brought him to New Mexico where he met Mabel Dodge Luhan and her husband Tony. At their recommendation, he made several paintings of Pueblo Indians.

Roerich left the United States, probably late in 1924, to return to London from where he embarked for a voyage to India and Central Asia in the spring of 1925. It is curious that he took a route which scholars have attributed to Gurdjieff more than a quarter century earlier. He travelled through the Suez Canal to Colombo in Ceylon (now Sri Lanka). He went northward to Calcutta and Darjeeling. Then he went east and north, skirting Nepal and the Himalayas to Srinagar, capital

---

[15] "From what Gurdjieff said once or twice in 1949, it seems that in 1935 he made a trip to Asia - he said "Persia," which might include Turkestan.... Presumably the purpose was to consult with persons he trusted about the next phase of his life" (Bennett, p. 182).
[16] James Moore, *Gurdjieff: A Biography. The Anatomy of a Myth* (Shaftesbury, Dorset and Rockport, MA: Element, 1991), p. 64.

Gurdjieff's Meetings and Non-Meetings

of Kashmir and to Leh nearby, before arriving in Ladahk in present-day Pakistan. He trekked northeastward from there to Khotan (Hotien) and into Tibet (Sinkiang) along the Cherchem Darya and Terim rivers, stopping at the monasteries Maulbek and Lamayura. Roerich proceeded north to Jarkend, Kashgen, Umruchi and, finally, through the Gobi Desert to Irkutsk on Lake Baikal on the trail of the legendary Shambhala, the earthly link with heaven that he heard of so often in the legends of the area. This route, almost identical to Gurdjieff's own route to the Gobi and Lake Baikal, James Moore calls a "secret path" that "does not cross with those of the great geographers of the epoch."[17]

Roerich returned to the West by way of Delhi, Bombay and Calcutta. Instead of returning to the United States, he went to Moscow and convinced the Soviet authorities to authorize him to explore the regions north of Tibet. With his wife Helena and his two sons, Georgii and Svetoslav, Roerich left by land on 13 July 1926. They crossed the Urals and went on to the Altai Mountain range in Mongolia, where they made camp on the 26 August 1926.[18] They sat out the long winter to come nearby, and on 27 July 1927, passed over the range (known often in the West as the Humboldt Range) to Lhasa. Unfortunately, they were ill received and imprisoned for the winter in the Tibetan capital. In March 1928, they were able to leave Tibet and proceed south to Gangtok and Darjeeling before returning to the West.[19]

Back in New York in the fall of 1928, Roerich associated himself with Claude Bragdon, friend of Orage and editor of the English translation of Ouspensky's *Tertium Organum*, to establish an academy of the arts. That year Roerich opened a Museum in his house on East 103 Street, overlooking the Hudson River in Manhattan. Bragdon agreed to edit translations of Roerich's work. Orage probably knew of Roerich in London in 1918, where he worked for a time with Diaghilev. Roerich attended at least one of Orage's talks in the autumn of 1924, and listened to Orage in 1928 and 1929. Orage and Jesse were in attendance at the opening of the Roerich museum. Though it is entirely possible that Roerich heard from Orage about Gurdjieff's earlier travels to Central Asia, there is evidence that Roerich and Gurdjieff were together in Central Asia in the first decade of the century.[20]

---

[17] Moore, *Gurdjieff*, p. 31. In the pages following he traces Gurdjieff's peregrinations in Central Asia See
James Webb's map of Gurdjieff s travels, *The Harmonious Circle*, p. 74.
[18] See *Altai Himalaya* (Brookfell, CT: Arun Press, 1983), with Introduction by Claude Bragdon.
[19] Jacqueline Decter, *Nicholas Roerich, The Life and Art of a Russian Master* (London: Thames and Hudson, 1989), p. 158, reproduces the map of the 1923-1928, expeditions which resembles Webb's map (*The Harmonious Circle*, p 74.), of Gurdjieff's travels there thirty years earlier, described in *Meetings*, pp.
165-76.
[20] During the Stalinist purge trials, G. I. Bokii confessed that he had joined a Masonic lodge in 1909 that had been founded by Gurdjieff and included N. K Roerich and his wife, Dr. K N. Riabinin, B. Stomoniakov, I. M Moskvin and S. D. Mercurov (Gurdjieff's "cousin").

Since his arrival in the States, Roerich had been thinking of an international program to protect cultural artefacts, and in 1928 he drew up a pact to present to international authorities. The Roerich pact was known as "Banners of Peace," and renown gained its author a nomination for the Nobel Peace Prize (Frank Billings Kellogg, American Secretary of State, was the eventual recipient). A short time later Roerich began a collaboration with Henry Asgard Wallace, whom Franklin Delano Roosevelt appointed Secretary of Agriculture in 1933, and the two were in Orage's audience for a series of lectures on Social Credit in the spring of 1931. Wallace had been drawn to Orage's economic theory as a possible solution for the monetary problems caused by the Great Depression of the thirties and with Roerich's agricultural account of the Gobi where drought resistant grasses grew beneath the desert sands. Wallace hired Roerich for the Department. While Svetoslav stayed behind to pursue his studies, at Columbia University, Roerich, Helena, and their son George[21] went to Central Asia in the summer of 1934 where he remained until the autumn of 1935 to search for drought-resistant grasses.

Well before Roerich succeeded in convincing Wallace that there was organic life beneath the sands of the Gobi Desert, Orage had completed his translation of *Meetings with Remarkable Men* in which Gurdjieff speaks of the possible utilization of vegetable materials in and under the sands of the Gobi (p. 168) and recounts that he and his fellow seekers discovered a map of pre-sands Egypt. In *Beelzebub's Tales*, Gurdjieff has his hero Beelzebub visit pre-sands Egypt during his second descent to Earth and both works imply that under present-day deserts lie vestiges of ancient civilizations.[22] Roerich claimed that cultural artefacts remained there attesting to ancient civilizations in the Gobi. He proposed to uncover cultural objects to be protected by treaty. During his absence from the United States in the spring of 1935, the Roerich Pact was approved and signed by the United States and twenty-one other countries.

Meanwhile, however, Wallace was becoming suspicious of another purpose for the Roerichs' voyages, and he removed them from his department in 1936 as soon as Roerich returned to the United States. Leaving his museum behind, Roerich moved to India where he died in 1947. What exactly the deeper purpose was that Wallace suspected has not been explained. The press exposed him as a meddling and manipulative mystic[23] and wondered pointedly how Roerich maintained relations with Soviet authorities that allowed him free access to remote areas of the Soviet Union.

---

[21] Later known for his translation of the Tibetan *Blue Annals*.

[22] Such grasses are known today as love grass (genus *erogrostis*) and sand love grass (genus *tricodes*), and are used for forage and ground cover in the Southwest of the United States.

[23] See Edward L. and Frederick H. Schapsmeier, *Henry A. Wallace of Iowa: The Agrarian Years, 1910-1940* (Ames: Iowa State UP, 1968), and *The Price of Vision: The Diary of Henry A. Wallace 1942-1946*, ed. John Morton Blum (Boston: Houghton Mifflin, 1973), p. 358. In an attempt to slander Wallace at the time he was running for president in 1948, the columnist Westbrook Pegler revealed Wallace's relationship with Roerich in the so-called "Guru Letters" that were to prove Wallace's dangerous mystical affinities. Decter, *Nicholas Roerich*, points out that his interest in mystical symbolism is manifested in the Great Pyramid design on the one dollar bill which he persuaded Roosevelt to have placed there.

A quarter century earlier, in the midst of revolution, Gurdjieff had also maintained favourable relations with Soviet powers with exemplary cunning; and, he might have thought of exercising them in his overture to Soviet officials in Washington in May 1935. Though he received only a conditional approval to return to Russia, it is assumed he might have returned to Russian Central Asia to "test the terrain."[24] Knowledge of Roerich's whereabouts and influence in the Soviet Union at the time would have been of great value to him, and the Roerichs were precisely where Gurdjieff had reason to be. In *Life is real only then, when I am*, (pp. 108 and 134), written shortly before he disappeared Gurdjieff says that an Essene school still exists in Central Asia where he still had pupils.

There are over-riding questions that force themselves upon our attention. First, how much did these two men with comparable itineraries for their lives, know of each other? Roerich's trek through Central Asia between 1925 and 1927 seems charted on a Gurdjieffian map. Roerich's own psycho-philosophy of life, *The Invincible*,[25] first published in Riga in 1936, is replete with material echoing Gurdjieff's teaching; but, then again, such correspondences are found in many writings of the decade. Secondly, what was Gurdjieff looking for in Central Asia? If the Soviet government banned him from teaching, then he must have gone to Central Asia for other reasons, and these would be connected to his earlier visits there that he represents in *Meetings*. Perhaps Gurdjieff was looking again for Sarmoung, the putative source of his esoteric knowledge. Perhaps he would join the brotherhood there and end his life as had his beloved mentor Prince Yuri Lubovedsky.[26]

There is ancillary circumstantial evidence that this might have been so. A Soviet psychiatrist in Novosibirsk visited Kuiya, just north of the Nenia River on the northwestern slopes of the Altai where she experienced *kamlani*, shaman magic. The shamans of the area spoke of Belevodia and Beloushka as a mythic sacred mountain, corresponding to the Sufi Hurqayla, Tibetan Shambhala and Gurdjieff's Sarmoung.[27] As Gurdjieff could, the Altai shamans had the power to absorb negative energies.[28] The psychiatrist is told that the mystical gate of Hurqalya has a passage entered through a time wheel, and that listening to music of the circles incites a mystical

---

[24] Moore, *Gurdjieff*, p. 258.
[25] New York: Nicholas Roerich Museum, 1974.
[26] Whereas Gurdjieff says that he arrived at the secret monastery of Sarmoung, Roerich was drawn the famed Shambhala, whose putative ruler was Rigden Djapo (Rig reflects the Indo-European root for "king"). In *Altai Himalaya*, Roerich speaks of the monastery of Takur Gundla in terms that echo Gurdjieff's description of Sarmoung. If the name *Sarmoung* derives from a Tocharian nominal compound, it could be represent an Indo-European juncture of *sar*, "self" and *moung* "image."
[27] Olga Kharitidi, *Siberian Wisdom Discovered by a Russian Psychiatrist* (San Francisco: Harper, 1996). pp. 78-83. 217-18, relates a discussion she had with a doctor who tells her that those pupils of Gurdjieff who stayed behind in the Soviet Union, were still active in the Altai area in search of the Time Wheel.
[28] Op. cit, p. 193.

experience. She is told that Gurdjieff's pupils who remained in the USSR continued his search for the Time Wheel.[29]

Whether or not he found what he had hoped for in Central Asia, Gurdjieff returned to Paris in September 1935, about the time Roerich was returning to New York. Neither seems to have achieved exactly what each sought, and how much their fates were intertwined remains a mystery for the time being.[30] Back in Dmitri's apartment at 6, Rue des Colonels Renard, just down the slope of Avenue Carnot from the Arc de Triomphe, facing Rue d'Armaille, Gurdjieff resumed his teaching to a few pupils, who included the members of the old female Paris group, now re-christened "The Rope.": Margaret Anderson, Jane Heap, Georgette Leblanc, Solita Solano, all of whom had begun their work earlier with Orage. Kathryn Hulme joined the group;[31] and a number of French, including René Daumal, Luc Dietrich and Henri Tracol in the late thirties were delegated to Mme de Salzmann for instruction. Nonetheless, Gurdjieff's hopes of re-establishing the Institute had faded for the moment. He was low on money and, apparently, down on his luck, but he persevered and earned wages once again as a medical practitioner.

In the spring of 1939, he took one last pre-war trip to the States, but failed to attract much interest or money. The timing was bad. The American economy had not yet recovered its essential vitality, interest in his presence was not encouragingly enthusiastic, and war was in the air. Disdaining offers by some of his old pupils to remain in the United States, he returned to Paris in May. When war was declared in September, most of his pupils left. Jane Heap set up a group in London, and Margaret Anderson, went into seclusion before fleeing to America. Gurdjieff sent requests to his American followers to find means for him to find refuge in the United States. A letter over the signatures of Donald Whitcomb, Israel Solon and Fred Leighton circulated among the New York group, asking everyone to send money to Gurdjieff, explaining that $200 had already reached him, enough for a visa to Cuba, and that Gurdjieff approved. The letter suggested Mexico as an alternative, and estimated that $1000 would suffice to get him there. The money was pledged, but before it was sent to Gurdjieff, word was received that all was well. Gurdjieff was content to stay in his brother's apartment in Paris. German and French authorities alike tolerated his presence.

What had changed his situation? Perhaps the cares and conditions of age prompted him to sit out a difficult situation rather than undertake a new exile. Or, it might have been that Gurdjieff found his presence tolerated, or even made secure and comfortable by local authorities as well as by the occupying forces. Perhaps he had found a benefactor to assure his financial well-being. This latter supposition is confirmed in the story of the well known hotelier and horse breeder François Dupré,

---

[29] Op. cit, pp. 217-18.

[30] Roerich's Russian diaries are in the archives of the Sterling Library at Yale University.

[31] Margaret Anderson traces this teaching in *The Unknowable Gurdjieff* (London: Routledge & Kegan Paul, 1962). More recently, William Patrick Patterson, *Ladies of the Rope* (Fairfax, CA: Arete Communications, 1999), puts together Solano's account with pieces of others, and provides a helpful commentary. Curiously, Gurdjieff's own visiting card when he moved to the area of the Etoile misspells the street name "6, rue du Colonel-Renard" (rue des Colonels-Renard).

who, curiously, like Cutting before him, had never set eyes upon Gurdjieff. Unlike Cutting, however, he took utmost pains to avoid seeing Gurdjieff; and unlike Cutting he advanced a considerable sum of money to maintain him.

Dupré, born in 1888, served honorably in WWI as an officer in the French Army. He was seriously wounded at Verdun and, during his recovery, contracted mumps, the after effects of which left him sterile. Thanks to a considerable fortune left him by the Singer family (automobiles, sewing machines), he invested in hotels and by the mid-thirties he could boast owning the prestigious George V, the luxurious Plaza Athenée off the Champs-Elysees, and the luxurious Ritz in Montréal. He owned residences off the Avenue Foch in the Square du Bois du Boulogne in Paris, and houses in Montréal and Jamaica.

Besides these, he had acquired a large stable of horses in Arras, and though he took little interest in racing himself, he was eminently successful and well-known as a breeder of horses.

After a first marriage had ended in divorce, in 1937 Dupré met a Serbo-Hungarian, named Anna Stefanna Nagy, then twenty-five and a chambermaid on board the CGT Normandie. They were married a year later in Montréal, but Dupré kept his infirmity from Anci, as she was known familiarly. Their marriage went well, and even the occupation of France did not disturb the relative luxury of their life, since Dupré's hotels were commandeered as billets for high-ranking German officers, which put money into his coffers. Shortly before the war broke out, Anci came down with intestinal problems. Local doctors diagnosed a tumor which, because of its location at the base of the liver, they felt was inoperable. In discomfort, she looked for advice elsewhere, and an acquaintance of her husband, the poet and essayist René Daumal, sent her to Gurdjieff. Gurdjieff felt about her abdominal and thoracic regions and then held the palm of his right hand over the tumor. He told her to return if the pain persisted.[32]

Within a day, the pain and signs of the tumor had disappeared. She became devoted to Gurdjieff and in gratitude, with the encouragement of Jeanne de Salzmann, to whom Gurdjieff had entrusted Daumal and his young Jewish wife, Vera Milanova, she offered to support Gurdjieff financially.[33] With Jeanne de Salzmann, who spent most of her time during the Occupation in Geneva, Evian and Peyvoux, she approached Dupré for continued support for Gurdjieff. Dupré wanted nothing to do with Gurdjieff himself, though he was willing to satisfy his wife's wishes in the matter. At the time, Gurdjieff had a few French pupils, among whom were Henri Tracol and his wife, Rene Daumal and his friend Philippe Lavastine (who later married Jeanne de Salzmann's daughter Natalie), Lanza del Vasto (pseudonym of the Sicilian-born Joseph Jean Lanza di Trabra-Branciforte, a devotee of Mahatma Gandhi), Louis Le Prudomme, René Zuber and Luc Dietrich

---

[32] This account was told me by my sister, Eve Chevalier, who had served as Anci's traveling companion in 1950 and 1951, confirmed by my mother, Edith Taylor who had known Franqois Dupré since World War I.

[33] The story of Anci and Frangois Dupré that follows is documented by Jacqueline Decour of Veyrier Switzerland whose mother was Dupré's first cousin.

(whose confessional novel, *L'Apprentisage de la Ville* encodes a tribute to Gurdjieff). Daumal, the most talented of the French group, went into exile in the Savoy Alps during much of the war, not only because of his tuberculosis, but because his wife was Jewish. He died in 1944, before the end of hostilities and before he completed *Mont Analogue*, his personal tribute to Gurdjieff's teaching. His younger friend, Dietrich, disciple of Lanza del Vasta, died as well before the liberation of Paris. None of these, however, had influence over the authorities sufficient to protect Gurdjieff against charges of hoarding. Gurdjieff's own explanation, reputedly told to Fritz Peters, was: "I make deal with Germans, with policemen, with all kinds idealistic people who make 'black market.' Result: I eat well and continue have tobacco, liquor, and what is necessary for me and for many others."[34]

Dupré's acquiescence in his wife's support of Gurdjieff was threatened when, on New Years' Eve, 1942, with expectations of his pleasure in the fact, Anci announced to her husband that she was pregnant. After disclosing the secret of his infirmity, he stormed out of the house and, despite the curfew, managed to reach his mother's apartment where he spent the night. He had his personal belongings moved out of the Square du Bois de Boulogne the next day and renounced his wife. Her lover, almost certainly Luc Dietrich, had no means to take her in.[35] Dupré ordered her to have an abortion, but outside of France. He would arrange for necessary papers, so she contacted Jeanne de Salzmann and René Daumal who were, for the moment, living in Peyvoux in the Alps. They had Anci come to Evian, where they furnished her names of a doctor and a "safe house" in Geneva where she could be lodged. She crossed the border into Switzerland through German border controls with an *Ausweiss* her husband procured from German authorities, and underwent an abortion in her fifth month of pregnancy.

Back in Paris, she and Dupré reached an amicable agreement, to the effect that she would remain his wife and occupy the Square du Bois, and he would move into the George V. She continued to finance Gurdjieff throughout the war with her husband's money. Through Dupré's influence in authoritative quarters, Gurdjieff kept his person and his limited teaching unscathed; though it was no secret to the authorities and Gurdjieff's neighbours that his larder was full of contraband foodstuffs. Gurdjieff's larder and obvious financial security lasted from the time the Germans

---

[34] Peters, *Gurdjieff Remembered*, pp. 92-93. Moore, p.281, names the most prominent of Gurdjieff's French group during the war. René Daumal mentions the names of his associates in Mme de Salzmann's group in a letter to Vera Daumal 13 September 1938 (*René Daumal, Correspondance III, 1933-1944* (Paris: Gallimard, 1996), p. 129. In late 1944, Roger Manchester, serving in the USAF, visited Gurdjieff and took note of his comfortable circumstances. So did Fritz Peters, but his account in *Gurdjieff Remembered* is considered by many to be more fiction than fact. In 1946 Nick Putnam and Philip Lasell succeeded in getting to Paris, and both reported back to America that Gurdjieff was in fine form. Nick was there primarily to recover his wife, Dmitri's daughter Lida [Lydia] Gurdjieff, while Lasell sought Gurdjieff's help for his opium dependency.

[35] A sculpture of the joined hands of Anci and Luc Dietrich is extant. Dupré was unable to initiate divorce proceedings because his Canadian marriage was never registered in France.

entered Paris in June to the end of the Occupation. He was generous with its contents and with money to others in the area who came to him for help. The story he told, repeated in the biographies, is that he secured credit from local merchants by claiming that he owned Texas oil wells whose income would be sent to him at war's end.[36] As his biographer remarks, "Gurdjieff - despite his commercial transactions with German 'idealists' - was wholly indemnified by his grandfatherly humanity and his support of Jewish group members."[37] No one seems to know precisely what his deals with the Germans and French police consisted of. Some have speculated that he was protected by the Germans because of his German contacts (made in Hellerau?) or German sympathy with his teaching (this was known). Perhaps his anti-Bolshevik views were a factor, though where and to whom he expressed them is unknown. Anci's contribution consisted of her husband's money, but more important was her husband's business connections with the German Occupation authorities.

Following the Liberation, it was, ironically, Dupré who was imprisoned for collaboration, simply because he had abetted Occupation forces by billeting the Werhmacht (as if he had much of a choice in the matter). He regained freedom only after paying an exorbitant fine to the French. Meanwhile, Gurdjieff was seized one afternoon after the Liberation for illegal possession of foreign currency found under his bed, but he was released almost immediately on the grounds that he was a poor old man who did not understand his crime.

This account, then, is a story of Gurdjieff's capacity for survival, an account of his dogged determination to fulfil what he had foreseen at the turn of the century as a threefold mission to serve himself, his pupils, and the world at large. What made Gurdjieff's survival through the economic depression of the thirties and the duration of WWII was, finally, his almost uncanny ability to draw upon the energies of others whose lives he touched, and to leave those people sincerely grateful for the value his presence added to their lives. Neither Toomer, Orage, Wright, Mabel Dodge Luhan, nor Anci Dupré completed their own lives without a deep sense of moral debt to Georgivanich.

---

[36] Patterson, *Ladies of the Rope*, p. 174.
[37] Moore, p. 283. It was Dupré's influence and money that provided Gurdjieff with means to protect a number of Jews. When Gurdjieff returned to New York in 1948, he said that all his French debt had been liquidated It is assumed (Patterson, p. 183) that Ouspensky's former group paid the debt, but it was Dupré's money once more. After Gurdjieff's death, Anci put forward the balance of funds demanded by Harcourt-Brace for the publication of *All and Everything*.

All & Everything Conference 2002

Bibliography

Anderson, Margaret. *The Unknowable Gurdjieff.* London: Routledge & Kegan Paul, 1962.
Bennett, John Godolphin. *Gurdjieff: Making a New World.* London: Turnstone, 1973.
Blum, John Morton, ed. *The Price of Vision: The Diary of Henry A. Wallace 1942-1946.* Boston: Houghton Mifflin, 1973
Daumal, René. *Correspondance.* 3 vols. Paris: Gallimard, 1996.
Decter, Jacqueline. *Nicholas Roerich, The Life and Art of a Russian Master.* London: Thames and Hudson, 1989.
Gill, Brendan. *Many Masks.* New York: Da Capo, 1998.
Kharitidi, Olga *Siberian Wisdom Discovered by a Russian Psychiatrist.* San Francisco: Harper, 1996.
Lowitt, Richard. *Bronson M. Cutting.* Albuquerque: University of New Mexico Press, 1992.
McCorkle, Beth. *The Gurdjieff Years 1929-1949: Recollections of Louise March.* Walworth, New York: The Work Study Association, 1990.
Moore, James. *Gurdjieff, a Biography: The Anatomy of a Myth.* Shaftesbury, Dorset: Element, 1991.
Peters, Fritz. *Boyhood With Gurdjieff.* London: Gollanz, 1964.
 - *Gurdjieff Remembered.* London: Gollanz, 1969.
Roerich, Nicholas. *Altai Himalaya.* Brookfell, CT: Arun Press, 1983 (with Introduction by Bragdon). (see www.roerich.org)
 - *Shambhala.* NY: Nicholas Roerich Museum, 1985.
 - *The Invincible.* NY: Nicholas Roerich Museum, 1974 (translated from the original 1936 Riga edition).
Edward L. and Frederick H. Schapsmeier, Edward L. and Frederick H.. *Henry A. Wallace of Iowa: The Agrarian Years, 1910-1940.* Ames: Iowa State UP, 1968
Webb, James. *The Harmonious Circle: The Lives and Works of G. I. Gurdjieff, P. D. Ouspensky and Their Followers.* London: Thames and Hudson, 1980.

© Copyright 2002 - Professor Paul Beekman Taylor - All Rights Reserved

Gurdjieff's Meetings and Non-Meetings with Remarkable and Unremarkable Men and Women 1935-1949 - Questions & Answers

Question: "From what you have said, many of the rumours we have read are somehow substantiated. What about the stories linking Gurdjieff with Hitler and Stalin?

Paul Taylor: These stories from Louis Pauwels' *The Dawn of the Magicians* and his anthology of essays on Gurdjieff have flooded web sites in the United States, but I have no idea where he got his information. He has since retracted most of these stories, like that of the Tibetan monks under Gurdjieff's influence who defended the Berlin bunker and so forth. The Stalin connection is more complex since good authority has located the common birthplace of Gurdjieff's mother and Stalin in Gori. Gurdjieff and his brother Dmitri may well have been considered by Stalin as members of his Georgian political clan. Since Gurdjieff does not allude to Stalin in *Tales*, but does treat Lenin and Trotsky negatively, it may be that he spares Stalin, but then again, Gurdjieff was writing before the Stalinist purges in the late twenties. It is clear that Stalin's daughter Svetlana, who married Wesley Peters, the husband earlier of Svetlana Hinzenberg and daughter of Olgivanna Wright, knew a good deal about Gurdjieff before she went into exile in the United States.

Question: You seem to characterize a number of people who turned their backs on Gurdjieff. Isn't true, however, that Gurdjieff, like other gurus, pushed pupils away from him after a while. He threw de Hartmann and de Salzmann out.

Paul Taylor: There are relative points of view on this point. I don't believe any one turned his back on Gurdjieff, but withdrew from serving as agents or representatives for raising money. Orage and Toomer withdrew from Gurdjieff after the Depression set in and people had less money to spare. After Orage left, few Americans visited the Prieuré. Both Orage and Toomer returned to their "ordinary lives," and this is what Gurdjieff had said pupils should so. Back in St. Petersburg, Gurdjieff vaunted his "system" as one that did not require withdrawal from the world. He wanted to train people to go out and teach. He wanted an American base for instruction.

Question: Why the United States?

Paul Taylor: I don't know exactly what he knew of the United States (which he called "America," the term I prefer also to use in this context). He could not teach in England for political reasons, and because Ouspensky had his groups there. He left Germany after a year or so because the political climate was growing unhealthy. He did find an American there, Rosemary Lilliard, who later married Stanley Nott, and she had important American connections. She was sponsored in Germany by Imogene Hogg, one of the richest persons in Houston and a leading sponsor of the arts, Texas, the daughter of "Big Jim" Hogg, former governor of Texas. Imogene visited Rosemary at the Prieuré in 1923, one of the first American visitors. Gurdjieff himself said that he went to America both to spread his ideas there and to take a tourist break from his hectic schedule of activities in France. But, I don't see where he rested.

Question: You said that Gurdjieff administered shock treatments in Paris. What kind of shock treatments?

Paul Taylor: Gurdjieff said in "The Material Question" that he had made money in Paris in 1922 and 1923 treating drug addiction and alcoholism, and he may have used electrical currents to alter bodily flows of energy. In "The Bokharian Dervish" he speaks of electricity in this fashion. Later, in 1935 to 1938 he used electricity and injections in his treatments. I don't know what kind of electrical machinery he used, but it is said that he designed it himself.

Question: You spoke of Gurdjieff's connections with Roerich. Was Roerich a pupil of Gurdjieff's?

Paul Taylor: He was not a pupil in the sense the term is used of those who were at the Prieuré. I don't know if we should trust the purge-trial testimony in the Soviet Union that identified Roerich, his wife and Mercourov as members of a Masonic Lodge in Central Asia in 1909. If true, however, then they were associates of a sort. There is evidence that Roerich listened to Orage in New York. Further, the route Roerich took to Central Asia follows very closely the lines Webb traces for Gurdjieff's journeys there, the one that leads north from Ceylon.

Question: Where did Gurdjieff "disappear to?" You said the Altai Mountains. Where are they?

Paul Taylor: I was referring to the range of mountains southeast of Novosibirsk, near Lake Baikal, in an area adjacent to Russian Buryat. Gurdjieff referred often to the fact that he had pupils still in that area as late as 1935.

Question: What about Ethel Merston?

Paul Taylor: All I know is that Ethel Merston went to India after the Prieuré closed, and she corresponded from there with Jessmin Howarth. Dushka Howarth has these letters in New York City.

Question: I find it difficult to understand, with all his power, why Gurdjieff had so much trouble with money.

Paul Taylor: I don't think he had "trouble" with money. He seemed always to be able to get what he needed. Even in the case of the loss of the Prieuré because of an unpaid coal bill, it might have been simply that Gurdjieff used that occasion to change directions. He raised a good deal of money between 1926 and 1929, and then the Depression limited amounts he could get from America. I never saw him express genuine anxiety about money. He never had any or he always had access to it. Money was a source of stories. It was a joke; the "dirty dollar question" was a symptom of a weakness in Western Civilization, and he was able to adjust to it, exploit it, master it, if you will. For example, when he came to America with melons in his baggage, and customs officials wanted to confiscate them. He told them that he was doing important agricultural research, and they let him pass. Gurdjieff seemed to enjoy the psychology of money, particularly in America.

Triads and Laws

Ana Fragomeni

I will talk about the Law of Three. My studies are based on Bennett's *Dramatic Universe II* (DU) and on Gurdjieff's *Beelzebub's Tales* (BT). That's not a definitive position, so I bring this for us to discuss here.

The first question of the Law of Three is why it is the second in BT - Gurdjieff say it is the second of the fundamental cosmic laws, and before he said it was the first. And I think that both these laws, they work together, but for us to study them, we need to separate them.

From our point of view, the Law of Three can be the second, because the Law of Seven for us is given, like a structure in time, and we must only know where the intervals are, in order to know when to act, but how to act is the work of the Law of Three.

The Law of Three consists of three independent forces and the process Harnelmiatznel. I first thought this part of the definition, on BT[1] was a redundancy, but it is not. It if necessary for us to remember if we are going down or up. By the same process, we can be going up or down.

---

[1] *Beelzebub's Tales*, vol II, p.343 (Chapter 39). "The higher blends with the lower in order to actualize the middle and thus becomes either higher for the preceding lower, or lower for the succeeding higher."

Triads and Laws

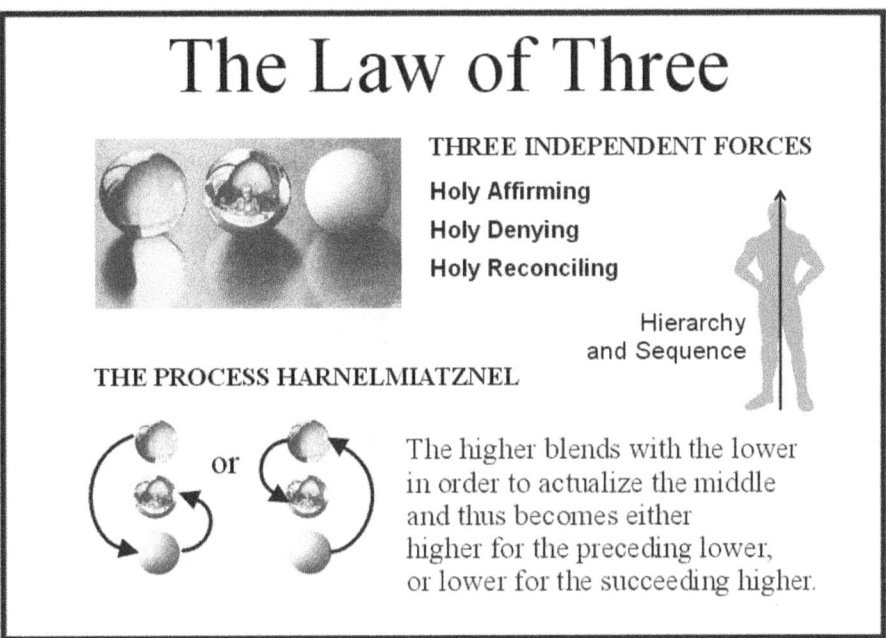

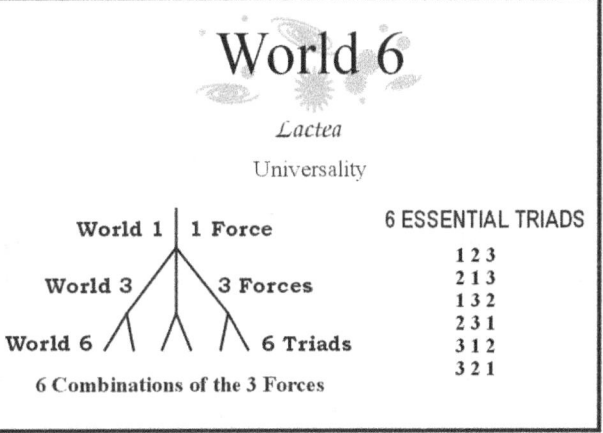

The Law of Three in higher worlds is very difficult for us to understand, because in Worlds 1 there is just one law: it is the mystery of the Holy Trinity, three forces in one, then, in World 3 they are separated and it is also difficult to understand. We begin to have some clues only in World 6, with the combination of the three forces, that forms six Essential triads.

All & Everything Conference 2002

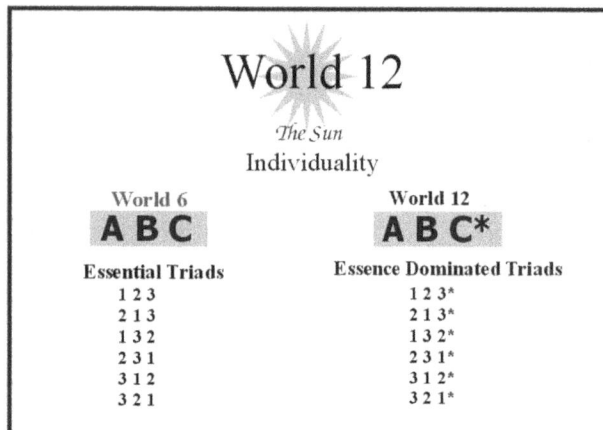

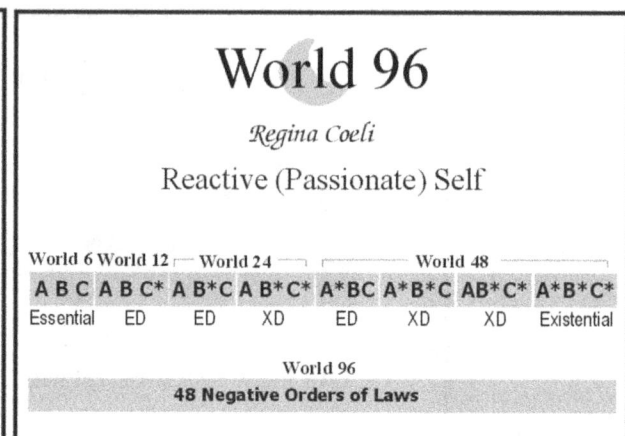

So, I need to present some of the worlds here because when we read in the books that talk about triads, they talk about these triads, but these are Essential triads, in the level of Lactea, not on our level.

We have no Essential forces. We do not use these forces because from World 6 below, when there begin the laws of the Sun, each world emanates its own forces, so at each world that is created the laws are duplicated. Another thing: triads are laws. And not only this: they are orders of laws, many laws.

I show here the World 12, because here there some forces become Existential forces. So, these new triads are not completely essential, but only Essence Dominated, because the results of the acts of the Sun enter Existence and begin to be limited by existence conditions.

We finish here in the World 96, where we see the 48 laws of the Earth - that is called "Mixtus Orbis" in the Ray of Creation because of the balance, a mixture, between Essential and Existential laws. Continuing the have its 48 laws and then the Moon duplicates it with 48 negative orders of laws.

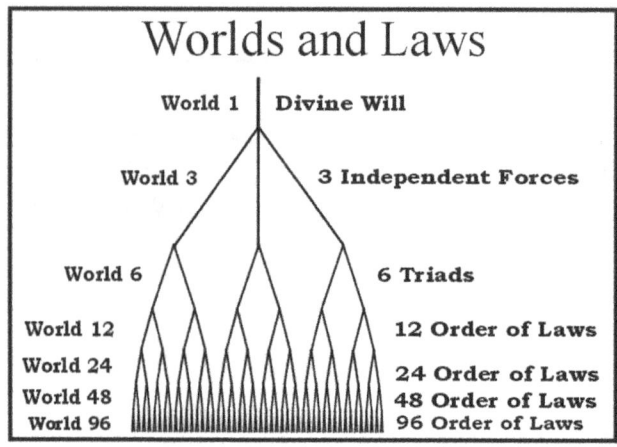

With so many laws, we may think we live in a deterministic universe. Even Einstein, at the beginning, he didn't accept the quantum mechanics and uncertainty principle, because he didn't want to accept that the electron could goes where it wants. Even the electron has some limited will. Everything has some will.

Einstein asked if God played dice. And I say that He does, and the electron also.

It is interesting, because dice have six faces, like the prototype triads. We can study the six triads and make the compensation to understand the laws where we live. But in life we don't play dice, exactly, we play chess. Life is a strategic game, a heuristic game, like chess. At each move you must make your choice and, maintaining your aim, and change or adapt your strategy at each moment.

That's why it is so important for us to learn the rules, to know how to play.

"The road to hell is paved with good intentions." If we don't know we cannot help anyone.

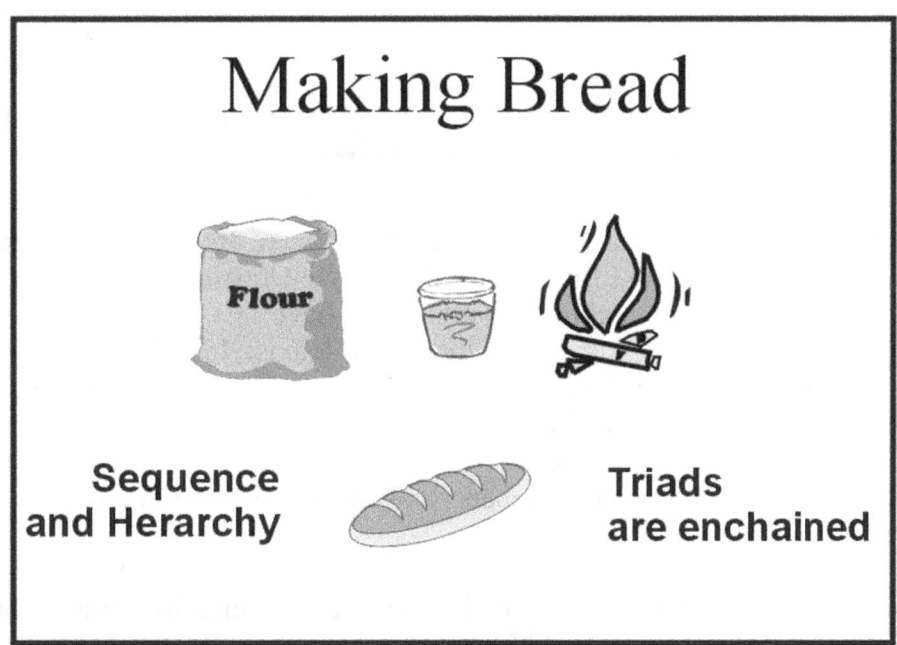

This is a triad Gurdjieff liked to teach. He talked a lot about this in his books: making bread. First of all, we see that there is a sequence: we cannot put water in the fire and then the flour; and we cannot put fire in the flour then the water. We must follow the right sequence. If we don't begin with the right force, the result will be probably the contrary.

And there is hierarchy also: the flour commands the triad. Beginning with the quantity and quality of the four, I must adjust the water and the fire. This is a denying force, a resistance force, but it is commanding the triad. All triad that goes up begins with the denying force. That is why the first element is so important in the triad. How to begin - see the yellow paper I distributed[2].

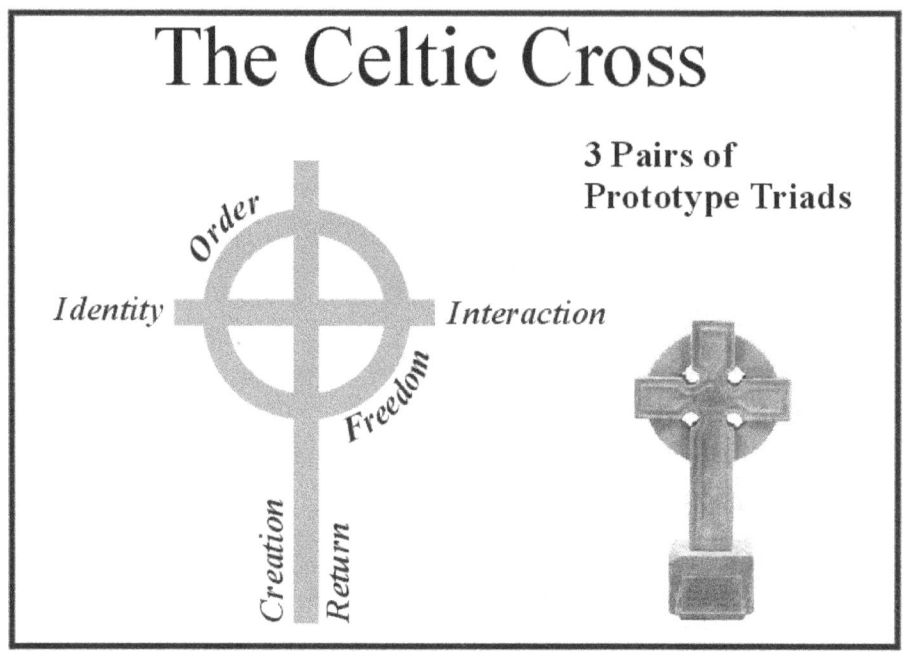

This is the way I like to study the triads: **the Celtic Cross**. There are a lot of ways to study them. I prefer two pairs of prototype triads. I find this symbol very interesting, an ancient knowledge. The Celtic, roman, gothic and orthodox churches, almost all have this cross. We have here the two fundamental triads: Creation and Return, in the vertical axis; Identity and Interaction in the horizontal axis, and order and Freedom, that make a movement contraclockwise and clockwise. The names of the triads, we can discuss later.

Here we have the correspondence with numbers: 1 as the Affirmative Force, 2 the Passive Force and 3 the Reconciling Force.

This approach is according the position of the Reconciling Impulse. When the Reconciling Impulse is at the last position, I call them Metabolic Triads; these are the fundamental triads. We will discuss this in the following transparencies. Existential triads are in the horizontal axis, where the two opposite forces 1 and 2 are not in direct contact, so they need a mediator. And

---

[2] *Beelzebub's Tales*, Chapter 1, p.4. "However that may be, I begin... But begin with what? Oh, THE DEVIL! Will there indeed be repeated that same exceedingly unpleasant and highly strange sensation which it befell me to experience when about THREE WEEKS ago I was composing in my thoughts the SCHEME AND SEQUENCE of the ideas destined by me for publication and did not know then how to begin either?"

Triads and Laws

Transcendental triads are when the Reconciling Impulse begins and commands the triad - these are a kind of magic triads. Now we will see the three pairs.

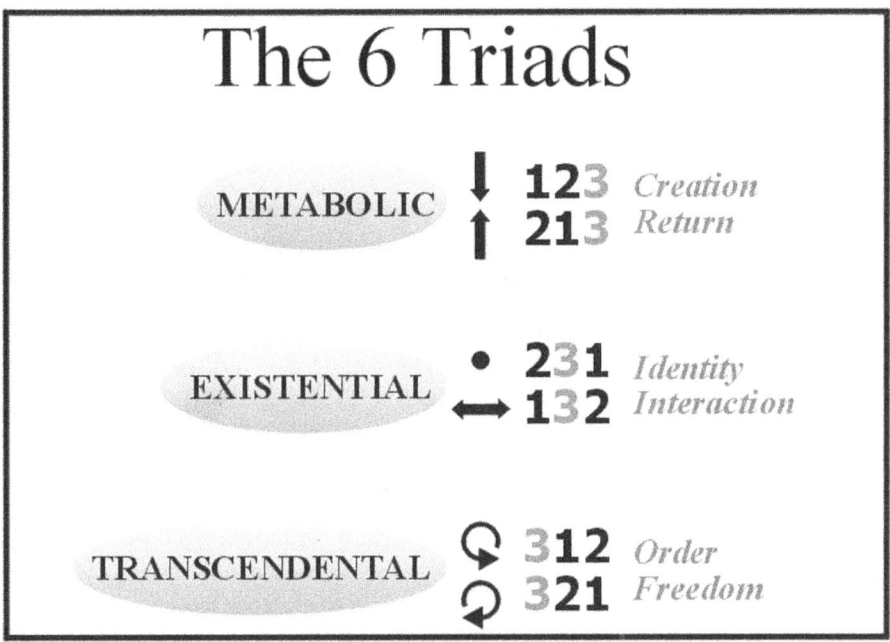

These I call Metabolic triads because they are about exchange of energy. This one (Creation 123) transforms pure energy or power in matter, and the other (Return 213) transforms matter in energy, coming back.

(Creation 123) This is like the Second Law of Thermodynamics: here the entropy increases. At the top we can say we have God, and at the bottom, we can say we have God, also, and in the middle we have another God. Do you remember the prayer in BT?[3]: *"Holy God, Holy Firm, Holy Immortal, Have mercy on us"*?

We can say also that her (the top) is God and here (the bottom) is Devil. Here is Affirmation, and here Denying. Only Denying, the Devil, pushes us up. God has a big force, and pushes everything down. BT is to push us up, to send us up to God.

When Gurdjieff says, *"Begin with what?"* - It is very important to know how to begin - he says begin with *"Oh, the devil!"*

Here, we have an asymmetry, because this triad down is very, very strong and is the natural process and the natural preference of Nature. If I do nothing, and I just stand still, Nature puts me

---

[3] *Beelzebub's Tales*, vol II, p. 344 (Chapter 39).

down. Just to be here, I must make some effort, a lot of effort. This (Creation 123) is the natural and automatic triad. Everything, left to itself, goes down, like the Ray of Creation.

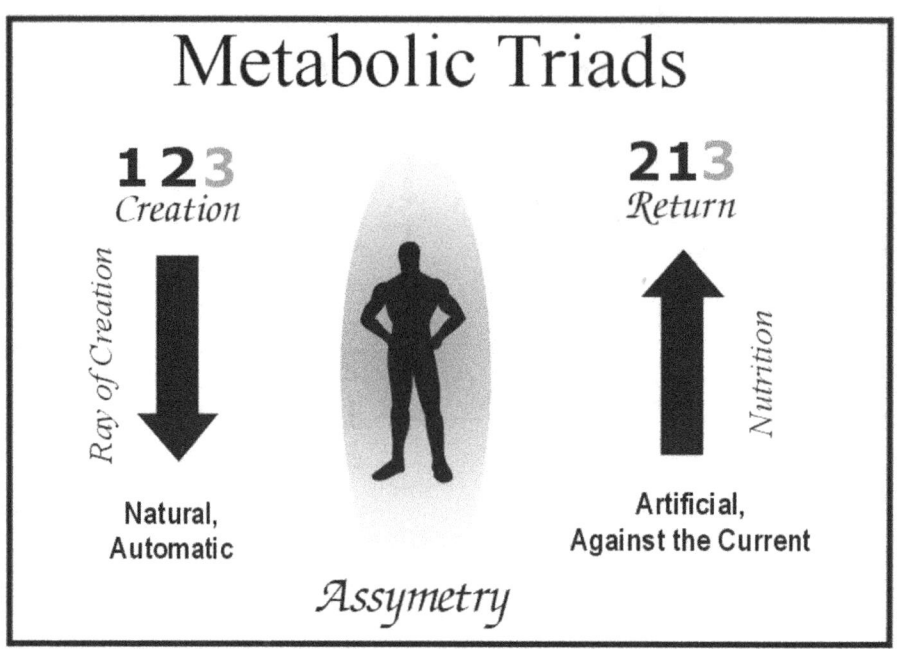

Nutrition (Return 213) is the mechanism, the device His Endlessness put in the world, when he changed the laws, to make us want to go up, by the needs. So by the needs of food - we must strive to get everyday, three or four times a day - we must remember ourselves at least on these occasions. I have needs, so I exist. If I did not have I could forget. So, I think needs are the device to push us up.

On the horizontal axis are the triads balanced by inside. The first, Identity (231) - the name Bennett uses, and he explains it very well in his book - is like thinghood, just to be. This table, just to be, is making an effort; all its atoms are shaking and dynamically moving to make this table be. And also, it has (the table) a dependence from the context. This is a table because it has a size and a scale that is useful for me, a "usefulness". A stone could be a table here, and a stone could not be a table in another environment and conditions. So, that is a dependence.

And now, Interaction (132). It is interesting, that these triads, I think, are like "Love thy neighbour as thyself". It is interesting also that if I can lift some weight with one hand, with the two hands together I can lift more than the double. If we are two persons together, we can bear too much more than the double than one person alone. So it is very important this interaction.

Triads and Laws

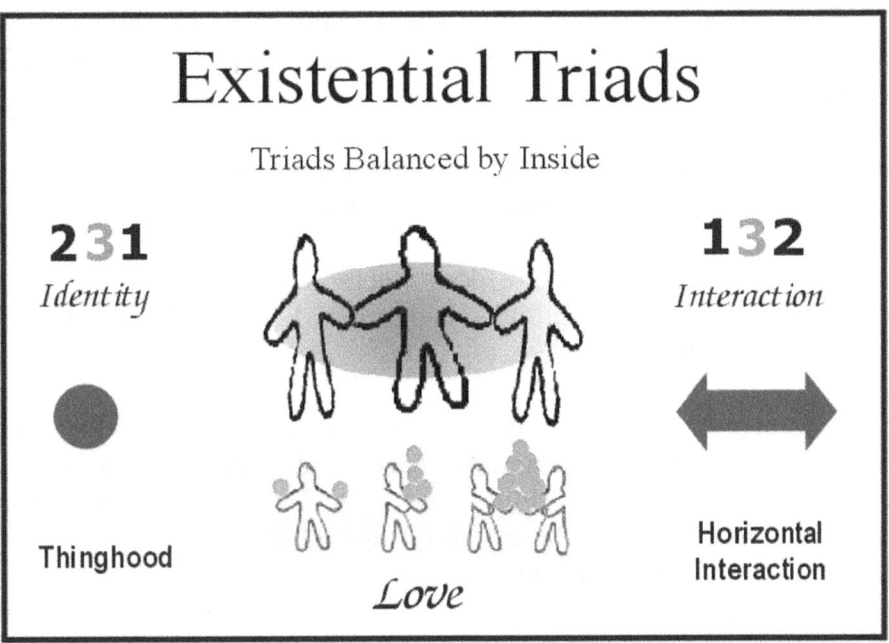

About the Transcendental triads, one triad (Order 312) looks for keep order, keep everything as it is. It is forbidden to change; it is very difficult to change, because this triad is very powerful, like Creation (123). So, Nature does this. If someone wants to make something different, like coming to this Conference, his hard-drive will crash and his telephone line will go off, he will find all kind of difficulty to be different and to change.

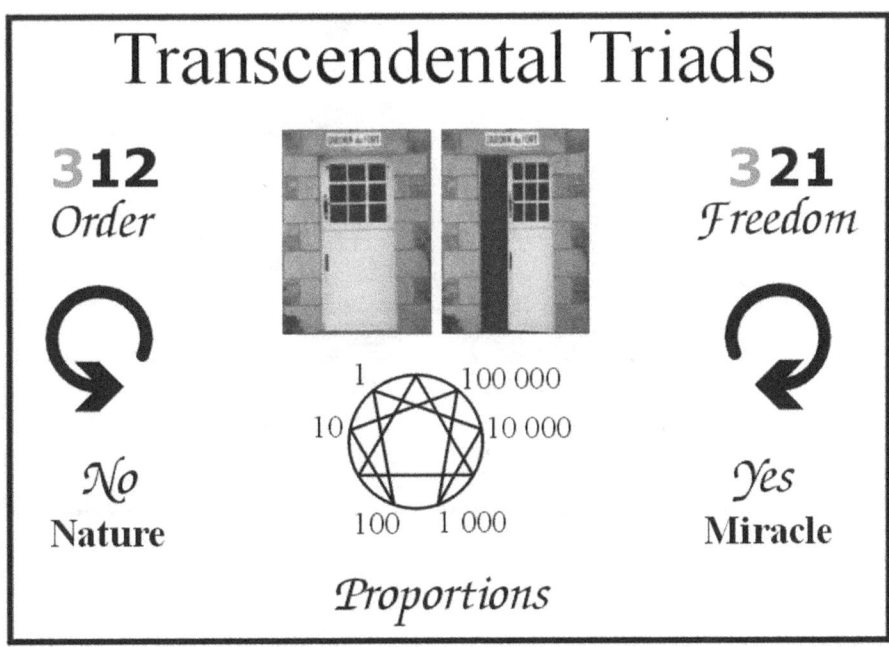

All & Everything Conference 2002

This triad (Order 312) works with masses of people, and this triad Freedom (321) is an individual triad. Only individual or small groups can pass trough this triad. Bennett said that Freedom "is the door God left opened" - I find this beautiful.

This has something to do with proportions, because these two laws are the regulators of the movement of the universe, basically, the movement of energy.

If everything is going too much down, Freedom enters and provides some help. If Freedom is freeing so much people, Order comes and puts them down. So, if we begin a Gurdjieff group with 100,000 people at the end it will be just one.

But it is interesting in everything in life, because if you see, an orchestra, for example, have only one maestro, but needs lot of musicians, a lot of teachers for these musicians, and a lot of people to hear the music, and a lot of people to build the theatre, and one architect to plan the building. So, if for an orchestra, at one moment, there are two or three maestros, two won't succeed because there's only place for one. They can be very good, but that's an accounting, and it is forbidden to have more than one at that place. So, we see, Christ said he was the vine and we were the branches[4]. The tree is more important than the branches. Sometimes we think of ourselves as important, but the important is the whole.

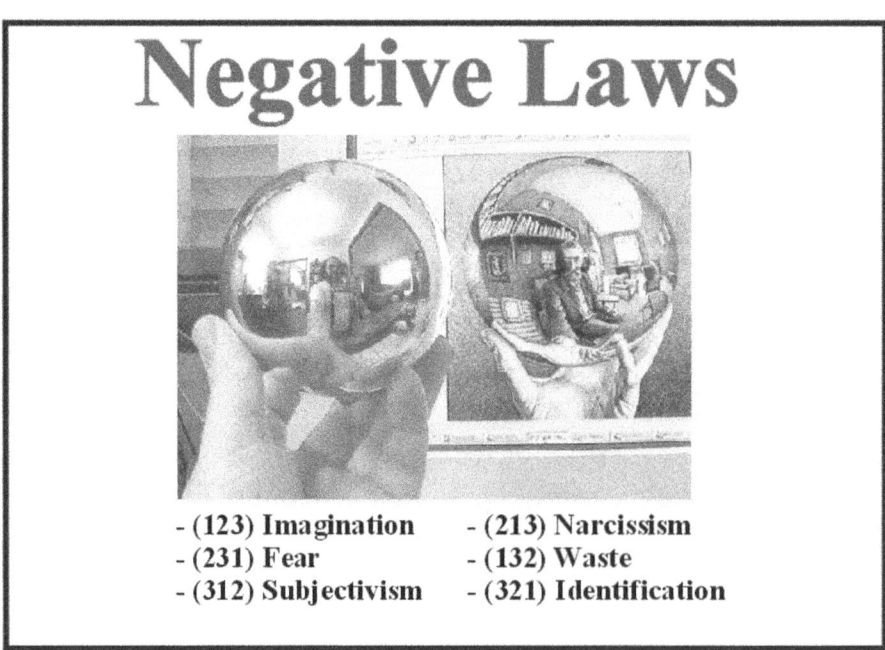

---

[4] John 15, 5. "I am the vine, ye are the branches: He that abideth in me, and I in him, the same bringeth forth much fruit: for without me ye can do nothing."

As I said about the laws, that are existential forces working, sometimes these laws appear in our life, but there are not that magical forces come from above; they can be from below, or from myself and be not so magic at all.

In practice, in our life, I think that the most important about the laws is to learn about the negative laws. Here, not only existential forces come to work, limited by existence, and we don't know how to distinguish between them, but also even the whole triad of Creation can be imagination, only imagination. A triad may be Waste, identification...

As an example, how can we domesticate an elephant? We take the baby elephant and tie him to a small wooden pole, with a rope. He tries to free himself, and he cannot. He tries again, and again and again. Then he gives up. He doesn't try anymore. He grows up, he becomes very strong, but at the circus the elephants are tied to a small pole, and they don't try to escape.

Paul says in Corinthians 1: *"When I was a child"* [5], I used to speak like a child, but now I am not a child anymore... And a lot of times we react to things that happened to us when we were a child; we forget that we change, situations change and the laws change, so from certain laws it is very easy to be free.

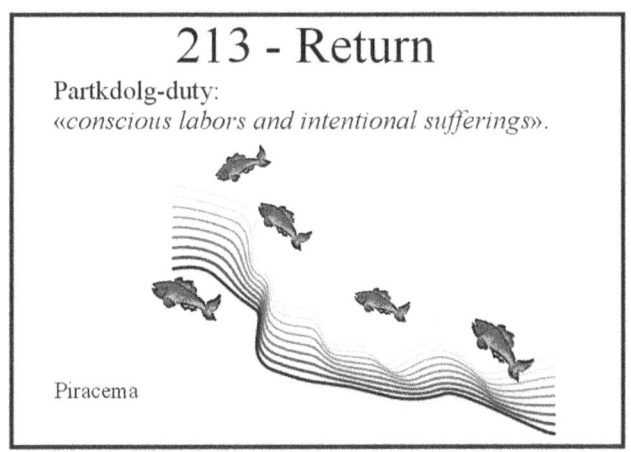

Now, I think that the most important triad is the Return (213). Bennett calls it Evolution. The most difficult thing in this study is the words. You see, Darwin talks about "human evolution". When the stars create the elements and the red giant blows up. Scientists call this "stars evolution". But it is not, it is "involution" (123), because energy is becoming matter." So, I prefer to say "Return".

Fish in the river, must make effort just to stay in the river. To maintain their species, they must swim against the current, to the head of the river, to put their eggs. In Brazil we call this "Piracema" - I don't know how to say this in English. So, like in Piracema, in the Bible Jacob wrestled God, and have his name changed to Israel, because he had changed. That is what we must do: to fight with God - although it sounds very strange.

---

[5] 1 Corinthians 13, 11. "When I was a child, I spake as a child, I understood as a child, I thought as a child: but when I became a man, I put away childish things."

All & Everything Conference 2002

I like these two enneagrams side by side. In reality, they should be superposed, because the things go all together; all the laws are here. Creation and Interaction, and Freedom and everything are here. I think these two examples are very important for us to know.

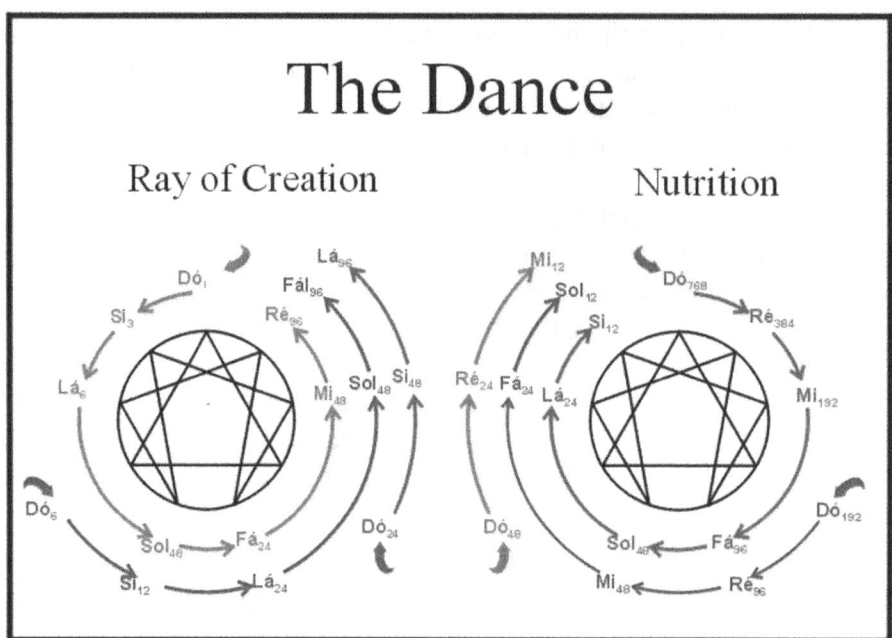

We call this one (SS) Order (312), the counterclockwise law. The name is very difficult to understand. I discussed this name with Nick Tereshchenko, I wanted to change it with Nature, but he didn't agree easily, so I continued to call this triad like Bennett did in *Dramatic Universe*.[6] Nick said me that Bennett in former works used these names on the contrary, calling 312 Freedom and order 321, but the last was *Dramatic Universe*. That's why I think we must not to attach ourselves too much on words, and it is better to work with symbols.

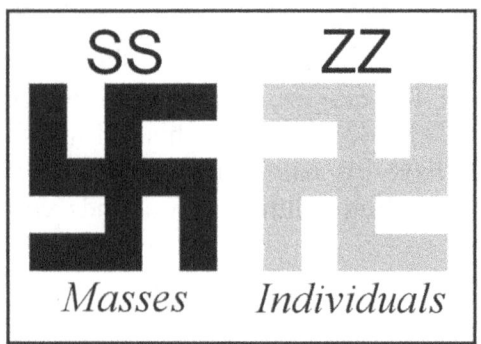

We can notice that Hitler's swastika was an "SS"[7], counterclockwise. This deals with masses. I used to ask myself why Lenin, with all his charm, everybody liked him, like everybody liked Hitler at the beginning, and Mussolini too, why didn't they put their charisma at work for a constructive aims, to make good things? Why didn't they say to people: "Go to agriculture, go to your houses and work for everybody"? - Because it is impossible.

---

[6] *Dramatic Universe,* vol II.
[7] The Schutzstaffel.

Triads and Laws

If you have a group of adolescents and say to them: "Put fire on a house!" they like it and they do it. But if you say: "Let's build a house!" they would say: "Oh, no, I am tired now…" because everything that goes up requires a lot of effort. And I see my major sin, laziness, is the major for almost everybody, because we don't want to make effort.

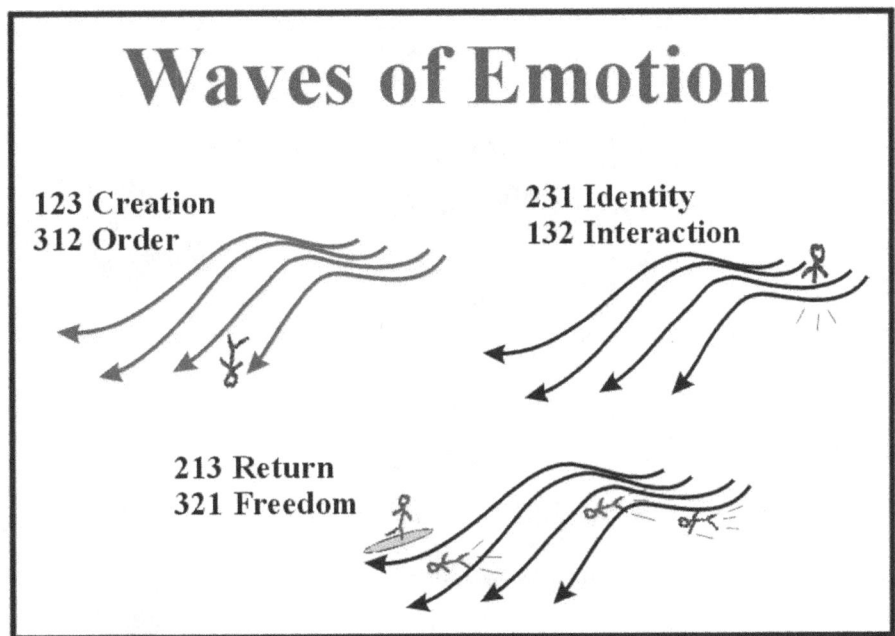

Well, to build a house you must do this movement (clockwise), and each individual brick must have some part of consciousness.

There are three ways we deal with emotions, in an analogy with the waves on the sea. If you do nothing, no effort, the waves carry you down. The emotion can be anger, impulsiveness. You see that Affirmation is here (123, 312) and Affirmation is submitting the other impulses. When Affirmation comes first it pushes things down. If you say to your children: "You must study, because I want you to study", they would do study. They must recognize that they NEED to study. Study is a triad like Nutrition (213) that refines energies.

The other situation is when I strive to stay with my head out of the water. It is very difficult already. So, I make a lot of effort and I stay at the same place, but it is better than going with the impulsive emotion. Because this emotion can be love, also - "I love you and I want to help you!" - but I am ignorant; I don't know anything, so I will only disturb you. My love is not a pure one, for I am contaminated by existence, so it is not good.

And the third example is when I stop, and then I act, and I learn how to use the force of emotion and I can swim or surf in the emotion. For example, it is very strong the force of anger - when I want to do something difficult, I can call my anger, I must be angry with that disorder, to put order on it. So, anger can be very useful, if I don't let it have me.

To finish, as we want to achieve Freedom, we can make an analogy with Robotics, be compared with tools and robots.

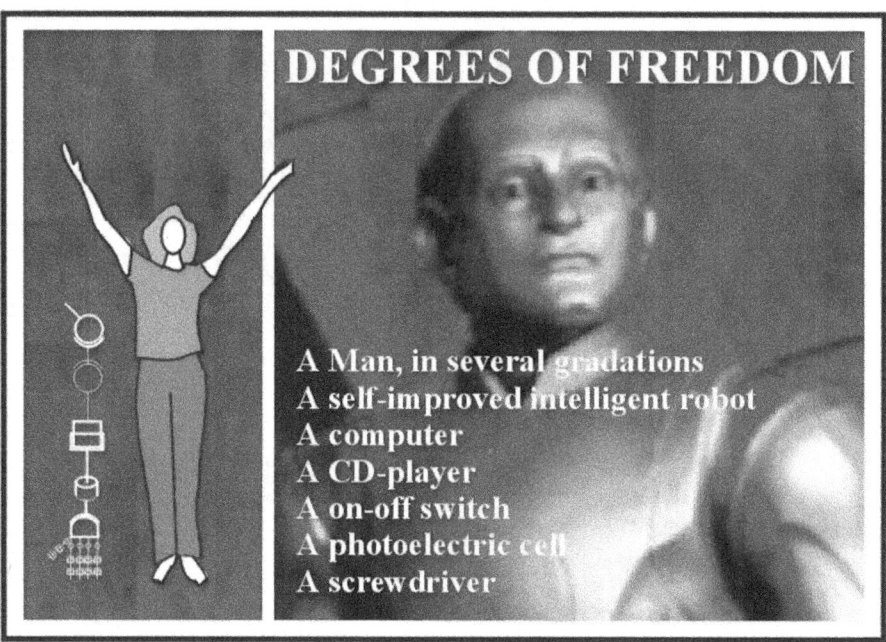

First of all, we can be a screwdriver, a tool for anyone, then we can be a photoelectric cell, that only recognizes one aspect, light. An on-off switch, that only answers with two reactions. Then we can be a CD-player - like I am being now… Then, we can be a computer and think that we think. Or we can be a self-improved intelligent robot, but not yet a man.

Then, when we begin to be a man, there are several gradations. And here is interesting, because in robotics and industrial automation, good robots must have only six degrees of freedom. And an arm is a good robot. Sometimes, you see, the finger, it has one degree of freedom, but it think it is free, then all the fingers think they are free, but the hand carries them. Then the wrist carries the hand, the elbow carries the shoulder and the shoulder carries them all. But "I" carry the shoulder, it is the same with us; a lot of times we think we are free and we are not.

I think it is this, and I thank you for listening.

© Copyright 2002 - Ana Fragomeni - All Rights Reserved

Triads and Laws - Questions & Answers

Questioner 1: I want you please to explain the difference between how you see what you said as existential from essential. I want you to explain why the six triads of existential are doubled again as six triads of essential. And I want you to tell the difference between the six triads from what you call the negative triads.

Ana Fragomeni: I don't know... Not very well. Well, I think that at the level of the galaxy there is pure Will. The Will of God is different from ours. And from the sun and from the planets. So, I have a kind of Will that is contaminated by existence. When I have this body, I have some kind of will or desire, and if I had not this body I would not have this kind of Will, that is not needed in higher levels, but here I need this. So, I think there is a gradation of Will. And the negative laws...

Questioner 1: So, on the side of essence you think that Will is more pure.

Ana Fragomeni: Yes. I think the Will down is more "dirty", not so pure. It is existence, not so bad, in a moral judgement, but we are more separated. So, my Will is something for ME, separated from YOU, and this not good for the universe as a whole. The moment when I am separated, I am contaminated by existence. Gurdjieff said that we can only judge the whole if we pick three worlds at the same time. We live in three worlds, at least, because we have three kinds of food, three kinds of bodies, even if not completed, but I cannot judge separately my earthly body, my material body.

And about the negative laws, I don't understand exactly the theory, but in practice, I see it is like the problem of the elephant. If you domesticate a flea, you put it in a bottle and close the bottle. It wants go get out of the bottle and jumps but cannot free itself. It begins to jump lower and lower, so you can open the bottle and it will not get out ever more.

So, in practice I see negative laws only like imagination. Internal consideration, for example, I think that you think... only imagination. Identification: sometimes I study the triads so much that I become the triads, then I think I am Bennett... imagination ... I must stop this.

Questioner 1: Why are your laws of existence different from the negative laws? I see that existence has a negativity and essence...

Ana Fragomeni: No, no! I don't think as existence as negative. Existence is real, but negative laws are not real. If I imagine something, it is like a mirror. You saw the picture here for the negative laws - that is an image on a mirror - it is the contrary of the real. I think that something exists, but it does not exist. Even the worlds closest to us are mirrors. We must put away the mirrors, to find the real.

Questioner 2: I am quite familiar with Bennett, but I have an insoluble difficulty. If you take, for example... (tape inaudible) in 213... Can you translate the numbers into a situation to make us understand what is a triad and what is not?

Ana Fragomeni: Yes. It is difficult, I think, because, first because of the words - the "words", not the "worlds"... One, two, three - we say it in numbers. We can make analogies, but these are dangerous also. I can say that 123 is "the male, the female and the child". But it is not always like this. We can say that man is the Affirmative force and woman the Denying force, but it is a symbolism, because I can be more affirmative than you in some situations. But it is interesting this triad Creation: with pure forces it creates things in the world. If I have a child, I am passive, receptive to the affirming power, but it is God that is creating the child, not me; I am just a tool, a passive tool for the child to be born. Nobody here knows how to make a child. Here, 213: this is like Nutrition and like Studying. Here (Creation 123): the thing that is produced is less intelligent than the one that have the Will. And here (Return 213): I produce more intelligent things. Creation is the Nature's preference: by photosynthesis the plants, with the help of light, make a potato, that is less intelligent than light. Than, in this triad (Return 213) I eat the potato, that is matter, and I make en effort with my organism and I transform the potato into feelings and thoughts, so I am elevating the level of that matter.

But no triad works alone, they are always in chains. So, when you see, for instance, Darwin "evolution" and "selection" of species, that is not one triad that is making this: there are a lot of triads playing together, all triads, essential and existential triads playing together. Even to eat a potato, in my organism, a lot of triads work, enchained. I am showing a great simplification, but we must begin with a few things that fit our head, than go through complication. Bennett explains all this very well in *Dramatic Universe*, but I read first *Deeper Man*, were he talks a lot of "father, mother and child", and this way is very difficult. More difficult is to study the Holy Trinity, mixing the analogies: where is the woman, who is the Holy Ghost? So, it is better to study with numbers. Did you receive these papers? In the green paper we have Napoleon, a powerful leader, saying that by force we cannot get anything good - it is historical. The leaders that used force, like Hitler, Mussolini and Lenin, had put everything down. And the leaders that pushed up, like the Dalai-Lama, Gurdjieff, Christ, were individuals with few followers - and they suffered a lot. But people under Hitler suffered a lot also. Everybody suffer, but if you choose the good suffering you pay before and the result is better.

Questioner 3: Interesting, when you talk about the powerful ... (tape inaudible) in travels he took with him a (tape inaudible) the symbol of the Sarmoung, the sun connection ... (tape inaudible). For example, he organized for the ... (tape inaudible) ... ancient Egypt - and not in accordance with history.

The other thing is on the living triads... When he told about the three forces, active, passive - and you use the term negative, I like to use the term "enabling" force. And the other though it that we need to recognize as you work down trough the Ray of Creation trough the universe, is comes unto the Second Law or Thermodynamics, in which everything goes downhill from up to lower levels. Once you get a living material, a living cell, a living organism, it goes against the Second Law or Thermodynamics. And it comes that you cannot go uphill, and this is why they need an interacting system. There are these two aspects: the living and the non-living, that interact with one another.

Ana Fragomeni: Thank you very much; I forgot one transparency.

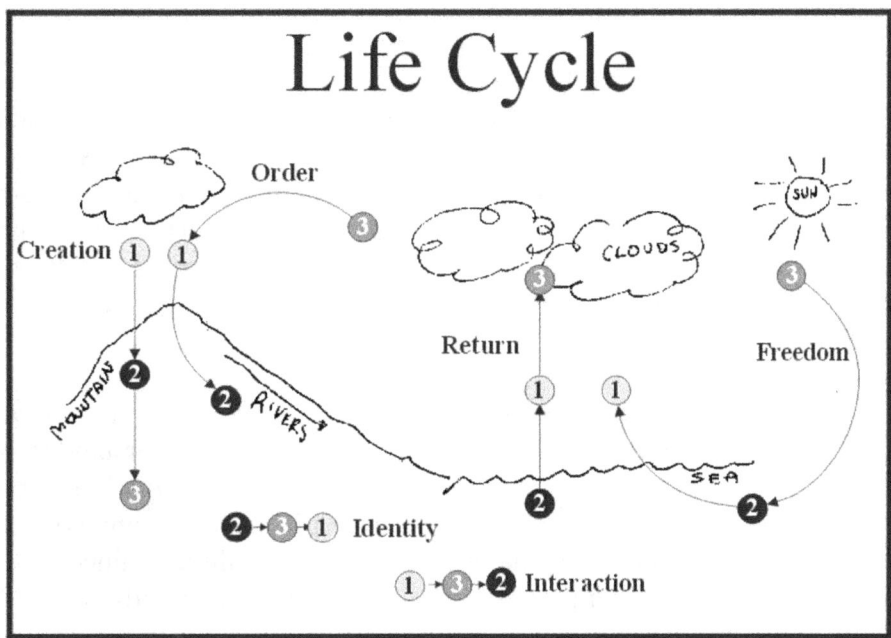

Here you see that for the clouds to drop in rain, it is easy, and the water goes down in the rivers to the sea. The second Law of Thermodynamics says that any isolated system, left by its own, goes down, to complexity and to disorder, increasing entropy. It is easy for the water to go down, but if I wish to push the water up, it is very, very difficult. Another thing that is very important and I have forgotten is the Return, 213, always leaves a waste. It is not possible that everybody go up at the same time, so there is a recycling. Here there is the Identity (231) of the molecules of water in the sea and the Interaction (132) between them. And to come back, there is need for help from outside. Always, to return, we need help from outside.

That's why the laws were changed to make this union. We cannot go up without help from another system: I cannot help myself - it is the law.

So, I thank you very much for remembering this.

Seminar 1 - Chapters 8, 9 & 10 of Beelzebub's Tales to His Grandson

Facilitator: Keith Buzzell

Facilitator: In "The Arousing of Thought" Gurdjieff emphasizes that he is going to speak to both our waking consciousness and the subconscious. In part he does this by his 'sensation picturings', images that enter and influence each of our three brains. Here in chapters 8, 9 and 10 we have, among other things, slimy slugs, planetary tremors, asphyxiating sticks, and catastrophic bursting planets… We also have miscalculations, possibilities and 'glories to chance'. We have peculiarities and queerness; we have pictures of other beings, of ravens and of three brained beings with tails and hoofs. What do we make of these 'sensation picturings' and this abundance of ideas? Who would like to begin?

Participant 1: I'd like to begin. Look at the title of the book, *An Objectively Impartial Criticism of the Life of Man*. It is actually the primary title of his book as far as I understand it, because he puts that before '*Beelzebub's Tales to His Grandson*', after '*All and Everything*'. The book is rife with criticisms which most people have thought about but haven't blessed. Somehow we assume, or I assume, as a human being, that I am in the natural state of what a three brained being would sound like, what he would look like. If I simply look at the book as a space odyssey, - then here's this traveller, these travellers, and he is going to speak to Hassein about these strange three-brained beings that have taken his fancy and it's obvious that he would naturally see us as having a slimy epidermis. So I simply want to speak to that in a general way without getting into any subtleties right now. If someone were coming and visiting this planet, or viewing from the planet Mars, maybe somebody from the star system Sirius might very well look at us very strange three-brained beings and call us slugs simply because of how we appear to them.

Participant 2: That reminds me of the film E.T. E.T. is in the cupboard and the young girl opens the cupboard. E.T. screams.

Participant 3: The reference to the slugs appears in another chapter before, and I can't quite remember the context which creates and uses it, because Hassein asks him, 'what about those slugs that you mentioned' and in the book, in a previous chapter, Gurdjieff talks about the slugs.

Participant 4: With this expression, 'slugs', Gurdjieff also puts a very heavy weight on his relationship with humanity, so to speak. 'I call you slugs'. On the one hand, as Sy said, he expressed criticism that many people thought of expressing but didn't. When one grows up, in no matter what country, often I suppose he has the feeling of disgust with the way society is set up. So in a way, I think also that slugs are just an expression of this vehement position against that, the

Seminar 1 - Chapters 3, 4 & 5 of Beelzebub's Tales to His Grandson

way things are. At the same time whoever reads a book by somebody called Gurdjieff and comes across this expression in the very first chapter, it's as if this heavy weight that Gurdjieff puts in his relationship with mankind hits him in a negative way. So Gurdjieff has distanced himself, in a way, making it impossible to be accepted by mass culture. I suppose that would be a mistrusting of Gurdjieff. I'm talking about the main culture again, the main culture mistrusting Gurdjieff. It has to do with this slug expression in that particular chapter and whatever is entailed throughout the book, this book as criticism, because in a way all the criticism kind of hangs from there, emanating from this expression. It is a very strange thing for me if I see myself as being part of humanity, so to speak, it puts me in a very strange light. I think that society is unacceptable but on the other hand what do I do, it's as if I have to keep Gurdjieff a secret in my life. I don't know if you understand what I'm talking about. If I ever try to speak with people about Gurdjieff, then the question will come very often, very soon, 'How do you place yourself against this kind of characterization of humanity'?

Participant 2: My impression when I read this is, what is a slug and a slug after all is pretty much a digestive tract, it just kind of moves along and it eats, digests some of what it eats to just be able to exist and then it eliminates. A little bit further on when Gurdjieff says, Beelzebub laughed and he said surely, 'you are surely asking about those beings who breed on the planet Earth and who call themselves men'. So it seems it was a pretty accurate picture that Hassein picked up from what his grandfather was telling him about these three-brained beings on the planet Earth. We call ourselves men, but in fact all we do is maintain our physical existence and that's it. But the possibilities are so much greater. That is how I understood it.

Participant 3: The reference to slimy beings is in Chapter three where he is talking about different qualities of beings on the other planets, then he says, "on the just-mentioned planet Earth also Three-Brained-Beings are formed and they also contain all the data for coating higher being bodies in themselves, but the "strength of spirit" they do not begin to compare with beings breeding on the little planet aforementioned. The external coatings of the three-brained beings of that planet Earth closely resemble our own, only, first of all, their skin is a little slimier than ours, and then, secondly, they have no tail" and they even wear boots etc., etc. That is the reference which Hassein picks up. He picks it up and describes men as slugs.

Participant 6: I may have missed something. I would be interested in the three most important ideas in these three chapters, which I may be wrong about, but slugs doesn't seem to me to be the most important; which are the formation of the moon and Anulios, no small matter. The Ilnosoparnian process to enable the formation of Askokin to help the moon, (no small matter) and the nature of Kundabuffer, or the establishment of the nature of Kundabuffer. It's fascinating that the humanities already divert us from the key issues.

Participant 4: Do you think it's a small issue? I think it's a very big issue, what kind of relationship that humanity has with Gurdjieff and how people see Gurdjieff.

Participant 6: I was touched by it and I looked up in Purgatory where he talks about the fifth Stopinder, the possibility came of Tetartocosmoses moving about and this description which has always seemed to be like a slug. I never related it to the earlier part but I do find it very interesting, because for me a very important moment is when he writes that the Common Father could use these Tetartocosmoses, make use of it, for help in administration of the enlarging world. This image of something tactile, I'm trying to speak to another part of us, and that set me on to it, and so of course the three mentioned subjects are very important but I think also being a slug on the planet actually might not be less in significance. It might be a very big thing to be able to move and this is maybe one of the important qualities of an individual. We may not think very highly of slugs but... So I just wanted to come up with this (from BT):

"Without constant individual tension the possibility appeared of the independent automatic moving from one place to another on the surface of the given planet."

Facilitator: If you follow the syntax of the sentence, at least as I understand it, what Endlessness is seeing as a possibility of making use of is not the being but the capacity for automatic independent motion. It is the *motion* that he suddenly sees, not the being, not the creature. To me that's a really important thing, 'automatic independent motion'. It raises all manner of questions related to Heropass.

Participant 7: If this were my first reading, of just these three chapters, the whole issue of slugs he kind of lets that go by and, for me, in that first chapter, what made an impression was Beelzebub taking the opportunity to point out some of the aspects of what kind of observation it takes to draw some objective conclusions about these people. This pretty much boils down to what knowing entails. Gurdjieff takes the context, the origin, sustained in intimate impartial observation and actual involvement with his descents. Mostly he tells Hassein in this chapter about how he has come to know them so well in this respect. Because in the next two chapters that follow he didn't cover this slug thing, in respect of taking these three chapters as a unit, that didn't seem to be the primary thing, but he uses it as an opportunity to say how he came to know that.

Participant 8: Toward the end of our readings for today, page 91, he's starting on one of his big duties, about the 3rd or 4th paragraph down. He's observed these things which were never done by three-brained beings on other planets, namely they would "suddenly, without rhyme or reason begin destroying one another's existence". Which is, of course, repeated in most chapters of the book, reciprocal destruction. In all these early chapters he plants ideas; he doesn't necessarily develop each idea. Chris brought up a lot of things that obviously are not all developed.

Participant 9: To me it's an important idea in these three chapters that you just brought up, mainly that they suddenly without rhyme or reason begin destroying one another's existence. The only planet in the whole of the universe to behave in this manner, because of Kundabuffer and properties associated with that. How is it that you understand this - do we tackle such big ideas here?

Seminar 1 - Chapters 3, 4 & 5 of Beelzebub's Tales to His Grandson

Facilitator: It may be of some importance if we also note here how he introduces reciprocal destruction. What is the explanation that Beelzebub gives for this very strange phenomena? What is the explanation that he offers first? How does he explain it?

Participant 9: That the population was increasing?

Participant 4: These properties must be given to the organ Kundabuffer. That's the only explanation that he can give to himself at that stage. Later, he gets quite a lot of ideas.

Facilitator: He aligns it directly with some high law - that this was inevitably a requirement within the cosmic order. That's how he sees it there.

Participant 10: ...seeing reality topsy turvy or how you say it 'upside-down'?

Facilitator: This is very early, it is perhaps important to see that as, we will find out in respect to Askokin, there is this mention we come upon here but he does not speak about Abrustdonis and Helkdonis until 'Form and Sequence' - nearly the end of the book. And then he takes it up in detail. I think it's important that here we have a representation that infers what Askokin is and what it's going to do but it isn't taken up until much later. And he admits it. That's my point. He mentions that 'I did not understand this for a very long time, I only recently learned in detail about it.' There's an inference here that something similar that's going on with respect to the understanding of why these peculiar beings suddenly begin destroying each other. He looks at that and says it must be a simple unfolding of the law. That's the level of understanding he has then. Not what comes later but what is here first. Chris asked the question of what kind of being is a slug and I think this is something useful to at least pause on. Slugs are one-brained beings and that may have something to connect up with what Dimitri said. This is an accusation, perhaps, that human beings as they ordinarily function, (the first impression is that they function as one-brained beings!) That's a very insulting kind of proposition that this is the way we are, or the way we appear to be.

Participant 12: I also think that a young immature, inexperienced, not yet educated, - how Hassein perceives, you know that men are slugs and I think that we can find ourselves in this way, that we tend to have a poor opinion of our fellow man. You know, we see them as slugs, or whatever type of slugs we see. At the beginning we think that has something to do with our perception of our fellow men. We see the rest of mankind as slugs, in an uneducated and immature kind of way. But it's not all, as Dimitri was speaking. Beelzebub recognizes that he is actually talking about men when he says he existed among them for a long time and even made friends with many of those terrestrial three brained beings. These aren't slugs anymore. In a few paragraphs, from one-brain beings that don't articulate or manipulate anything, they consume or excrete a slight trail and move along it. There's this difference between the way Hassein perceives human beings and the way that Beelzebub perceives them as three-brained beings.

Participant 7: That is why he just touches on but does not develop - at the beginning of page 2nd paragraph he talks about love, the idea that you teach with love, and then Beelzebub says no, "you yourself ask what interests you most of all. It would give me at the present moment much pleasure to tell you about just whatever particularly you wish to know". In teaching it's been proven that if you teach in an area in which the pupil is interested in and of course if you teach with love they're going to learn a lot and that of course is developed again and again in the book.

Facilitator: It's an important point, one of the absolute underpinnings of Oskiano, proper Oskiano. He gives us this great forcible example. 'What are you interested in!?'

Participant 4: Does he say no anywhere else in the book?

Facilitator: I don't remember.

Participant 4: Any other time when he simply just said no?

Participant 2: Is that a reference to slugs? I don't know where else it's mentioned. It's on page 630 and without getting into the issue of that particular paragraph he speaks about the group of beings in which he includes "slugs, snails, lice, mole crickets, and many other parasites who destroy everything good". There are some issues but he's not happy about this group of, I'm not sure they are all parasites; I don't believe snails are parasites.

Participant 3: Oh, yes.

Participant 2: Snails are parasites?

Participant 3: They're the same family as slugs, but it doesn't require living on another organic being.

Participant 2: But slugs don't either, but they do occasionally.

Participant 3: As opposed to a louse for example.

Participant 2: I don't know about lice, but I have unfortunately a long history of unfortunate contacts with snails. Snails eat each others dead bodies. They will roam almost anywhere like slugs. They have the same habits as slugs.

Participant 3: Maybe they're parasites, maybe they're not, but that's not really the issue.

Participant 2: No they're not parasitic in the sense they live off, they're not really slugs.

Participant 3: But what I was really getting at, he takes this category of beings and he is very negative about them. Now maybe a stretch, maybe he's using slugs differently there than he is in

Seminar 1 - Chapters 3, 4 & 5 of Beelzebub's Tales to His Grandson

the chapter we're looking at. I just wanted to call it to our attention because he says that they destroy everything good and if three-brained beings are equated to slugs, maybe that's another way of telling us how we are.

Participant 2: I don't want to anticipate what I'm going to say later, but in the late fall of 1922 and early 1923 the Prieuré was infested with slugs and Gurdjieff sent out children with little buckets to collect them. They came back with buckets and buckets full of them because they were destroying the gardens. So, just another context, we're talking about the way Gurdjieff felt about slugs having destroyed that which is good.

Participant 3: That's useful, because a biologist might not consider a slug or a snail as a destroyer of everything good. He may see them as having a very useful function in the eco-system, but he's using them in that way because of that particular event.

Participant 6: I think biologically a slug population depends on the vegetation available. He sent someone out with buckets to collect slugs but there are lots of undeveloped slugs to replace the slugs you have taken away. So they exist in a kind of quasi state of equilibrium, and the more the supply, the more of them there are.

Participant 2: Does anyone know what animal eats slugs and will keep your garden clean?

Participant 7: Ducks.

Participant 2: Yes, and he cultivated hedgehogs also. You can't poison the slugs because you might poison the hedgehogs.

Participant 10: I think what's interesting about the paragraph that Sy has brought our attention to is the fact that he does mention this destruction and slugs and in the previous chapter it also mentions slugs and the destruction or war. So there appears to be a correlation there.

Participant 11: And then it's interesting about their size. They eat so many plants, as little as they are, so small they are.

Facilitator: Interesting also, I think, in the context of what I was trying to emphasize at the opening about sensation-picturings. Just think, here we have spent this time essentially around this very evocative sensation-picturing that has so many interesting levels to it. But we also have two other chapters here and we do have Ilnosoparno! Anyone have any comments relative to what's going on here.

Participant 12: The thing that strikes me about this reference is that he is saying nasty stuff about what is on the planet like us with our slimy skins, and in a way I came away from thinking that he almost seems to make an excuse for men's behavior in the order that he finishes up about how men behave in this extraordinary way about killing, about the way they kill each other at certain

59

times. It's almost as though he's saying, well, this happens because it's not what you might call a law conformable thing, that if one uses reason, there is no way this can be justified and he perhaps explains it in a way because he said man isn't as he should be because we interfered with him, we interfered or brought him into being for a specific purpose of the cosmos. In the process we degraded him inadvertently, but deliberately, by introducing Kundabuffer. The result of this is that man is not as he ought to be and cannot be as he ought to be because he's got these traits that continue. In my own way I tie that up with Mr. Bennett's book called The First Liberation which is a liberation from like and dislike. You can see in all these chapters that man's behavior is not reasonable. It's bent on like and dislike, on prejudice which is not reasonable but mechanically emotional. As we know, when people are bound to each other, it's usually not because there's any reason to it. It is because of like or dislike, not for reason. Therefore it may well be that having explained how man is as he is, having this great weight on him for which he is not entirely responsible, - he (man) has landed in a position where he must do something drastic of his own accord to overcome this reliance on emotion and like and dislike. I think Bennett very much hoped for it.

Participant 5: Going back to Ilnosoparno. For me it's a little bit difficult for me to imagine how you can have those two laws functioning separately but not altogether separated. That is, as quoted from the *Tales*, page 84,

"This sacred substance can be formed on planets only when both fundamental cosmic laws operating in them, the sacred 'Heptaparaparshinokh,' and the sacred 'Triamazikamno,' function, as this is called, 'Ilnosoparno,' that is to say, when the said sacred cosmic laws in the given cosmic concentration are deflected independently and also manifest on its surface independently - of course independently only within certain limits."

What I was going to go on to say about 'independently within certain limits'. In a sense this is not totally in order to produce this Askokin which takes the kind of energy that is formed when something dies. You have to have - it's almost like - sorry, I don't have the words for it.

Participant 12: There is this astonishing thing on page 122 about Ilnosoparno which is equated with 'day': "As I have already told you, the cosmic process called 'Ilnosoparnian' is actualized - that 'Trogoautoegocratic' process which we call 'kshtatsavacht' periodically proceeds; and they also call this cosmic phenomenon 'daylight'." Light, organic light, he's talking about. Is that what we're saying, that two laws have the possibility of relative independence and this is in the very creation relative to the light.

Facilitator: Ilnosoparno seems to be a process once it has been instituted. Certain things flow from it. It might be worthwhile to go back and see that something is initiated here and now there is a lawful unfolding. I understand this as an enormously important thing for us to see. Early on in the *Tales*, Gurdjieff is saying something of colossal importance in developing perspective. Ilnosoparno, instituted from Above with the approval of Endlessness, is a process that is lawful, Trogoautoegocratic etc. And once it is initiated, what happens? The unfolding of what?

Seminar 1 - Chapters 3, 4 & 5 of Beelzebub's Tales to His Grandson

Participant: I'm not terribly good on Genesis, but isn't one of the early acts of Creation the separation between light and darkness? Isn't there in this chapter a suggestion, I mean in some way there is a separation?

Participant: In reference to Genesis light and dark doesn't refer to day and night. That comes much later.

Participant: Light and dark as cosmic principles. In some way, which is not at the moment explained, in order to connect this Ilnosoparnian process to its purpose, possibly something is being separated which would otherwise be acting in some way very closely allied. It seems to be very important in this chapter. We're beginning to see cracks appearing in the infinite. One of the cracks is this business of the moon; another crack is the separation of the laws. So in a sense it is being shown by creating cracks in the seamless web of the laws. Can we go this route?

Participant: If I stay with that, then another crack that appears for me in these chapters is that the Sacred Individuals themselves are capable of error and that by their anticipation in situations they may cause worse errors. That would be of the same order, another thing that makes things every so often not work or be a surprise, shock, hazard.

Participant: That brings diversity into being through the process of the octave of creation.

Facilitator: This is the initiating event in all of the *Tales*. The collision of the comet Kondoor, everything in the *Tales* follows from the collision, however we understand Kondoor and the unified Earth. Everything follows from that, the imbalance, the moon, Anulios, the necessity for Ilnosoparno, the necessity for Askokin to bind them together, the necessity for Kundabuffer. Everything flows from this. So it's a primordial idea, however we come to understand Kondoor, the comet. This is the first thing. You pointed to things that happened via Sacred Individuals, yes, it was one of the highest beings concerned with world creation and maintenance with the Comet. However we see this miscalculation it is the introduction of the first crack relative to life on earth, relative to the Earth itself. This is not a cosmic-cosmic event. Very carefully he separates that off. This is something that affects Earth, not even the other planets of our solar system; it is something that specifically affects Earth.

Participant: Is Earth the only planet that has to produce Askokin? I guess what I'm a little confused about all the laws of reciprocal maintenance. It seems like the universe was set up in a way that everything is dependent on something else, that it's a huge interconnected thing. So it seems in that the order of things that this planet would have to provide food for the planet that comes, the ones that are becoming, and be food for the ones that are becoming, you know, like the sun, let us say. So it seems like that's a universal principle that there is this reciprocal maintenance. What I don't understand is - is Askokin an exception to that? Is it a slightly different variation on that? All of the planets are in different relationships of becoming, I assume.

Participant: But it turned out this event had local effects. At first they were alarmed but it didn't have cosmic effects, it had local effects.

Participant: Isn't there a cosmic, a universal principle of this reciprocal maintenance between everything that exists, so is this an exception?

(tape change)

Participant 2: I was blocked when Chris and Bert came in and I had asked the question 'how do you separate light from darkness?' I don't understand what that means. What are you separating, - when you separate you take away *unity*. What are you doing? How do you separate light from darkness? Where is light to begin with, to be separated? I know I'm dense, obtuse here but I just would like to understand because what, in a way, one way of doing that is saying, all right, it's the Big Bang out of the black hole there comes light, right? By a conservation of energy, - but what does the Bible mean, separation of light from darkness? I have no idea what that means. This perhaps deals with everything we're talking about in this flow of time, of Heropass, from a beginning. The first instance of Gurdjieff's Universe is not unlike the first one billionth of a second of the Big Bang theory. And scientists are tracing the consequences and defining the elements and defining the laws of creation and uniqueness and so is Gurdjieff. But is it relevant to worry about where does this light come from?

Participant 8: I think that the book of Genesis points to the becoming of awareness or we become aware of a difference between light and dark. Later comes the sun and the moon. But the other thing that gives significance to the comet is the idea of a comet traditionally being a carrier of disaster.

Participant: I'm not a great scholar when it comes to immanent and eminent and that sort of thing. But there is in high theology a very clear distinction made between the manifested and unmanifested deity. It's a huge transition from the complete mystery that nothing could ever penetrate to the moment when time, matter, everything begins to exist. He shows himself part of this. At this point something must be enabled to interact, so there must have been at some point, a start to a separation of something. To me, what the Bible is saying is that symbolically. You know you can call it anything you like, but light and darkness is a pretty good sort of stab at symbolically describing the first act of separation of the creation of something from, in a sense, nothing. You have absolutely free everything and that, I think, is as good as you get…

Participant: That's a good stab. I'm thinking of Augustine who spent eight years worrying about all his commentary on Genesis.

Participant: Then I'm in good company!

Participant: He takes that up but he doesn't see it the same way you do. He says that God is the greatest invisibilium. The Universe is the greatest visible and the two never mix. There are other

Seminar 1 - Chapters 3, 4 & 5 of Beelzebub's Tales to His Grandson

ways of looking at this if we are talking about manifest and unmanifest. That's the way Augustine looked at it. The theological question of 'What did God do before the Creation'?

Participant: It's irrelevant because before the Universe was created there was no space or time. Big Bang, which is generally accepted and makes sense to modern science has a problem because we forget the stage of an expanding Universe and the Suns could not form from that, it would have to become *non-uniform*. It did but we do not know how that happened. So the next stage of the big bang is for the universe to become corresponding in non-uniform centers of individuality.

Participant 2: Yes the point is completely overdrawn on this idea of the gradually expanding Universe so I think actually Hawkins, as you know, Hawkins has other ideas.

Participant 7: I would like to say something and I'm sorry for all of the theological upsets that what I say might create. Now, if I'm not mistaken, nobody in that book, (the *Tales*) we're reading, actually sees God. There are references to God.

Participant: You mean His Endlessness?

Participant: Yes.

Participant: …"the gaze of his endlessness falls upon the...."

Participant: Yes, but there's no indication of face to face

(tape gap)

Participant: What does he mean, never allowing one to sleep in peace?

Participant: This is quite different from other mythologies where there is a pretty gross encounter with God or Gods. Now this is… let me put my thoughts in order here. We speak about 'God created' and by using the word God we have a reference to God being some place else. I'm going to ask the question, where is God now? When is the light separated from the darkness? I think light separated from darkness when *'I'* separate light from darkness. Consciousness and I can only know consciousness in me. I think this is pretty significant that nobody sees God in Beelzebub. The thrust of creation, so to speak, that passes through me is God. Everything exists, is created, when I am aware of it. Somehow I bear the history of the Universe on the shoulders of my consciousness, if I may use such weighty expressions. If this could be the case, then the descriptions that have to do with cosmologies, with cosmology in general, is the description of my being aware of the cosmos, my being aware of the things that cosmology speaks about. So everything in these descriptions as a way for me to perceive my world is helped by Gurdjieff... through a book to help me perceive my world. The references tonight to light and darkness are references to the moments when these things become concepts - I am aware of it.

All & Everything Conference 2002

Participant: I was just going to say, I can imagine a comet to come and split off a section of the earth and it becomes a moon and Anulios. These are images and external cosmology is only an image for my own inner cosmology. What's clear to me from this book is that when the moon splits up from me that it is my *feeling* center, not my emotional center which is completely different but is inactive. My feeling center now is detached from the place where it should be and is now spread out throughout my body. Because of my reaction to explain passions my body reacts and that's because mechanically my feelings are spread throughout my body. My body has to pay for that. So when I'm doing this, tapping a foot and scratching, that's my feelings manifested through my body. That's what I get from this book. So the cosmology doesn't make much sense because how can I experience that? This I can experience and I understand that where my feelings are now, they have to be brought back in place in the proper center and Anulios is to me my magnetic center. I have to get in touch with my magnetic center in order for it to function for me and I can't do that unless I have been talking to my magnetic center and only an objective, possibly, can make that connection. That's what I get from this.

Facilitator: This is interesting because what I hear in this exchange that Nick is putting forward, is exactly what he was saying seven years ago when he said everything that we read about in this book must have an analogousness in our life. This book is written for us, about us. I would stretch it a little bit further than that. The similar strain may have many levels of meaning and certainly the mythic dimensions of this opening here could apply to history, could apply to the cosmos in some way, could apply to an individual conceptus when suddenly a one has to divide into three in order to become a being; also to the moment of birth. These are all ways of relating it to our experience and that seems to be what you're emphasizing. As a Work book this has got to have some way of resonating in us. This is the 'sensation picturings' part, speaking to the subconscious, evoking something in us that is more than just the waking, linear logical, historical etc. It has to go deeper, has to evoke something from us that does have to do with our inner life.

Participant: I wonder at the roots of the word Kondoor. I thought there must be something to it... the Comet and all.

Facilitator: I asked Nick Tereshchenko. He couldn't help me. He said there's nothing in Russian.

Participant: So we have some other words.

Participant: Anyone have any other idea?

Participant: A high flying bird. It's a high flying bird of prey.

Participant: The condor.

Participant: In South America, yes.

Seminar 1 - Chapters 3, 4 & 5 of Beelzebub's Tales to His Grandson

Participant: We're all saying it started with Kondoor but he also says that it is as a result of the erroneous calculations of a certain Sacred Individual concerned with matters of world creation and world maintenance, the time of the passing of each of these concentrations etc. So it wasn't just calculation, it wasn't just... isn't that what it says here? It wasn't just Kondoor doing his thing; it was a miscalculation by an individual.

Facilitator: But it's a miscalculation, a temporal not a spatial error.

Participant: I know, in time it's still a miscalculation. Kondoor isn't the primary source. It was the miscalculation that was the source.

Facilitator: Yes, Miscalculation in time. It raises a very interesting question.

Participant: Tell us about that.

Facilitator: This appears to have so many things to do with the reconciliation of Heropass. We are left at the very opening of the Tales with this enigmatic circumstance. It starts with this, and it wasn't perfect - in time. Because of that everything else flows from the miscalculation. Something about that is very important.

Participant: I'd like to elaborate on this configuration about myth that Nick spoke about seven years ago - and, in a sense, what Dimitri was just speaking about. As I understood what you are speaking about is that this book really describes *us* in a way you talk about when I can become aware. What I got out of that is - that level of awareness is when we know we are the Absolute, - as opposed to all this separateness. I think that is the direction of the myth of the whole book, that this book describes us as God. Nick, is that where you were going with it?

Participant: The book is meant to destroy mercilessly without any compromise whatsoever etc. etc. And for me it is such a creative image. And... it's great. Because the more I work with this book the more something is shed away and yes there is a thrill in putting two things together. There is something else going on which is so important because we really are filled up with the most extraordinary amount of stuff. And that is what he says and it looks very crude, the way it's put here. It's a very important concept. I want to understand and believe but at the same time we go deeper so that we can shed it to become freer.

Participant: We can't go deeper without shedding.

Participant: A question concerning the erroneous calculations. I think that somehow I have come into the world with a very early sort of erroneous, implicit error that I have lived out from the beginning, that I didn't create - but came from something that was not me personally, like heredity. I don't think that I created it, but I have lived with it and so that's the connection I made with that for myself. To have uncovered that error is very difficult for me. To name the error has been important, though.

Facilitator: I recently reread Bennett's *Hazard*. I think it had a different name in its first printing. Tony Blake wrote a new preface to it I think. In there the issue, that you just phrased for me, is the entry of true Hazard into our life. I see a possible resonance - that the first event that is going to qualify the state of unity of the Earth is Hazard. Something entered here mainly from miscalculation. This is, perhaps, the entry of Hazard into everything that comes later - everything, and it starts not from something that is secure but something that has intrinsically in it already the possibility that it might not work out this way. And sure enough it didn't.

Participant: I think that Mr. Bennett said he called it the 'Dramatic Universe' because it was hazardous.

Facilitator: We haven't talked about Kundabuffer yet.

Participant: That must have been like a shock, because the atmosphere of the earth was not completely formed and that is like the slug. So the earth was a baby. So all these errors occur when we are very small. So the Earth was not yet formed - mankind was not present yet. The atmosphere was not well formed because if it was more formed it would stand as a buffer to defend and we have no defense, with the 'thin' skin like the slug. So we are sensitive to this kind of problem.

Facilitator: If we take it historically than the myth can also be understood, at one level, as Gurdjieff's projection of history. We're going back four billion years, long before life of any kind because it describes the appearance of life as coming much later (three years in objective time calculations). In that context it just raises some interesting questions - another level of seeing myth that isn't my personal life, but maybe, what he wants to project is that something changed, something was altered, namely the Comet - before life appeared. That's a really interesting question. Is Gurdjieff pointing in that direction? Did something happen, as he understood it, in this solar system relative to this earth, to the state of unity long before life appeared that in a sense qualifies something into the whole future of the earth. That there will be now an Earth, a Moon, and Anulios. There will be a disproportion and it is a disproportion long before life appears. That means this disproportion is going to influence the appearance of life, the appearance of Tetartocosmos, the appearance of brained beings and so forth. So it seems like a big idea.

Participant: You see, going down hill is easy. This started the going downhill and there is just one obstruction - the deviation is much later.

Participant: The question you're addressing - this is relatively recent in the myth when the parts break off of Earth. To get back to the beginning thing when something happened you have to go through the whole planet Purgatory chapter where it is describing how the laws actually were changed.

Facilitator: That's earlier yet.

Seminar 1 - Chapters 3, 4 & 5 of Beelzebub's Tales to His Grandson

Participant: That's what I'm saying. It is much, much earlier. Something changed things, it's Kondoor that represents something but that may be simply a manifestation of what changed it at the beginning.

Facilitator: Exactly. That's the point. That's where Hazard is built into the whole Universe through Trogoautoegocrat. We are simply seeing, in this specific solar system, one manifestation of that hazard and that is a comet. He says it's an error of miscalculation etc., but…

Participant: For me to think when I first read this chapter because I couldn't accept that a sacred individual could make a mistake. I was much annoyed! And so here I am and of course at the beginning I read, Gurdjieff says, "To destroy mercilessly the beliefs and views…"

Facilitator: The big one!

Participant: Yes, the big one, and I still believe that a sacred individual cannot make a mistake. It's like I said, I don't believe deeply in my heart that I make mistakes, but I say that I make mistakes - but how deeply I believe - I do not understand.

Participant: But surely the higher up you go in the order, the more freedom you have, the more freedom the more responsibility but also the more freedom and more possibility there is of error. You're getting away from something that's predetermined, something that has possibilities and potential and if you have possibilities and potential you've got that possibility of the hazard.

Participant: I'm saying something else. I have an icon - a picture of the world - Sacred individuals don't make mistakes, they are right.

Participant: Because the higher the individuals are the more the slightest deviation will matter. A little deviation of the comet is a great mistake.

Participant: Why is that ego?

Facilitator: I get the sense that you are misunderstanding Stefan. Stefan is talking about a very important subjective insight. And it has nothing to do with a logical confrontation of that, from knowing that Hazard is present. You are speaking, 'this is what I think and it keeps recurring and the more I keep thinking about it, still this feeling is right there.'

Participant: That's our conviction. This book is about ourselves, right? And if this Sacred individual made a mistake, - Who in this room does not feel that they're right?

Participant: Absolutely.

Participant: Isn't that our Sacred individual? We all think we're right. I can't really get my mind around that.

Participant: Well, it helps if we accept that we all lie continuously, particularly to ourselves.

Participant: I was going to say that what Stefan was saying gets even worse when, for me anyway, they came back and if they hadn't come back a year later, you know (laughter). Besides that it gets even worse. In any event "if only for the sake of their own reassurance". The highest level that anyone of us can reach or is possible in creation and it is still acting from a self-centered place, instead of looking at the whole picture and saying 'you know what' the consequences, it is not a cosmic event anymore. Let's wait a little longer. Let's see what happens. Instead, just to make sure for their own sakes - that is the worst. The stupendous terror for the three brained beings is the result of this.

Participant: It's a pretty good story, isn't it?

Participant: What you just said, the topic of conversation, fits in my mind with other things we have said tonight. There's a man who says 'I'm Beelzebub, you are slug. You're a mistake, big mistake food'. I have to make a decision. I pick up this book and let it help me or not. And I think that there's a dramatic push in there, by Gurdjieff, to confront one's responsibilities. Who is the person who says 'yes, you are Beelzebub and I am slack and everything is a mistake', and does one accept it? Does one accept to be helped by such views? And I think that this puts me, again I say, because of this responsibility, and I think this is the thing that needs to be done in individual people's lives. This is the missing link between what we do and our work - to accept the responsibility. We can not shake off our shoulders this responsibility. There's no way we can kind of let ourselves go to believing or becoming followers of any kind in this type of endeavor, in Work. To Work means to be responsible, and I think it just comes again and again Gurdjieff says and then you will learn to be responsible. It keeps you away from being a follower, by being in so heavy a predicament by the book throwing such a heavy stone.

Facilitator: Hassein is certainly helped throughout and guided throughout. But as Beelzebub himself says in other places, 'I have not placed an opinion in front of you' - (arguably) I wanted to present factual circumstances so that you could draw your own conclusions, come to your own answer. Is that what you meant?

Participant: Yes, yes.

Facilitator: But that takes up the whole of the *Tales* and takes the wisdom and guidance and cleverness of Gurdjieff to help us. So to some degree we walk this tightrope of having to follow because I don't know, and here is this marvellous aid and the following to me is 'following along'. I go along and I try to perceive and try to understand and try to apply and so on. Then it is corrected in the context of the book so while I'm not a blind follower I must admit that I need guidance and help.

Participant: First of all, I think we must be very cautious about going too far down the line of Nick's - that this is just about man's inner world. I think that would belittle the book. I think it's

Seminar 1 - Chapters 3, 4 & 5 of Beelzebub's Tales to His Grandson

much more than that. There is a real moon. There is a series of concentric meanings and it's obviously got an inner meaning to our psychology, but it's got other meanings as well. Coming round to one of the psychological meanings, I think, something that I'd like to share with you, is my interest in the bottom of page 86, where it talks about "beginning gradually to be spiritualized by what is called being-instincts", and on page 88 it says "you must know that by the time of the second descent of the Most High Commission, there had already gradually been engendered in them - as is proper to three-brained beings - what is called 'mechanical instinct'." I would have to look up the Russian to make sure we are dealing with different adjectives here, but let us assume that there are allied meanings here with the key word *instinct*. Actually I've been studying the references to instinct through the book which are incredibly interesting, taking it far beyond the Ouspenskian definition in *Fragments*. Gurdjieff uses it in very particular way, indicates some sacred organic ferment that appears within beings and I actually think it's probably fundamental to true human evolution - this fact of reconnecting with instinct and thereby with conscience.

Participant: It's an interesting conclusion.

Participant: Doesn't he say somewhere that there is an instinct for self perfection?

Participant: Of course it does. It's in the Strivings. It's exactly that kind of thing. What is that instinct to self perfection? They are already beginning to get it through instinct and then of course Kundabuffer comes along and bang! So I just wanted to share with you my interest in that.

Participant: Instinctive, for me, links it to the collective unconscious and with conscious efforts.

Participant: Is Beelzebub talking about how we have to, somehow or other, either acknowledge or get rid of things that are interfering. You pick up the book and the first thing he does is call you a slug, right? So you can actually throw away the book and go about your way or you can say, well, am I? Isn't that really a definition of prejudice? It's a very simple definition of how we make up our minds so quickly, based on prejudice most of the time in our physical and psychological experience of the universe. It seems to me, to get at something like instinct you have to clear these paths and I think that's what this chapter is about. What are the things in our way to seeing anything?

Facilitator: I have made an error. (Laughter) I've run over time. We'll have a break.

(coffee break)

Facilitator: Five o'clock is, by the schedule, when we were to stop. Let's go to about ten past, that will give us half an hour from now to continue with chapters 8, 9 and 10.

Participant: Where we were was that Anulios is forgotten and the name which is Kimespai, the other name for Anulios. That is what they called Anulios then and the later, which are the more modern beings, also forgets. We also forgot, because that is a cosmological thing and we also forgot in ourselves the placement of Kundabuffer. So I think may be a connection between Anulios, which is forgotten and as a name and as a thing in the personal sense also the influence of Kundabuffer is also forgotten. That's what I think the group is all the time doing, all those levels. We reached the point, if the chronology is correct, where the name gets changed to Kimespai because of the early effects of Kundabuffer and finally it disappears altogether, even to the point where we forget the name and then it isn't even referred to in grandmother's fairy tales. All that seems to be connected up with the consequences of Kundabuffer, which links them that much closer together. When we finally forget Anulios altogether. We see it, if at all, as an aerolite or a meteorite flashing in the sky and then it is gone in our experience, in our life experience. Whatever it is that Anulios may represent, it is not present in our experience it seems. But it becomes that because of the consequences of Kundabuffer. In Atlantis they named it and knew it and could find it and then the early influences of the consequences of Kundabuffer, early influences lead to Kimespai. Even that deceives us, then we can sleep without being disturbed.

Participant: I think that he's intimating that, as we don't see Anulios, that Anulios is the third force, and in the resultant third force blindness.

Facilitator: Anyone interested in pursuing that? Do you see any analogy or correspondence between the third force blindness as Gurdjieff emphasizes so often and this disappearance of Anulios?

Participant: Well, I would think first, in theory yes, but I would think if Anulios is magnetic center that its magnetic center that brings us into the world. So its not entirely lost because it's a part of us that we may get in touch with that brings us here or brings us into the wish for spiritual development. Or to understand our situation. Because that wouldn't come from personality, that would come from something different. That would make a 'flashing' and it may be strong enough for us to pursue it in a way that would make us go and buy a book or read or join a group. And I think then, once Anulios becomes a magnetic center we begin to make an effort. Then it will not allow you to sleep in peace.

Participant: Are you actually going to accept the statement that Anulios is magnetic center? Can we live with that? I can't.

Participant: For myself, I had thought of Anulios as conscience, because it has broken away from us, we are no longer in touch with it. To be in touch with conscience we can't be self-calming, you can't rest easy on anything. Everything is a question and I think this is unseen in today's world and certainly the result of Kundabuffer. Then the whole thing with the moon, that we only see it because it reflects the sun. We see it at night. When we are in the dark there is a part that is thought to be dead, but because it is empty it is capable of reflecting and reflecting the sun which is the center of our solar system. That's what I have done with that so far.

Participant: I want to make things more complicated. There is a second moon. It has been found astronomically about fifteen years ago. Just to thicken the plot and I remember also reading some

Seminar 1 - Chapters 3, 4 & 5 of Beelzebub's Tales to His Grandson

place and for people who remembered it as well it was the conversation when Mr. Gurdjieff insisted that people did indeed have tails at one point. There was a period when they did have some such organ. Does anybody remember this except myself? Not in the book, but in a conversation he insisted that he meant it. There was a period in evolution, that the human race went back and had tails actually.

Participant: I thought he said it was at the base of where the tails should have been.

Participant: Oh yeah, so I put these two things together and I wondered to the extent to which the year of Anulios (and in parenthesis Kundabuffer) not the consequences but the organ itself, could in anyway be a reference to things existing in a material way, because the second moon does exist.

Participant: I have found that just about everything that Gurdjieff refers to has a basis in fact, in astronomy, in biology, in anthropology it does, but to me he uses those facts in a mythological sense which means that it's a symbol. I don't think he's trying to teach us the natural sciences. I think he is assuming that we have some knowledge of this in our own way or that whether we do or not he's using (interrupted)

Participant: ... we discussed this before. The only thing I'm saying is this has bothered me, not bothered me but I have thought of it and it has amazed me that there is a possibility that Gurdjieff knew that there was a second moon. Just the fact that if he indeed know this is an amazing thing that somehow such knowledge has been preserved. Nobody seemed to know that such a heavenly body existed up until about fifteen years ago. If he indeed knew it maybe he used it allegorically, maybe he didn't, I do not know, maybe it was very important that he did. But if he knew it there is also a very interesting dimension in that. Somehow he had knowledge of this very factual nature.

Participant: Like the Gilgamesh quotation.

Participant: Yes, like that for example.

Participant: The word itself is interesting in what it might mean. Linguists here may know more than I do, I would relate it to the word null, nothing and in relation to what Dorothy said about the third force blind and the third force is a property presumably of the real world, Gurdjieff tells us that. As I understand the real world in metaphysical terms, it is that there isn't anything, there's nothing. It's in every tradition. All there really is the Absolute, which is who we are and in that respect when we discover and see Anulios, then we are in that state, that state of unification. That's another way of putting it.

Participant: No, no

Participant: I just want to say in response to Chris, he asks if Anulios, I hope I said *if* Anulios is magnetic center.

All & Everything Conference 2002

Participant: Accepted.

Participant: Can I ask something about Kundabuffer? He talks about these two properties. "That they should perceive reality topsy-turvy and secondly, that every repeated impression from outside should crystallize in them data which would engender factors for evoking in them sensations of pleasure and enjoyment". My question is, when it comes to the first property I am definitely becoming convinced of the profundity of that reality, that in fact, I do perceive reality upside down and I feel that's a process I'm beginning to realize more and more. But the second one, I have noticed that, but it doesn't have the profundity of this perceiving the upside - down and I just want to know if you or anyone else, how do you understand this, this second property and why was this particular property in Kundabuffer supposed to aid humanity to not see reality? Why couldn't he have just done the first one? Why the second factor?

Participant: If we could substitute the word desire, which I think is a broader term.

Participant: Substitute the desire for what?

Participant: For pleasure and enjoyment. Again it is this sort of thing, and it's not just in the Gurdjieff tradition, it's in every tradition. That identification with fears on one side and desires on the other. That would keep us identified with this life rather than reality.

Participant: What about repeated. I'm just wondering how do you understand that 'repeated'?

Participant: I would just like to say, in the case of the second one, for pleasure and enjoyment, we're talking about sensation, so this is affecting your first body and the perception is our intellectual part and so the way that we perceive things as being topsy-turvy is a perception

Participant: It also feels connected to living in the moving parts of centers which repeat those things.

Participant: Can we also say it the other way around and say evoking in them the avoidance of sensations of suffering, particularly about oneself and one's complete lack of realism. Which ever way you look at it, we're really sick and I think if one takes it in that sort of light, and the fact that we cannot accept authentically seconds or minutes after the situation. It is very difficult to follow that with an honest, good heart. But the potency to be able to bear that has been seriously damaged - by what? I mean it's just a way of addressing that. I think it an incredible interesting question.

Participant: The question came up for me also, Todd, and at first when I was reading this book I looked at the property of the organ Kundabuffer, seeing things upside-down and would forget this repeated, this repetition of pleasure. The more I looked at that it seemed to me that that is what causes the crystallization in us of the properties of the organ Kundabuffer because it is repeated and repeated and repeated. Also that is confirmed by the fact that we try so hard with our tasks and different exercises to break that.

Seminar 1 - Chapters 3, 4 & 5 of Beelzebub's Tales to His Grandson

Facilitator: I don't know if it would be a helpful image or not, but five or six years ago at this conference I gave a particular perspective on Kundabuffer that involved an enneagramatic image that placed our lower intellectual activity at Re or 1 and then our sensory and motor function (in a mechanical sense) at 2 and 4 and, only when we get to 5 do we enter the world of ordinary emotion, 5 and 7, and go to the higher intellectual. So the intellectual would be at 8 and 1. The moving center activities would be at 2 and 4 and normal emotional activity would be at 5 and 7. Then if Kundabuffer is seen as something which then buffers and becomes a reflector and/or absorber of all of those things that are inherent in the word buffer. If that descends in the center then 1 moves to 4 moves to 2 and then moves toward 8 but bounces off of the mirror, bounces off of the buffer, back to 1, so we do repeat this lower intellectual, which is what Mandy was saying, 'topsy-turvy'. That's an intellectual process - we perceive the world and then it goes down to mechanical expression, lower expression and sensation and then can't get across, bounces back to topsy-turvy down to the generation of sensations that are repetitive.

Participant: Are you saying that cycle of repetition we begin to become addicted to or enjoy, it becomes pleasurable.

Facilitator: We're vulnerable to it. We can only suffer if we can get over to ordinary real emotion so we're vulnerable.

Participant: It's even a reflection of suffering, isn't it? The 1, 4, 2 is a reflection of real suffering because we are all miserable but we are so attached to it.

Facilitator: Something gets through there. It seems to me that we would not be able to be called even peculiar three-brained beings if we did not have some function - something gets through. It enters into the subconscious at 8, 5 and 7. That's all the subconscious. Then out of the subconscious coming through the line from 7 to 1, out of the subconscious which we don't see comes that activation of our intellectual topsy-turvy, so that all that should inform us about the world of real emotion, about suffering and effort and meaning and especially relationship, a whole world of relationship that to me seems to come out of the coalescence at 7. The whole of that state of relationship disappears.

Participant: For me, this has something to do with the opposite of the lack of Being-Partkdolg-duty and I'm interested in this difference between reason of understanding and reason of knowing, which is described in Form and Sequence because it is to me the possibility of trying to discern in myself what happens when I am really present or trying to be present and receive an impression. It's talking about impressions, in a way pulling a chair comes into us and so, if we live in this way, where we are passive in us when we receive, so the impressions enter willy-nilly or go to different parts. That kind of builds up our vanity, self-love, being sure that the world is like we think it is or being sure it is as horrible as we think it is. That is how it is for me. I think what we're saying is true, maybe what is relationship then of the second conscious shock. Turning that around and becoming active, receiving actively, which would be the opposite of just being a slave to the repetition of impressions. In order for anything to change for me, I must have access to something higher, which is above this. So whatever I think about it I cannot make change necessary unless I make (conscience?) possible. There is nothing in my personality which is going to change.

Facilitator: That's where I see it connected to the comet Kondoor.

Participant: I would like to say a few ideas about Kundabuffer. May I? I think it is one of the very difficult points in this book. Kundalini is accused of being the force, that puts people to sleep and there are traditions in the East that Kundalini is the awakening force. The use of Kundabuffer, what does it buffer? It buffers Kundalini. Then we read that Kundabuffer was implanted into the lower portion of the spine and we know that Gurdjieff said that in man the active force emanates from the brain, from what is in the head. The negative force is in the spine and the balancing force is in the solar plexus. What is this negative force that is in the spine, what does it have to do with Kundabuffer, that has something to do with the spine? What does Kundabuffer have to do with Kundalini, which is a force in the spine that is awakening according to Eastern tradition? There are people who believe so much in Eastern traditions in Kundalini. What are we faced with here? It is not a very simple thing that we are faced at all. Even mythologically we are just not used to exotic word to signify Kundabuffer. He uses Kunda and buffer and does not allow us to make any mistake that he is talking about Kundalini (?) and buffer and we know it as a fact that Kundalini, when come to the awakening, it uncoils, the serpent uncoiling into the spine so actually it is not buffer, to uncoil means to rise, Kundalini is rising. I think that this is a very difficult ground to take. I can. Do you want to say something?

Participant: When you finish.

Participant: Then the idea of the positive force being the brain and the negative being the spine - what does it mean? The positive force is issued from the brain and the negative in the spine and the balance in the solar plexus.

Participant: The automatisms of the body will result in crystallizations of behavior in the synapses of neural behavior, because it is in synapses that all the automatisms are actually condensed in the body. I personally believe that the idea of the positive force issues from the very means that man can wish, intellectually, but the minute that he tries to do, his behavior bounces off his automatisms which are actually in the ganglia in the spine. I think this is a very concrete image there and I think this is a buffer to freedom, so to speak. I have studied a little bit of Kundalini according to Eastern traditions and I believe in what Gurdjieff says. I believe that what they call Kundalini is very often a very negative hypnotizing force. I believe that Gurdjieff is talking about exactly the same force only on another level. I believe that when Gurdjieff says Kundabuffer, it means a buffer of Kundalini, but if he is to use the word Kundalini he falls into what specific schools in the East called Kundalini which is lying. My personal opinion I believe that this happens exactly because the automatisms of behavior, what John called the moving parts of the centers. The center of gravity is in the spine.

Seminar 1 - Chapters 3, 4 & 5 of Beelzebub's Tales to His Grandson

Participant: What I was going to add to it is really to affirm what you're saying with this possible addition or elaboration on the Kunda. It's another example to me of this criticism objectively of the life of man because there are all kinds of people in Eastern traditions who have quote, 'raised their Kundalini'. It's an experience of vibrations up the spine. People can get a 'high' from it. I'm not at all saying that I'm a master of Kundalini, but I've had some experience like that. It's not what it's about. It's not what this teaching is about and I think he's using it exactly like you say, it's a buffer. It's another one of these things to prevent us from going toward the real thing.

Participant: I just want to say that it gets explained in chapter 21, page 250.

Participant: Do we have to stop?

Participant: Schedule 5:30. It's only 5:00 actually.

Participant: Page 250. Do you want me to read? Yes.

"It was just when they began wiseacring and inventing various forms of that famous 'suffering' of theirs that they also played their usual 'tricks' with this word."

"Namely, first of all, as the root of the second half of this word chanced to coincide with a word in the language of that time which meant 'Reflection,' and as they also had invented a means for destroying this material formation rapidly and not merely in the course of time as Saint Buddha had told them, they also wiseacred about this word according to the following rumination of their bob-tailed Reason. Of course, when this organ is in action, it ought to have in its name also the root of the word to 'reflect'; now, since we are destroying even its material basis, the name must end with a word whose root means 'former', and because 'former' in their current language was then pronounced 'lina', they changed the second half of this word, and instead of 'reflection', they stuck in the mentioned 'lina', so that instead of the word Kundabuffer, they obtained the word 'Kundalina.'"

So if you can understand that - Applause!

Facilitator: One of Gurdjieff's great constructions! Since Gurdjieff never puts everything in one place for any idea there is also this very careful definition in the law of three that Makary characterizes. I think there, when he talks about Holy Affirming as being the good coming from the source down, always involutional and then Holy Denying, then becomes evil. It also is that which crystallizes out when the Holy Affirming runs out of gas, if you will. It runs out of momentum. It also is the source of the striving to return. The third force then becomes the result of the clash, not the clash, but the results of the clash which clearly seems to identify something in Holy Denying that has a striving to return. You were talking about striving to return, something built in instinctively. It is in the law, in the law that there is something here even though it is now the crystallization, involutionally there is still something inside of it that has to strive to return.

Participant: We are talking about something pretty important here. May I go on a little bit? You see there's been something about the enneagram that has not been pointed out. That's the fact that on point #6 we put the negative force, right? 7 to 9 negative.

Participant: I thought that was always 9 to 3 as denying force. And at 6 is Holy Reconciling.

Participant: No, that's 9

Participant: A different form of the law.

Participant: The positive force is #3, the 9 is reconciling. 1, 2, 3.

Participant: This point is where we go to the bars. (Laughter)

Participant: Anyway, let me complete my thought. I am not listening to them right in the sense that there are many people who have put it differently. We also have the second conscious shock on 6 and there seems to be a contradiction there. The denying has the potential of the second conscious shock and the only way that one can get rid of this contradiction is what you just said, having the potential to return existing within negativity. I could go on speaking a long time, but it's not necessary. What I just said is that I agree with what you say because in my universe the positive force is on 3 and the negative force is on 6.

Facilitator: It's good that we wrapped that up! Thank you all.

End of Session

Gurdjieff's Enneagramatic View:
A Path for Superceding Modern Physic's and Chemistry's Understanding of Nature

Nathan Batalion

Introduction

I was very pleased to discover the existence of this forum, the *All and Everything International Humanities Conference*. For the ideas of Gurdjieff are close to my own. One of the peculiarities of my ideas is that I do *not* see nature's coherence as pointed to by our dominant mathematical language of modern science. It is my contention that modern civilization's use of this language over the last 400 years - namely as the final arbiter for nature's truths, and while effectively building technologies and harnessing certain energies - fails to deeply understand nature's real coherency. It misses the truer syntax and thus is implicated in our mounting ecological crises.

My vision is expressed using a different language of nature, one that still employs mathematics but subordinately - not as either the starting point or concluding arbiter of a presumably universal understanding. This other language turns out to be similar to Gurdjieff's. It is similar but not entirely the same. For Gurdjieff's designation of the enneagram as a universal hieroglyph is a way of pointing to nature's coherency within the limitations of a quantitative language as well, of geometry - of points making straight or curved lines usually drawn in black against a white background. However this particular choice of geometric forms is ultimately based on a pre-geometric understanding. Thus within the limitations of this language of geometry, the enneagram comes as close as possible to symbolizing an order that precedes its own form.

Consequently I prefer to use the enneagram only as a "left brain" (geometric/quantitative or linear) adjunct, one juxtaposed next to and subordinate to the more "right brain" symbol of the rainbow. With the rainbow, the color distinctions show the *identical* relationships - but now minus the drawback of permanent linearity. For its color separations dissolve to form a more integral oneness. This is not a matter of splitting hairs but of language becoming ever more faithful to what is real. From the start I make no apology for honoring, feeling at home and at the very same time diverging from and critiquing Gurdjieff's view and terminology. Those who only dogmatically copy his perspective, word for word, reveal that they have not dipped into their own original experience sufficiently, if at all. They have not developed enough means to judge where he soared to heights and where he still fell short.

All & Everything Conference 2002

What I learned grew out of a certain context. In my youth I was a math prodigy having passed university calculus exams at the age of 13. But at 17 I had a high fever that left me partly aphasic. This meant I was impaired in the ability to think, speak, or communicate in whole sentences. The condition abandoned me to a left-brain-hampered perception and literally threw me into another universe. But the positive result was that I develop a quite independent view and this autonomy was enhanced by coming into contact with Gurdjieff's ideas, methods, and perspectives. Thus I am immeasurably indebted to him. Ultimately this handicap became an advantage. But it also made me feel like an alien from another galaxy living in our modern culture - one who speaks an entirely different sounding and meaning tongue.

The Approach

Normally in modern science we start with postulates or hypotheses and then develop verified theorems or principles. The process is similar to drawing a map that points to a "road" (metaphorical for a pattern of thought, paradigm or thesis) in a "wilderness territory" (metaphorical for a region of our orderless senses). We don't know if the road actually exists until we compare the two - until some experience validates our hunch. With the *deductive method* we start with the left-brain (map-making) faculty as dominant and move to verify our chosen mapping technique in direct experience. However in the 17th century, Sir Francis Bacon critiqued this method. He offered an opposite *inductive* method. As he put it, ideas should be weighted by stones rather than given wings. We tend to find in our senses what our naïve preconceptions point to while ignoring or devaluating negating data. We then mistake the map for the territory, fall into deep illusions or what he called "idols." For Bacon, grounded sensory data was thus his primary starting point before conceptualizations. *One starts with no hypotheses and no postulates*. One of Bacon's chief symbols for this method was a ladder one climbs from the ground up to progressively higher generalizations of truth. At the very top we finally view the highest of all generalizations, something akin to the unity of nature.

A chief failing of Bacon's ideas was that he never climbed his own ladder to the very top. He offered a method without a unifying vision as a result. And this was at a critical time when the current vision of Christendom was challenged and falling asunder. The deductive method of Descartes filled the vacuum and triumphed to form the new philosophy of nature of modernity. It successfully (or so it seemed) offered a more unifying view, the mathematical, to vastly rebind consciousness with a higher level of integrity. It appeared to be less flawed than the revelatory view that by faith alone believed the earth was at the center of the universe.

However, a key problem transpired. Western civilization's new "enlightenment" period made, I contend, an unprecedented and immense mistake. It fell into yet deeper traps of illusions precisely by choosing this primary deductive tool. This again refers to the mathematical tool - which takes its place comfortably at the very top of Bacon's ladder - there integrating the inductive method into its fold. Thus we no longer need to climb upwards from our senses but rather can safely work our way down. If we think the world might be made up of indivisible atoms, for example, and to parallel how counting is built up by indivisible "1s" we prove this mathematically. We move down to our senses. The essence of the mathematical philosophy of nature was expressed by Galileo in a little tract called *Il Saggiatore* published in 1623.[1] Therein he claims that the symbols of quantification give us the master key to escape illusions. They point to the primary, inner, abiding, and non-illusionary perception of the world. Qualities we ordinarily experience give us only secondary, surface, non-abiding and thus fooling perceptions - the kind that created the illusion of geocentricity fooling the greatest of minds for centuries. The problem with this Galilean view is that it is itself an inversion. It now takes a great deal of effort to overturn Galileo and others to get back to our reality foundation stones. Why and how this "quantitative-over-qualitative view" is an inversion should become clearer later.

Right now we are merely addressing methods. Gurdjieff offered another methodology to follow - to retrace our steps back to root foundations, to the ground floor of Bacon's ladder and more purely. Using Gurdjieff's methods of self-observation we can start with an imaginary observer - as if looking from outside *all* the contents of our consciousness - whether right/left brain or mind/feeling/body contents - at whatever transpires. We thus begin with a pre-conceptual or trans-mental, trans-emotional, trans-physical overview. This is the same as what occurs and is seen in aphasia.

We get a sense of this method in certain disciplines. For example, Betty Edwards in her *Drawing on the Right Side of the Brain* gives one approach. Take a landscape artwork and turn it upside down. It should be such that you then *cannot* recognize its elements conceptually. This leaves you to copy and draw the picture as you actually see it - directly and nakedly - without the filter or bias of symbolic ideas.

Now the reader of this text might, right now, turn this page upside down to no longer be reading a conceptual document. Please do. We then switch brain polarities. What appears is just some white background with black marks on it - suspending the use of concepts of even "white," "black," "background," "marks" and so on. We then just see as is and in the present moment - with *mindlessness* but also the enhanced objectivity of a camera's eye. To maintain this, math-bound concepts are also not allowed to bias and shroud perceptions. Furthermore the moment contains not just a visual experience. One can also feel the texture of the paper one is touching, hear background sounds, smell background scents, and so on. One can further sense the presence of one's own body postural awareness - and again minus any and all concepts such as "texture," "paper," "sounds," "smells," "body," "sensations," and so on. What that experience culminates in is akin to the fruits of the Gurdjieffian method of self-awareness.

If we go to a university library we will find tens of thousands of books, and with a diversity of subject matters. The topics are expressed in billions if not trillions of words. Yet if we turn all these books upside down, we are again left with just a "primitive" view of black marks on white

---

[1] Stillman Drake, trans. Discoveries and Opinions of Galileo - Including the Starry Messenger (1610), Letter to the Grand Duchess Christina (1615), and Excerpts from Letters on Sunspots (1613), the Assayer (1623); Doubleday & Co, 1989.

backgrounds (with slight color variations and picture inserts in some). We usually pay no attention to this because this is a kind of ridiculous/meaningless view of an infant child - before being educated and acculturated. Yet it is my contention that this perception, including the "feel" of the difference between a smooth and a rough piece of paper - has a language of its own. It is a language of direct Baconian/Gurdjieffian experience - so that an infant child who has never learned a single word can still tell, for example, and by intonation alone, whether its mother's words of "I love you" convey love or something opposite, ingenuous and/or threatening. The intonation conveys its own meaning subliminally or pre-conceptually. That deeper and instinctive language of meaning, and what precedes thought, is not English or German, French, Italian, Spanish, Chinese or Latin. It is different *universala esperanto*. And its syntax, I contend, is displayed by the enneagram and the rainbow.

The Why of this Method and its Transcending of the Modern Vision

It is difficult to impossible for us to imagine that the present language of science could be transcended - given the successes of modern technology. In the 19th century, there was the sublime industrial revolution - the hammer replacing the sickle - with the arrival of the factories, lumber mills and early factory farms. Then came the steam engines, railroads, telegraphic and phone communications, soaring skyscrapers and massive engineered bridges. Later we saw the invention of cars, radios, TV's, motion pictures, home and office appliances, planes, jets, space ships, atomic weapons, missiles, - and now fax machines and computers. It all appears as if we are progressively "conquering and mastering" nature supremely for all times. But for me this is an illusion we have bought into and that attaches to the modern vision.

For example, I have met so many individuals and in all walks of life who have fallen prey to an ailment that is uniquely pervasive in our modern world - cancer. It virtually symbolizes a radical loss of control - why the thought of getting cancer is so frightening. And these individuals lost their battle with this ailment despite having available the best of treatments that modern technology and knowledge have to offer. Sometimes they were themselves prominent professors, engineers, or doctors - recognized experts in what we consider the best of "secrets or truths of nature" as revealed by physics, chemistry and its applications to medicine. Yet they fell just as hard and fully to this scourge. Cancer has decisively become an epidemic. In the US, about half of all men and nearly as many women can expect cancer in their lifetime. Other industrialized nations have similar statistics.

In this context I must add that when during the first half of the 20th century Gurdjieff brought his wisdom to the West, many primary conditions of life were different. Nowadays we have several unprecedented problems that can impact the survival of all life on our planet. This includes the proliferation of atomic weapons, the rise in cancer, and the avalanche of increasing environmental crises. In just this past winter we had the warmest climate ever recorded here in North America (since the weather bureau started keeping statistics in the late 19th century). Millions of fish that normally migrate from the northeast down to the Carolinas never made their trip this year. We are too dangerously upsetting the cycles of nature around us - and thus we don't have the luxury, I believe, of pursuing deeper understanding as just a personal matter. While Gurdjieff emphasized individual development, I contend, we are in a different age wherein this no longer suffices - and that the collective mind thus needs to evolve substantially if we are to survive.

Three Principles

Now pursuing the above described "purified Baconian" or Gurdjieffian approach to self-awareness leads, I contend, to the discovery of three primary principles. To explain these, I like to start with the rainbow as my key metaphor and with the enneagram following subordinately. When looking at the rainbow, it appears to the naked eye as semi-circular (actually fully circular when its arch is not blocked by the earth's contours). You will never find it to be elliptical, what might occur via the reflection of light around a physical surface. The circularity holds from all points of view because the rainbow is not a physical or three-dimensional object. It showcases, via colors, a set of pre-three dimensional relationships that hold, I claim, for larger terrains. This differs fundamentally from the Newtonian view. Newton mathematized the rainbow along with the rest of nature. He assigned numerical wavelengths to its colors. This assumed that mathematics per se forms the highest and centrally organizing paradigm of nature - as in his *Principia Naturalis Mathematica* - the *laws of nature as mathematical*. I generally reverse this view. This means that I outline how math symbol patterns are formed out of rainbowesque light rather than outlining how the rainbow's colors are defined by math symbols. The same holds true for quantum mechanics' description of light in terms of quanta. The reverse perspective yields an entirely different understanding of the world we live in - again, a right-brain dominant view.

The first of these principles is that of a dynamic indistinguishable oneness ("1-ness").

When we open our eyes each morning, we begin to experience a somewhat infinite diversity of forms. Is there just one single unity behind this? In some yoga practices, we begin meditation by concentrating on our breath, though invisible, and its goings in and out. Here we might do something similar. We make contact with an "indistinguishable oneness" underlying conscious and subconscious experience, even though it seems invisible, and again via the flowings in and out. This refers to the formation of any forms (mental, physical, and emotional) and their dissolving back into the same underlying oneness. The enneagram is a static display of this because it is expressed in mathematical/geometric (or separative/fixated) form. But the rainbow shows the same dynamically and therefore more faithfully - appearing out of thin air with its color separations and then disappearing again entirely - or going back into the same indistinguishableness.

When a rock falls on us by accident, thereby bruising or lacerating a limb, we might say instantaneously -" Oh… my God! It h-u-r-t-s!" Even if we are atheists, we might blurt out such sanctimonious words to bring a universally connective force into us to undo pain. But simultaneously inner awareness (inner rainbowesque light) travels to the injury to start the healing process or to bring wholeness to what is cut or bruised. This all happens instantaneously without any direction of the conscious or rational mind.

Thus contrary to contemporary methods in physics and chemistry (first measuring things or noting their separate beginning and end points), we instead begin by observing heightened connectivity - even to the extent of transcending our mind's separations. We start with what relates to indistinguishable oneness rather than the optimum distinguishing or sharpest separating forms of consciousness. For the simple symbol "1" in counting represents the root universally applicable symbol for a separate whole (the equivalent of a "point" in geometry) and again the main building block concept for the atomic view of indivisibles. By contrast, here we begin with the very opposite world view, one which is abidingly *pointless*. This starting pointlessness depicts an unfocused, passive, right brain dominant and ultimately, I contend, real view of the foundations of the world we live in.

The second principle is that of duality, separation, or distinction ("2-ness").

I also call this the primary pattern of illusion - the falling apart of the integrity of what is both inner and outer. It is a relationship that is thus more than physical - and therefore difficult to communicate as to just how universally it applies. A sense of this is gained by observing the infinity of all possible thoughts being reduced to only black and white marks on a printed page or computer screen. Again this duality manifests in a dynamic movement from 1'ness to 2'ness - a separation or distinction of forms.

This has two dimensions: the process and the end result or its active and passive aspects. Physically, we can actively lift a knife and cut something in *two* as an end result. But again prephysically there is a yet deeper digging separation that appears in our awareness as pre-three dimensional mental and emotional "distinctions" - namely seeing differences. For example, two people are in love. They get married and wear wedding bands. The circular rings symbolize their unity in spirit. The moment this relationship loses that unity is when they begin to see and give power to their differences. As a result they fight, and first over little things and then over much more major issues. The process of focusing on distinctions and then the consequent fighting is symbolic of the active separation or oppositional juxtapositioning. After a while, the stress of their fights is so overbearing that they burn out. They decide to divorce and live behind separate walls - sleeping in separate quarters or living in separate housing units. This is symbolic for an end result or passive separation.

Thus the active precedes the passive and is the more "connective" and self-conscious relationship.

Mathematical symbols represent the highest pointing tools or abstractions to guide the separation of all elements of consciousness - and therefore they point to separative relationships and the harnessing of separative energy releases (including atomic weapons) which manifest themselves via this view of reality. This gives the false sense of "conquering nature" - when actually we are focusing our collective consciousness on what is a systematic departure from a connective essence of nature. As mentioned, Galileo's philosophy represents a synthetic and ultimately anti-natural/anti-ecological inversion. In this regard, some elements of nature can be cleaved or separated harmlessly - like rocks. But organic forms, because they are the most connected, are ultimately harmed - and even multi-dimensionally to the point of extinction. Furthermore a society that organizes itself around money, a form of quantification as its "god" or ruling social paradigm, progressively forms competitive/oppositional, exploitative, and superficial/separative relationships - with the rising personal costs of stress, alienation, meaninglessness - and of loneliness and despair amid illusions of wealth. We no longer hear the cry of the 1960's, as with the Beatles' refrain of "all those lonely people." But modern society, like its alienated orientation to nature, lacks integrity.[2]

Ultimately we are building modern civilization on a quicksand form of consciousness that is non-sustainable. It will predictably collapse - just as the integrity of the inner ecology of our body collapses with systemic ailments. But we can reverse this, our foundation stones. We can retool uses of money and more generally math-bound applications using math/geometric symbols as pointing back to nature's underlying oneness - as with the enneagram. This is seen visually. Thus in geometry we might either draw a *corner* to represent active/oppositional separation or a rounded, cornerless figure, like the circle, which also has no breaks to symbolize oneness. All its points blend together connectively without opposition and as a whole.

A corner is simply the point where two lines meet - are connected - but in an "active separative" or oppositional way. Rub the corners of two rocks and rather than harmonize they release a spark of destructive fire. When we are exposed to a sharp edge - formed out of the opposition of two planes - this creates a cutting line (as with a knife or sword). Even the physical shape, the geometry of a postal envelope can cut a finger or lip. A serrated knife (with double cornered edges or in two plains) cuts more effectively. An electrified chain saw - combining a serrated edge with electricity (where electricity represents a sharp separation of positive, negative, neutral forms) cuts still more powerfully.

The above gives just a few and very brief examples of modes of duality relationships - mentally seeing differences, emotionally fighting and burning out, and physically cutting modes. They are infinite examples because these are universal principles forming a noetic (inner/outer as òne) view of the root nature of our world. Pre-three dimensionally, when light is focused, as with a laser, it also will cut into the fabric of light's forms - within and without. Concepts are guiding forms for the focusing/separating of inner light and thus by the mere act of focusing attention, conceptually (inner map) guided, we alter what we see. That is why pre-conceptual and unfocused perception sees more nakedly, more truthfully (and this is what the Gurdjieff's method tries to simulate - or what Gurdjieff refers to as an experience of what is more essential or "real"). With this understanding and in the laboratory, when a class of students all focus their attention under a microscope, and to see distinct elements in separate magnification levels brought into sharp focus 1x, 10x, 100x - for the act of focusing is the separating of consciousness - they then see non-objectively. Next when these same students are taught to measure the beginning and end points of what is seen, this then deepens the loss of objectivity. They are essentially taught an illusionary

---

[2] See discussion of the same in Jose Ortega y Gasset, *The Modern Theme*; Norton, 1933.

inversion. The reason we make this fundamental mistake is that the nature of consciousness is not thoroughly understood before we choose a form through which to enter the world of our senses. This was Galileo's mistake and thus the critical importance of starting with a purified inductive method.

I could write many more pages on this but I hope this gives a sufficient starting sense of how the principles of unity and duality interplay in this encompassing noetic dance - what then yields a different understanding of nature. This perspective is vital to know not only for itself, but in applications. While our math-bound view is at home in building machinery, things made of separate parts, the alternative view offers something more essential, the guiding of the healing process - mental, physical, or emotional - or a return from what is separative. Thus we unravel first the passive and then the active forms of separation (again whether physical, mental and emotional) and in reverse order to their initial course. Therefore a disease might begin with acute pain and fever, a shock or trauma and end in chronic numbness, unconsciousness, disability and death - moving through active to passive… or from acute to chronic and ultimately fatal stages. We then reverse the disease process via its originating paths. Also while the body falls prey to disease, consciousness experiences "illusions" - what represent the equivalent of an ill state or a falling apart of pre-three and three-dimensional awareness. The mathematical view, being the most separative, is thus the most illusionary - for it takes us systemically and systematically toward this direction (although the symbols again can be retooled to avoid this). From my perspective, the Galilean vision historically became dominant precisely because it harnesses entrancement, forming the least rather than the most objective vision (except in mechanical terrains). We see something similarly when a judge is given money on the side. He or she loses objectivity. Lastly there are *crossbridges*, a word used to designate the active and passive forms of separation coalescing, either enhancing each other or counteracting. Again this is a v-a-s-t subject. From a Gurdjieffian point of view, observing how a person falls "asleep" or becomes "mechanical," "identified," and with "crystallized habits" in daily life - all of these are contained in this subject matter. They are by-products of falling prey to the illusions of separative/surface appearance states of consciousness - with insufficient understanding of how to navigate commandingly in this terrain.

The third or triangulation principle is a connective return from both active and passive forms of duality, separation or distinction.

When dualities oppose or nullify each other the return out of illusions and ill health is but superficial. That is why with conventional cancer treatments - aggressively killing cancer cell with chemotherapy, radiation and surgery (allopathic methods based on separative/quantitative vision of nature of the 17th century) - this often heals only that which is local, acute, sitespecific and superficial - not that which is deeper, systemic or metastatic. What the third or triangulation principle represents is a path past separative/surface appearances to the causal or deeper, connective, systemic healing level of understanding. In my work with cancer patients, this principle underlies literally all effective remedies.

Gurdjieff's Enneagramatic View

Physically, and in ancient writings of the Sufis, Hawaiian Hunas, and I am thinking especially of the Essenes[3] who were early Judeo-Christian healers, water is one of many vital instruments for this principle of triangulation. Water unwinds oppositional separation when it rounds the sharp corners of rocks and puts out fire. Water brings out the rainbow and life or the connective/conscious relationship from every seed. Water forms spherical bubbles. Water soothes tensions. It sets up a triangulation in 1/3 =.333333 to infinity (the principle of integrity past division, remaining itself as 3 despite division). This relates to how water is the medium in homeopathy past progressively smaller divisions/separations of light into separate magnification levels. Therefore the triterations of homeopathic remedies have *real* effects past the atomic level of smallness (which is a cultural bias to focus on). In this context the atomic perception is seen as yet another fooling, anthropocentric view built around an illusionary starting point for deductive reasoning - the math-bound view of Galileo and his contemporaries.

The same overcoming of separations is displayed when we progressively divide a triangle by a line - which forms triangles to infinite smallness. Here again is a principle of depth integrity rather than of only surface or fooling appearance. The prism in this context, and via its triangulating form, also brings out the rainbow - the very same paradigm for the unity of colors in light and a metaphorical arching bridge between matter and mind. *"I draw my bow of rainbows, the continuum between minds and matters"* - a Hawaiian Huna song tells us. Amid the rainbow's colors[4] there are three essential colors of red, green, violet. They appear when the prism is tilted (as the seven colors condense into the three out of which they were formed). These three establish between themselves what Gurdjieff called the affirming, reconciling and denying principles - and they when pointed together reconnect integrally. This means they disappear into indistinguishable oneness or colorless light.

This returning or triangulation of duality forms is again not confined to that which is physical alone. It relates equally and with like power to what is mental, emotional, and physical. For example, with love we triangulate emotional differences - undoing hate, violence and self-centeredness. With mental synthesis we triangulate contradictions. When metaphorically "pouring water over words" we let go of sharp edges to yield expansive poetry. The three main chakras in some yoga practices representing three centers, as Gurdjieff might describe them - of mind, body and feelings. They can further be brought together to function, as Gurdjieff would say, *harmoniously*. We undo the main separative knots in the chakras of the rainbow/enneagramatic body. There is more to this as the rainbow and enneagram display not just three but seven relationships - but with the first three being the most essential and the other four simply derivative. Or as it is written in the *Dao De Jing*:[5]

---

[3] Edmond B. Szekely, trans. Essene Gospel of Peace - Book I; International Biogenic Society 1981
[4] The essentials of color relationships in the rainbow can be found in Colonel Dinshah P Ghadiali, *Spectro-Chrometry Encyclopedia* - Vol. 1-3; Spectro-Chrome Institute, 1939.
[5] Lao Tsu, Moss Roberts, trans. *Dao De Jing - The Book of the Way*; University California Press, 2001.

yi er	*Out of one came two,*
er san,	*Out of two, three*
san wan yi.	*Out of three, infinity.*

A few years ago I had the privilege to help found a clinic where cancer patients used alternative holistic means - where they could return from their "valley of the shadow" to light, health, and wholeness. This was immensely rewarding work to see many at the edge of death returning to health. However, it seemed each year still more fell prey to the same - dwarfing such efforts. Not only is this true for human beings, but the equivalent carcinomas are evident more widely in our environment as other life forms suffer equally. It is estimated in the next 50 years alone, and given the continuous "advance" of civilization, approximately $1/3^{rd}$ of all life forms will be threatened with extinction. It takes no genius to reason that we human beings might be next in line. Something needs to be done quite urgently and decisively. But the fuller healing of this dire state of affairs - with more than just a band-aid as conditions worsen - involves something *extremely* deep. This refers to uprooting our culture's quintessential or taproot worldview. Imagine that the "cure" triangulates the same, the originating steps of the mathematical/mechanical vision of nature - unravelling its entrancing separative illusions, stopping its engulfing cultural valleys of the shadow and re-guiding a return.

The seemingly childish spectacle of a rainbow and of the enneagram point to a way.

Lastly, turning to Gurdjieff's words for a concluding perspective: "Speaking in general it must be understood that the enneagram is a universal symbol. All knowledge can be included in the enneagram and with the help of the enneagram it can be interpreted. And in this connection only what a man is able to put into the enneagram does he actually know, that is, understand. What he cannot put into the enneagram he does not understand. For the man who is able to make use of it, the enneagram makes books and libraries entirely unnecessary. Everything can be included and read in the enneagram. A man may be quite alone in the desert and he can trace the enneagram in the sand and in it read the eternal laws of the universe. And every time he can learn something new, something he did not know before.

If two men who have been in different schools meet, they will draw the enneagram and with its help they will be able at once to establish which of them knows more and which, consequently, stands upon which step, that is to say, which is the elder, which is the teacher and which the pupil. The enneagram is the fundamental hieroglyph of a universal language which has as many different meanings as there are levels of men."[6]

© Copyright 2002 - Nathan Batalion - All Rights Reserved

---

[6] Gurdjieff, as quoted in Ouspensky, *In Search of the Miraculous*, p. 294.

Gurdjieff's Enneagramatic View - Questions & Answers

Keith Buzzell: Reading this paper is unusual at A&E, in the formal sense, as it is the first time we've read a paper submitted by an author quite unknown to any of us. We've had several papers presented where the authors were not here, but they were quite well known to a number of us.

Questioner 1: Here, it seems, he emphasizes that it is important not to buy the abstract idea but rather to learn via hands on, or phenomenological experience. You have only small representative things which you perceive, out of which you conceive an abstraction - that is, the 'thing' precedes the idea. But then, I was confused when it was followed by the idea of the whole, the totality, which, according to the Nominal is you never get to, you can't get to. There is no abstract core in the totality. No matter how much your phenomenological experience touches different aspects of life you cannot posit the whole from any inductive movement up the ladder - because you can never get to the top! As a medievalist I'm quite familiar with the inductive empiricist method. (As with Bacon) That goes nowhere by itself- it only goes somewhere if we can attach it to Gurdjieff. My idea about that is that Gurdjieff accepted *both* sides, rejected none - but agreed with none. There had to be a collaboration between induction and conceptualization of experience. Both conceptual and literal. But I may be wrong there, and I was wondering if you thought, in reading this, that he was going in that direction, not in denying conceptualization or deduction or going totally with the inductive empiricist view, or whether he was coming to what you might call a unitive view. That's what I always admired about Gurdjieff. He left *both* paths and took one right between the two. Depending on the individual - there are people who cannot be inductive, there are people who cannot be conceptual. That's the way I thought Gurdjieff looked at this.

Questioner 2: Have you finished reading the paper? Did he mention how this connects up specifically with the Gurdjieff Work?

Keith Buzzell: One of my questions was that I didn't understand the specific relationship between the rainbow and the Enneagram. As best I could understand it is that the enneagram was, for him, a geometric expression - and therefore is a symbolic abstraction. This results when you use a left brain, linear approach. A more real approach, relative to the actual phenomena, would be to see the enneagram in the contextual background of a prism showing the differentiation of light, which is really one. He does mention in the paper that Newton for instance comes up with a description of wave lengths that then describe the light and he ascribes the light to the wavelength, when in the actual phenomenon it is quite the reverse. You start with the actual phenomena (the prism) and the light blends together into one and becomes white light. Becomes *white* light, not red, orange or whatever. So there seems to be something here where he is pointing to what was his life experience that was predominantly, if you will, a classic right brain sort of thing - where he sees emotionally, he gains a whole impression of phenomena sensorily and inductively based on that and not on an abstraction. That seemed to be the main point that he was driving at. I do not have a clear idea what his Work experience is. I agree with Paul that Gurdjieff is right in the middle - he uses whatever is there in the moment - in reality.

Questioner 1: By the way, you know, when you are talking about an Indian abstraction it is a tricky business. I have spent many years studying Native American art. When you paint a sand painting, as part of a ceremonial cure, a blessing way or whatever the design that you make is extraordinarily complex and very often enneagramic-like and is hardly considered by those who use it as abstract. It is really 'hands-on' real and that's why it has to be destroyed. What really hurts - many of you have been in the southwest - and they *sell*, for God's sake, sand paintings. Now the true sand paintings have to be destroyed because it has a specific blessing or is a specific ceremony.

The enneagram is very much a ceremony too - imagine what I would think if I never knew anything about the enneagram and then read all these descriptions on the websites, all the sort of biorhythms and everything else that is attached to the enneagram - that's another way of looking at 'real'. Abstract is a funny term to use in terms of Gurdjieff, that's all I meant. I don't think Gurdjieff saw it that way and I admire this chap for going at it the way he does - but the terminology is always difficult. It is hard to say Gurdjieff is this or Gurdjieff is that or is not that. I have made a fool of myself in the past over a line in Gurdjieff's writings, that tried to pin him down. Gurdjieff is this *and* that.

Keith Buzzell: The impression I get is that Nathan has had some contact with one of the Nyland groups. But he didn't speak about it in reference to any period of time. My impression in talking to him on the telephone around this kind of thing (where I tried to get him to give a little clearer notion) was that his primary acquaintance is through the ideas, then, from his own life experience of having gone through this very difficult time he found that when he did become acquainted with Gurdjieff that he said, "finally someone understands". There is a teaching here that really recognized that life is this whole perceptual process that leads to this unity. Then he kind of sees it this way, talking about the ladder and stays pretty much with the imagery.

Questioner 3: How was he over the phone?

Keith Buzzell: Very articulate. He's now, I think, about 28-29 years old He seems to have no difficulty functioning in a logical left brain manner in terms of his verbal capacity.

Questioner 3: You know there's something I want to say along the lines Paul mentioned. From another angle - not Gurdjieffian. Many people get acquainted with philosophical ideas and schools and what they represent. They don't understand the kind of effort that people in philosophy have put sometimes, that they have tried to define their terms much more sharply. A philosopher would have all the objections that Paul has and then some. If one wants to make this kind of effort at philosophy he should be much better prepared.

Questioner 4: What I heard you read that seemed important to me was not about the enneagram so much. It has to do with self awareness. You read something there about self observation. It's hard to know just from that but I got the impression that he came to something himself because of the aphasic condition which had to do with this, and then when he came across the Gurdjieff teaching, whether it was through the Nyland group or whatever just like you said, he says "here's someone who finally understands my experience". And his self awareness experience when traced inward back to the root you might say, being aware, - being aware of being aware - would be this experiential direction - this experience of wholeness. Now we can't know his experience so it really requires him to be here to tell us and that's the problem.

Keith Buzzell: Unfortunately, I didn't read out in any detail his three principles. What his three principles confirmed (the point I think you emphasized) - what he sees here that is so true is that in the process of self observation naming is the worst thing you can do. If you start categorizing things and write out a diary and say this is an instance of this etc., then we are missing the point because we may not 'see' in the experience, we may not *experience* the feeling or the sensation and it's the feeling with the sensation. It's not the name that we give to the feeling or the sensation and he seems to clearly be able to separate those and to me that's important.

Questioner 5: Yes, because that's what we are striving for, searching for, to describe objectively. So real self awareness must be objective. So it can't be a calculation or analysis or description. There is no objectivity in that. Objectivity, in Gurdjieffian terms, must be that, must be no description.

Questioner 1: But remember the first thing that any one did when he went to the Institute - he was asked to do just that - to use language to help resolve it. That's the challenge. He was to fit the word to the condition. Now its true that gave an additional leverage to teachers of challenging the relationship between the terms and the conditions that they were put into. But you had to use the names. If you couldn't then you couldn't make that first step into what you might call deconstruction of your own problems. I seem to be contradicting something that is fundamental, but all Gurdjieff teachers in those days said you had to start with finding the names. The names always wrong, - of course they were wrong, but you had to go through that experience.

Questioner 6: I think I have a different impression from anybody else. I think I heard you say was that he had this unitive experience when he perceived without distinction or description or analysis of his perception and then something happened, as it were, and things separated and then you said something happened whereby he managed to restore himself to the unitive...

Keith Buzzell: What he calls the triangulation. I wouldn't differ from Paul but I think the description there is: first the experience, he put the name and anticipated the experience and then we get it backwards.

Questioner 6: But then what was it that happened to enable him to reconcile or to return to some sense of the unitive experience - after it had fragmented.

Keith Buzzell: I asked him and it seemed to go back to these images that he created with the deductive theme - essentially starting from up here and going down through the abstract/conceptual and applying that through mathematical symbolization and so forth and then apply it to the individual instance *or* you start here from the deductive, the actual experience of observation, the gathering of data. And then at the top of that ladder he mentions that you add the mathematical. The mathematical is then the top step of that rather than the beginning step. It is something that you gradually work up to. So it isn't that he denies the fusion into the abstract, he says how do you build into the abstract. You build into it from experience, trying not to name but then naming the experience, but having the experience first and not getting lost in feelings of jealousy or rage or sadness or whatever happens to be. To have that as an *experience* - subjective, real experience unnamed *first* and then name it.

Questioner 7: When you talked to him on the telephone were you moved by his spirit, were you emotionally moved by his spirit, because what I hear is that he is a man who was cut off from the ordinary kind of perception that we have and he found in the Gurdjieff Work a connection, that is something that made sense to him. That must have been an extraordinary experience, apart from how to label it in the language we use. He connected it up again, to some extent, through the Gurdjieff Work. So what surprises me about the paper is that it is an extraordinary story, but I find myself not moved by it. We can talk about intellectual terminology and naming but if you were the one effected you are dealing with a world that is extremely different from what you have ever dealt with before. It is a shock, a complete shock and then you find a 'work' in which it connects you up again with things.

Keith Buzzell: I think that's how it happens. This circumstance that he went through happened at a young age, when he was only seventeen, and this goes on for several years - but it gets better. He doesn't say totally off base, he is partially off base. What this means I have no idea as to degree. He clearly states that he had difficulty putting sentences together in a linear logical fashion. That makes sense if you go back and really see that when we start talking out our linear logical language we are at the end of at least four levels of abstraction that have to do with the phonemes, the alphabet, with the word constructions that have meaning for us, that have to do with combining those word sequences into a meaningful context. So we have at least those four levels of abstraction that you and I never give a thought to. We just open our mouth and out it comes. But when you are constantly aphasic that process is thwarted in some way, shape or form and that's what happened to him for a while and then gradually he reached the point where he could re-institute that linear logic. He would have to speak slowly and think it out. Not that he wasn't cognitively aware of it. We're talking about language, about communication. His mind, as a whole would have been working just fine.

Questioner 6: But were you talking about it like it doesn't have any feeling attached to it? Like it was a newspaper report?

Keith Buzzell: He doesn't report but I may be making that error. He speaks about it very emotionally because it's right brain function and our right brain is emotionally interconnected with emotional center.

Questioner 6: Right. So what emotions were reflected from him when you talked to him? Where was he?

Keith Buzzell: I found him very interesting and wished that we had had time to take this much further before the conference.

Questioner 2: This is a minor point but I think he spoke about Roger Bacon not Francis Bacon. I made the same mistake, - a lot of people do. It's really the late Roger Bacon who apparently had this kind of experience as a twelfth century monk, who Paul mentioned and not the well known Francis Bacon of the 17th Century. Somehow he seems to be making a connection here with Roger Bacon.

Questioner 1: Was Gurdjieff all inductive? No, of course not. That's the whole point. There is hardly a trace of inductive reasoning, or inductive process. If you go to Orage, Toomer and Ouspensky - that's deduction from the word go! To begin with they would deduce a particular value and then go look for the particular. It isn't going through an experience and then saying 'this is adding up to a realization of a particular value'. That would be inductive. But when you deduce that there is a particular value, a secret learning or whatever you want to call it and then you look for the experience that will prove it, that is according to logic, that's deduction, not induction. The difference is that induction tends to be one way up the ladder but deduction is not one way because deduction does not have a linear, a vertical direction. The problem with deduction is that you have to go find a consistent pattern of experiences. It's a scattered horizontal as well as a vertical search and this is the weakness of deduction in the history of philosophy. That's why Bacon was so revolutionary in a way, when he said you can know nothing to begin with and you build your knowledge by your perceptual experience and thus you build your concept of the world. It tricks us in a way when we are categorizing all of this. It is really a problem. It's not only conceptual or perceptual but inductive as well. It doesn't work. These are Yale University whiffinpoof terms, not really well connected up with the real experience.

Questioner 5: You know, I think the point is well taken. Let me explain how I see this and how it relates. When the man speaks about being present, seeing unity, the world as a unit. I don't think he means that the world is a unit. I think that 'I' am the unity at this point. He is in a certain state as he sees the unity and somehow he doesn't really persuade us as to how he is. He jumps immediately into categorizing the specific knowledge, his experience.

Questioner 7: Is he not paying a price of what he enjoys or shares? The problem is not one of perception, it is one of communication. Not one of cognition, it is one of communication. It is certainly not that he is an average person.

Questioner 5: He is at a point, what we would say, 'He is present'. He observes. At this point he says, 'so my mind is inductive and not deductive'. And it is with my right brain, not my left brain that I use for what I see. It is the state that makes him see unity not the nature of the room. The room is over there.

Questioner 7: What I got from it was that what he experienced was something that he couldn't communicate, as John said, and I'm sure that everyone has had that experience in some sense and I've spent years babbling at people about it. Something happens and I suspect he was babbling at people in an attempt to communicate something that couldn't be communicated. Eventually I met a Sufi and I was just babbling on and he just said 'Sophia you are just talking about that time' and I thought, 'that was right'. So while I think that won't mean anything to you, to me it helped enormously. It was just an incommunicable experience, it occurred. That's the feeling I got from him. He had this experience which there isn't any communication about it possible, - it only happens. You said before that this about it being in time, it's not really, it's just that I've never been able to find any words for it.

Questioner 8: Of all the papers to read this is the one you would read like a person speaking.

Keith Buzzell: Yes. I think that's true. Another thing to keep in mind. I have spent a great deal of time reading in the neurophysiological literature about brain injuries. An immense variety - temporary and permanent seizure disorders, tumors, blood vessel maldevelopments, a whole host of pathologies. If we had time to go through them I am sure you would all be terribly shocked at what we are capable and incapable of when certain parts of our central nervous system don't function. It's startling stuff and you would say that's not possible. It *is* possible. There are these people, these poor patients who have these difficulties and part of it is being reflected here I think. When you see we can't do we can't, as we sit here, suddenly say, 'well we're not talking about words because our left cortex (if we are right handed) we can't avoid that in this moment. It's experiential, it's there and it functions as it does in our adulthood with our background and so forth. We have no way of turning it off. His got turned off, that's the point, - at least partially turned off. So he has a different experiential entry into the world. Every experience he has during the day, first of all, is very emotionally charged because he's got this much more direct linkage by image into his limbic brain. So he feels these things here (pointing to the chest) far more. That's a state image. He's in an inner state that has to do with his emotional world, with every single perception he has up there, but he doesn't *name* it. He doesn't necessarily put a name on it but it's no less a cognitive three brain state. It's just one that doesn't happen to get over into the temporal lobe of the left brain.

Questioner 4: If he didn't have this difficulty on the left side of his brain it wouldn't be so complete or rosy or perfect or obsolete that it seems to be for him. It would be compromised by the activity of the left side of the brain and not be so completely a question about communicating or not. He just doesn't have that faculty.

Keith Buzzell: It's partially aphasic. It is not a permanent thing, it is something that over a period of several years he slowly regains in function. So he has an opportunity that I've never had and that is, I can remember and go back to those experiences and he can't do that. He has experienced something when this one aspect wasn't as functional. So he says, 'What is the world out there, how do I take that world in?" And it's no less complete and it's fully charged with feeling and emotion but it's not arranged in the same way.

Questioner 7: I have heard much more about you and your enthusiasm and your interests than I have from the paper. And so I know you better, but not him.

Questioner 4: Assuming for the moment that he's had this experience his writing in that intellectual way may deprive us of the emotion that we're looking for. I'm not saying that's true. We don't have enough information, except for you Keith, because you've spoken to the man and maybe something was communicated in a way that doesn't come across with this sort of an intellectual presentation.

Questioner 7: I love your excitement over this.

Questioner 1: Has anyone here seen the recent film called "Kaypa"? Yes? That is a Gurdjieff film from beginning to end although it ends with eternal recurrence which unfortunately twists this to Ouspensky. Kaypa is the name of a planet (which stands for Karatas). And the hero is Beelzebub and he comes down and goes into different countries and of course he ends up in the insane asylum and Jeff Bridges plays the psychologist who has the question, "How does this man's mind work?" because he has that sophistication of depth and perception. But he is 'sick' so you see we are stuck with that same judgement of ordinary society and we also know or we learn that he's not only one person, because this is the Beelzebub who can be evolved out of a real human being as well as entering into a three brained being. He is mad according to the psychiatrist because he has gone through an extraordinary trauma which has made him aphasic. So he walks between these two worlds, which is absolutely impossible for the psychiatrist to deal with, and at the end of the film Beelzebub leaves, goes back, takes someone with him and what is left behind is the vestige or the residue of what psychiatry makes out of it, which is totally 'ill'. You ought to see it. I think it's an extraordinary Gurdjieff film.

Questioner 7: Didn't you bring it with you? ...How can you do this to us? (laughter)

Questioner 1: I saw it in early November. It was in New York City and I was just shaken by it. I've seen a lot of things which can remind you of Gurdjieff here and there, like a lot of films that do this, but this was absolutely extraordinary and it highlights just the same problem that he's talking about.

Questioner 8: Well, what it made me think of and I don't know how to go about it - but - I have been in other spiritual disciplines and we would have principles and those were different ways of learning where you would give up concept and then they would give us the result and we would have to create it. Or they would give us a bunch of materials and then we would have to create the form. So listening to this, it's like people who are architectural and learn differently and think differently. You know there are some of us who just learn differently. What it makes me think of is that maybe in the situation of this man was that he was forced to perceive and think differently. That is an opportunity.

Keith Buzzell: That's how he certainly saw it. I think that he was forced, because of what had happened to him, to make a different kind of effort and so he discovered that his view of the world was quite different. So he had to accommodate to that and then over time, as he does point out, he finally came to treasure that, because it opened up a whole arena that he never would have seen before.

Questioner 9: I just want to say well maybe we could… because we do every night. We go into another world which is radically different and at least, I've been sort of conditioned to think that, there can be work of a sort and maybe tomorrow one will have discovered something. I've become a little bit interested because I spent some time with some Tibetans who are very active in working with this kind of thing. I was surprised to find that some people do take that very, very seriously, namely, that you can meditate in your sleep. I thought about it and it struck me now because I see that there is something that is different. I can't describe the world but it suddenly is *different*, and it has to do with being in something that has to do with my feelings much more than my waking state. So it has to do with a different part of myself and to me it's clear that it is something which is part of the reality that is me but which I'm not allowing myself to be close to or really take in.

Keith Buzzell: Well, we are well over time and it is getting late. We start again early in the A.M. Thank you all.

The Kahunas and Gurdjieff's Three Brain Beings

Dr. H. J. Sharp

It seems to me that an important factor relating to Spiritual Healing and other Psychic Phenomena is the forgotten and suppressed knowledge of the Kahunas.

Our story starts with W. Reginald Stewart of Brighton. When he was a young man, working as a foreign correspondent, he had heard of a tribe of Berbers living in the Atlas Mountains in North Africa, across from Spain, who possessed a great knowledge of "Magic" and whose tribal traditions indicated that they had migrated westwards from Egypt.

Mr. Stewart found the tribe and in it there was only one individual who knew and could use the ancient system of magic. This was a woman whose title was Quahini This was not a Berber word but was found much later to be a variation of the Hawaiian kahuna wahine, meaning a woman kahuna.

Only a blood son was able to receive the training in the knowledge and so after many difficulties Stewart managed to get himself adopted by the woman after going through much ceremony and ritual. Together with the daughter of the woman kahuna he began his training, being first taught the general theory of the ancient system of psychology and religion. His teacher explained that the instruction could only be given in what she called "the sacred language". This was not the Berber dialect and Stewart had great difficulty getting the meaning of the words translated into Berber and French, French being familiar to him and his teacher. He made a list of the important words. His training was halted by the death of the teacher from a stray bullet during a clash between two of the local tribes.

Mean while Max Freedom Long[1] had begun to investigate the ancient knowledge of the Huna in Hawaii around 1918. He quickly made a friend of Dr. William Tufts Bingham, who had been the Curator of the British Museum in Honolulu for many years and had been observing and recording the performance of miracles of healing by the Kahunas.

Dr Aubrey Westlake, whom I lived close by many years ago, also made the teaching of the Kahunas an important part of his work on alternative medicine.[2]

---

[1] The Secret Science at Work. Max Freedom Long. Devorss Publications. 1953.
[2] The Pattern of Health. Aubrey T. Westlake. Element Books. 1985.

The Hawaiian Islands had been isolated from the rest of the known world for centuries until Captain Cook discovered them in 1778. The inhabitants were considered to be primitive but of high intelligence. They had come across the vast Pacific from some other lands as their legends tell, sailing their outrigger canoes, guided by their knowledge of the stars. Their original home has not been proved, but many now believe it was in the Near East, migrating by way of India. Hence the connection with the Berbers discovered by Reginald Stewart.

There is an alternative but more complicated possibility. This is mentioned at the end of this paper. They brought with them as legends accounts similar to the Garden of Eden story, the Flood, Jonah and the Whale, The Epic of Gilgamesh, and many Old Testament stories. There was no story concerning Jesus which indicates that the migrations were begun before the time of Jesus. Some time after the discovery of Hawaii by Captain Cook, the missionaries came and suppressed all their traditional culture and beliefs. It is only as a result of the painstaking investigations of Max Freedom Long and Aubrey Westlake that their original culture has now been uncovered.

Max Freedom Long's research led to nothing in the early stages. He concluded that the Hawaiians and the Kahunas were irrevocably pledged to secrecy. He gave up in 1931 and left Hawaii. In 1934 he awoke one night with an idea, that the clues were all in the native language. So he looked for words which might have something to do with man's mental and spiritual nature.

Eventually, when Max Freedom Long began to publish some of his material, it was picked up by Reginald Stewart and they found that there was a correlation between the special words on his list and those of Freedom Long.

The most convincing proof that the ancient knowledge was originally well known and used in the Near east, was the fact that in many parts of the Old Testament, from Genesis on, there are Huna teachings mentioned and accounts given of the miracles performed by initiates. In the New Testament is to be found the same code. Jesus strove to spread the same basic beliefs in the same symbols. He performed the typical miracles of the Kahunas and observed the ancient cult of secrecy. He gave the disciples the Huna, or mystery, teachings concerning the "Kingdom of Heaven", so that they to could perform miracles and understand the hidden truths.

The key words which run through our story as it unfolds are creative imagination, aspiration, effort, honesty and will. We will gradually explore the significance of these words in particular as we proceed. At this stage, meanwhile, we can link aspiration, creative imagination and effort with prayer. The two basic forms of prayer are prayer of contemplation and prayer of petition. The most usual form of prayer we all indulge in from time to time is prayer of petition. We want something so we ask for it. Unfortunately such prayers are rarely answered. This may be because although prayers of petition are the most common, we are not properly taught how to make such prayers. Most of our religious instructors do not know anyway. But there have been people who know. One such group was the Kahuna of Hawaii.

The Kahunas and Gurdjieff's Three Brain Beings

Kahuna, pronounced kah - hoo" - nah, means "keeper of the secret". The basis of the teaching uncovered could be described as an acceptance of the human being a Three Brained Being. This, together with a number of other aspects makes a close parallel with the teaching of Gurdjieff which was also based on ancient knowledge. The long isolation of the Hawaiians makes the situation even more interesting and indicates a common root source of great antiquity.

The Kahuna consider that in each of us there are three separate entities or selves which they call the aka bodies. These depend upon the manna of vital force. For manna sometimes the word wai, meaning water, is used. So water is a symbol for manna. The three aka bodies are the low self, the middle self and the High Self.

The manna, the vital force, is generated by the low self from the foods and air it consumes. Using the symbol for manna, water, the water raised to overflowing as a fountain, is a symbol for the accumulated vital force as a surcharge by the lower self.

The vital force of the High Self, originally taken from the low self along the connecting aka cord, is symbolised by clouds and mist of fine droplets. These when falling symbolise the return of the vital force, transformed to carry the blessings of the High Self, as they fall on the middle and lower selves to help and heal. This in many ways is similar to the Mevlevi. They turn with the right hand uppermost palm open to receive the power from on high and with the left arm down, palm down to scatter the transformed energies on the earth.

The human can only be completely integrated when the three selves work harmoniously together. The High Self already works correctly. The task is to put the low and middle selves in order, in particular the low self, by trying to help the lower two selves evolve to higher levels. In this way the low self can lose some of its animal nature. This surely this is an accurate description of Man No. 1, 2, and 3 as the low self with Man No. 4 as the middle self.

The word for the low self is Uhinipili. This means a separate and conscious spirit or entity; a lesser God in the making. Its role is to act as a servant of the middle self as a younger brother. It has control of all the processes of the physical body, of everything but the voluntary muscles. In its aka body it can slide into and out of the physical body. It impregnates every cell and tissue of the body and brain. It alone is the seat of the emotions.

The major job of the middle self is to learn to control the low self and prevent it running off with the human. The low self manufactures all the vital force or manna for the three selves. Normally it shares the manna with the middle self who can use it at will.

The task of the middle self is to teach and guide the low self; to bring it along in its evolutionary growth and help it to be less animal and more human, just as the High Self offers help and guidance to the middle self.

Another task of the middle self is to learn to work consciously and properly with both the low self and the High Self. In addition to its basic instincts, its ability to remember, and its ability to use the five senses, the low self has the ability to sense radiation from things; has the ability to fasten to a person or thing, once contact has been made, an invisible thread of aka or ectoplasmic substance of the shadowy body or the low self, the Uhinipili; has the ability to use these established aka threads. For example, the aka finger can carry with it a portion of the aka duplication of the sense organs. Impressions can not only be sent back to the middle self, but also sent forward as thought forms, as "thought form clusters". This is in effect telepathy.

The Kahunas take the view that all prayer is telepathic. The High Self, like God, is a spirit and has no ears or other senses and so our only way of getting a message through is by thought form clusters. Prayer is simply asking the High Self to take its proper part in creating the desired conditions for which we pray. All three selves in a human have their part to play in creative prayer, that is to say, prayer of petition.

The High self is Aumakua, the utterly trustworthy parental spirit, the God who is father. Au, the action of mind, a flow of current in the sea, a cord. Makua, parent, a father.

The Kahunas believed that as a man has a trinity of spirits, so there must be a trinity of beings making up the next highest God. These are called Ku, Kan and Kanaloa. They considered that there must be a hierarchy of lesser Gods bridging the enormous gap between the spirits in man and the ultimate God himself. This is their "Ray of Creation".

If the High Self, to whom all prayer must first go, was not able to being about the conditions requested, it could at its discretion, carry the prayer on to higher beings. The High selves also lived in close association called the Poe Aumakua, the great Company of Aumakuas, all ready to help each other. Is this a reference to the Conscious Circle, to the masters of Wisdom?

Jesus said: "The Kingdom of heaven is within you".[3]

The Kahunas used another title for the High Self: Akua noho, a God who dwells with or within one. Isaiah sets down the Kahuna idea of the High Self as "Wonderful Counsellor"; "everlasting father".

In Kahuna the one great sin is hurting another. The High Self is beyond hurt, in other words beyond the union of opposites, but the low self can hurt others, mentally or physically and itself by excesses. Such things we are aware of and so can stop. Successful prayer, properly addressed to God by way of the High Self, or "in my name" as Jesus taught, cannot be made while one is still guilty of having hurt others. One must first make retribution.

The High self is symbolised as light - Ao or Io - Light and truth, or "The real Truth and Reality".

---

[3] Luke. Ch.17. v.21.

The Kahunas and Gurdjieff's Three Brain Beings

Prayer was often addressed to Ala -"The Anointed One" - or "The Way" - "The Path" - symbol of the aka cord running from the low self to the High Self. Jesus said; "I am the Way, the truth and the Life". Life in this sense is the manna transformed by the Higher self and returned to the low self and middle self as a healing and blessing force.

One who succeeds in uniting frequently with the High Self by means of contact made by the low self along the aka cord, is symbolically "Yoked to the Lord High Self". Jesus, speaking of the Father, taught: "My yoke is easy, My burden is light".[4]

A cup can symbolise the thought form cluster used to make the prayer by the low self and middle self and sent telepathically along the aka cord to the High Self. The filling of the cup symbolises the answering of the prayer by the High Self. In Egypt and India, the cup was replaced by the golden lotus which is itself a cup. The lotus rises on a long stem from the pool, representing the aka cord. The floating on the water is a symbol of the low self manna.

Another symbol is the seed. A cluster of seeds could be sent to the High Self along a manna flow along the cord. The daily sending of a surcharge of manna is the watering of the seeds planted in the Garden of Eden. For the Kahunas, the seed had the meaning of something which changed the state of things or changed the present conditions.

The thought form clusters sent must be of the desired condition and not of the present condition that needs to be changed. So the image of a broken leg is not sent, but an image of a healed leg. Ano-ano - a likeness or image of the desired condition. It is the meaning contained in the words of the prayer as they are spoken aloud while the prayer is being sent at the same instant by the low self telepathically. It is something set apart for a special purpose - consecrated. The same word - ano - is used for now, and this enables us to understand the strange practice advised by Jesus when he said: "Ask, believing that ye have received it now". The seed is the mental picture of the thing desired, not of the present imperfect condition.

"Therefore I say unto you, What things soever ye desire, when ye pray, believe ye receive them, and ye shall have them.

And when ye stand praying, forgive, it ye have ought against any: that your Father also which is in heaven may forgive you your trespasses".[5]

"And all things, whatsoever ye shall ask in prayer, believing, ye shall receive".[6]

So our only way to get our prayers to the High Self, Higher Emotional and Higher Intellectual Mind, is by the telepathic sending of thought form clusters of the ideas embodying the things for

---

[4] Matthew. Ch. 11. v. 30.
[5] Mark. Ch. 11. v. 24-25.
[6] Matthew. Ch. 21. v. 22.

which we pray. Therefore, according to the Kahunas, because only the low self can make contact with the High Self by extending an aka finger to follow the established aka thread to the High self - and, furthermore, because only the low self can make our prayer ideas or words into thought form clusters and send them along the activated aka cord - it follows that unless we train the low self to understand the use of this latent ability, and then to use it when we wish to send out a prayer, to get help from a higher level, nothing will be accomplished.

This is one of the greatest secrets of the Kahunas, and it explains what has always been the trouble when prayers are apparently unheard. If we wish to make sure our prayers of petition reach the High Self, and do not die on our lips as "empty words", we must put telepathy to use as well as creative imagination. As it is said, God created man in his own image. Men, humans, like God, have their creative ability, even if it be infinitesimal in comparison. God created by the use of the "Word" - by first deciding what was to be created, then by visualising it and causing it to take form, creative imagination. The human must decide what he or she wishes to create before beginning to pray.

Prayer is simply asking the Higher Self to take its proper part in creating the desired conditions for which we pray, and to use its superior mental and creative abilities to help bring about the desired state or conditions. So this is what we have learnt from the kahunas.

What are the Correspondences we can now Identify?

Perhaps the easiest is the High Self, which must surely correspond to Higher Emotional and Higher Intellectual mind, already functioning in us but at a level we are not conscious in. So that it is only when we achieve a special state that we have any awareness of it.

As such it has no direct connection with our organs of sense and can only be concerned with a direct knowing rather than knowing about. So information has to be fed to it in the form of thought form clusters and telepathically.

For us to produce the required thought form clusters we have to use our third brain with its creative imagination. So we have to consciously create an image of the condition we are trying to bring about, the person healed in body and mind.

At the same time we have to find out how to apply our personal unconscious mind in order to send forward telepathically the new situation we want to create. We already have conclusive evidence that in each of us at an unconscious level there is an entity of higher intelligence which we can learn to call upon. But this required a quietening of the personal conscious mind in order to begin to create a union of the personal unconscious and conscious minds. When this unity has been created a bridge is formed with Higher Mind and even the collective unconscious. This surely corresponds to the aka cord of the kahunas, and it is along this bridge that the thought form clusters and the telepathic thoughts can be sent.

The Kahunas and Gurdjieff's Three Brain Beings

A Final word on the migration of the Kahunas

To try and bring ourselves up to date with the origin of the Kahunas and the Polynesians we need to take note of the work of Bryan Sykes. While the correspondence of the special secret Huna language discovered in the Berber tribe in the Atlas Mountains and in Hawaii would indicate a connection. Bearing in mind that the tribal traditions of the Berbers indicate a migration west from Egypt, one would assume that this continued via India and across the Pacific Ocean going via Indonesia, Papua New Guinea and eventually to the Hawaiian Islands. Voyages must have been made to South America since that was the home of the sweet potato, now well established as a staple food throughout the Polynesian islands.

There is a problem, however, if one accepts the work of Bryan Sykes, using the technique of plotting migration using mitochondria DNA[7]. This work indicates that the Polynesians originated in Taiwan or the coasts of China around 30,000 years ago. The trail of their migrations then appears to have moved out into the Pacific to Hawaii in the North arriving around 1,500 years ago, to Rapanui, Easter Island, and Aotearoa, New Zealand in the far south around 1,200 years ago.

The sweet potato which originated as an Andean crop, but now thrives all over Polynesia, shows again how active at voyaging were the Polynesians. But how did they get to the Atlas Mountains? Maybe they sailed south of Australia and right across the Indian Ocean to Madagascar, which until relatively recently was uninhabited. It is now partially inhabited by people speaking a similar language. From there they could have sailed up the Red Sea to arrive in Egypt and from there to the Atlas Mountains and the Berber tribe.

© Copyright 2002 - Dr. H. J. Sharp - All Rights Reserved

---

[7] Bryan Sykes. The Seven Daughters of Eve. Bantam Press. 2001.

The Kahunas and Gurdjieff's Three Brain Beings - Questions & Answers

Questioner 1: Is there any mention by the researchers of any connection to the early Judaic esoteric teachings?

Bert Sharp: No, not to my knowledge

Questioner 1: Because Marlena and I were invited to a conference in Hawaii. The island of Kauai is the oldest and we were just so fortunate that the person who organised the conference attended by some 250 individuals involved in education, and she was able, she had lived in Hawaii and had a very close relationship with many Kahunas, and so on the second evening that we were there this group for the very first time, they had not done it before, this group of Hawaiians, there were three generations of women, a woman dressed in white, very elaborate, a woman in her mid eighties, statuesque and of such presence, and she came up and sat in the front, and finally was assisted on to the stage, and for the first time she announced that they were going to share with us certain aspects of Hawaiian culture, because they thought it was so important for the education of the children. And then she sang, and if ever I had experienced a discontinuity, it was when she opened her mouth because this voice was of a particular pitch, and so she sang and it was a blessing upon us. And then she left and I believe it was her daughter who is the present leader, teacher of this group, and she spoke about the Hawaiian culture. And she started by saying Aloha and she tracked through by allusion and never, she smiled a few times and she would kind of go off sideways. There were questions about the lost tribes and she said the ancient language as first written down was a mirror image of the ancient Jewish language, and Aloha is a derivative of Elohim and she gave a very clear explanation of the connection.

Bert Sharp: Very interesting indeed. These are things that need to be pursued I think. Incidentally to that, not wanting to take your comments away, which I think are very important, I spent a little time in Tahiti and I was surprised to find that it is a matriarchal society. The men are not allowed to own land or property or businesses. They are all owned by the women and the men do what they are told, and it is a different attitude to society to any I have experienced anywhere else, and this links with what you are saying about the power of the woman's voice.

Questioner 2: I have attended a small tourist type Kahuna lecture on the island of Hawaii. The word secret was never used and I do not know if it was inferred or not. There were women and men in very important jobs as a routine. The other thing was that they did have a connection to the ancient Judaic language and we thought it was a comment on the tourists because so many of them.

The Kahunas and Gurdjieff's Three Brain Beings - Questions & Answers

Bert Sharp: If you read this chap's book that was published only last year called *The Seven Daughters of Eve*, in which he uses mitochondrial DNA to race through the female line these migrations of the Polynesians. They were very busy over thousands of years migrating all over, virtually from China, across the whole of the Pacific and including the Atlas Mountains. It is quite an eye opener, the way in which they must have moved about and they must have been related to many other cultures.

Questioner 3: I wonder if you have come across anything?

Bert Sharp: No.

Questioner 1: One of the things that we were able to talk about which we found fascinating, and it was obvious that they were well into spiritual healing. Even the children as young as 4 or 5 are working in this direction.

Bert Sharp: What struck me was that there are correspondences with Gurdjieff's teaching and their teaching which is in secret.

Questioner 1: We also saw small children of 5 or 6 and they did special games. One with what looked like clubs, about a foot long and narrow at both ends with a bulbous part in the middle. They each held two of them. They faced each other in pairs and kept in rhythm with the music as they sang. And then they began to throw the clubs at each other right handed and then left handed and then cross ways. If I had to do that, I would have needed much practice. And then they had a weighted ball on a piece of string and they each had two of these and they would spin them over their heads and behind their backs and in front of them. I turned to Marlena and said, these are attention exercises. They all needed a great deal of focused attention.

Bert Sharp: This is all evidence of there being a common source, but perhaps at an unconscious level. This is my feeling about it all.

Questioner 2: I realise that your study is comparative in nature, it compares things ... but I have a question that perhaps you would like to comment or give your opinion upon if there is something in what you have studied that corresponds to answering me.

We say appeal to a higher level - pray, or something such...

Bert Sharp: Yes.

Questioner 2: What would happen if I appealed to the higher self to murder my opponent? Or to grant me a million pounds?

Bert Sharp: That is against the rules!

Questioner 2: Who makes the rules? What I mean to say by that is that the system seems to have a need for an internal structure as well, and that was not mentioned at all.

Bert Sharp: When you say "who makes the rules?" - Who decided on the pattern of the atomic structure of the elements? That is making the rules. This comes from the Absolute. In such a way it determines the way in which they will combine, which determines the way cells will form, which determines the way in which eventually sentient multi-cellular organisms like us evolve.

Questioner 2: OK I accept that, if you assume there is a natural order which trickles down from the structure of the Universe to the higher self. .. But it is ME who is asking. I'm in my lower self that is asking for these things and it could be mistaken, or it could be driven by evil or it could be driven by motives that are not so clear, so isn't there a need in such structures for ethics? If one puts ethics into it, how is one sure that the ethics abide with this descending physical structure from high up. Without becoming dogmatic, or becoming obscene?

Bert Sharp: I hear what you are saying and I have difficulty trying to answer it. But what comes to me about that is this relates to Swedenborg and the Doctrine of Uses which is a bit complex. It's as if it's all arranged beforehand, what is possible. We're given certain things which are possible. We're given the raw materials, like when we go into the DIY shop you can buy certain types of wood, certain preformed types of wood from which you can make other things. Something like that I think. But if you ask for a material or a shape or a tool which is not available for a very good reason, then you won't get it. I'm not giving you a good answer I know, but…

Questioner 2: Well the scary thing is what happens if you get it?

Bert Sharp: But you don't.

Questioner 2: You don't. OK.

(Inaudible section)

Bert Sharp: I don't know whether this helps as an answer which came to me about two years ago; that in effect (quotes) "and with these feelings came an absolute knowledge, a direct knowing that all was so arranged from the beginning that we individuals, when we are ready, we could of ourselves create the high level functioning of Heaven on Earth. Heaven as we call it exists in the world of ideas, beyond manifestation and the wonder of the Godhead is that it has not created it, but is cultivating us in our own time so that we create it ourselves. The direct knowledge came that all possibilities exist out of time and space so there is all we need to create what we are aligned to when we are ready and able. We have first to complete our own creation so that we are in proper order and correctly functioning". I don't know whether that makes any sense to you.

Questioner 2: It is a point of view, yeah.

The Kahunas and Gurdjieff's Three Brain Beings - Questions & Answers

Bert Sharp: It's not a point of view; it's something which came directly to me.

Questioner 2: Yes no, when I say point of view, the words, it came because reality was seen from a point of view, that's how it came directly. I wonder, how does this convince a poor criminal to get rid of his intentions? Of criminality's, of crimes?

Bert Sharp: I could not answer you. Can anyone else answer?

Questioner 4: I was just going to say that from the point of view of - I don't know if these Kahunas are similar, but European witchcraft, you certainly can ask for what you want.

Questioner 2: You can. Exactly.

Questioner 4: You can do what you want. As long as you bear the consequences. What you send out returns to you.

Questioner 5: That's very pat. I would tend to reply if a person is criminal, is not normal… (inaudible) maybe we're talking about two quite different types, that may be possible but maybe it just doesn't apply to this kind of work at all. It's a dangerous sort of power.

Questioner 2: I agree with what you say. Only the thing is that you are urged to pray, to ask for what you need; it is not to ask for what is proper. To receive the consequences if you make a mistake I understand. But that you are limited so that what you ask is going to be proper - you have to have a freedom of choice, even to screw up.

Questioner 5: That's right. There's a difference between an honest mistake and a criminal act.

Bert Sharp: As we are we have no freedom of choice do we, because we have no free will. We start off with a feeling that we have free will and that determines that we act as if we had it. And that feeds back into the system and reinforces the original feeling of free will so we go on acting as if we had it, but as we are we have no free will. And you can think of the fact that there are, to try and put if in very simple terms, there are if you like three forms of evolution: there is at the level of the elements and molecules, because of their combining power, the evolution of higher forms under the law of chance. Like the breakdown of radioactive material. Any particular atom of radioactive material might last for ever - or it might break down now. But is it is in a large mass, it then comes under the law of probabilities, so you can predict its half life. So at the molecular and cellular level, at the level of multi-cellular organisms it's under the law of destiny, but when the multi-cellular organism, a sentient organism such as a human, reaches the stage at which it psychologically develops to the higher level, to become what in effect you could call the god-human, then it has free will and it comes under evolution under the law of will because it has responsibility and it is sufficiently responsible to choose what is in the interests and what is determined, what is meant for the evolution of the totality. It's something like that, I think. But I know I am not making a lot of sense.

Questioner 6: Isn't this the apish theorem, where the ape is threatened (?) the point of having such a thing would be the transformation of the criminal or (?) other matter which is what presumably the lower self lifts them - I mean why should there be such a structure unless there is perhaps a return? What is return? Return is that change of levels, isn't it? So just is another view, if you like, of what prayer might be, to say that you have to sort of ask only good questions, ask the good and the right things occurs to me to be only part of the picture, in a way it means that is acting as spirit in conscious, thus creating an inner state where you are more refined but the (?) as such is surely about living everything that we experience, and...

Bert Sharp: I think that that is related to the level at which you've got, if you like. A family with children and perhaps one of the children becomes ill. One family may think well that is of no consequence, or sooner its dead the better and out of the way, it's a nuisance. But what we would think of as a more responsible family, a more developed family, would have compassion on that and wish to do what they could to ameliorate the suffering of the child and perhaps they would resort to prayer to try and change the situation for the benefit of the child. I think it is something like that.

Questioner 6: But in me there are both, there is the impetus to help that child and there is the impetus which frankly does not care. But I have both in me.

Bert Sharp: Well we see this now in the world today, isn't it, every day in the news. The destruction and lack of responsibility, the lack of thought for others. But we don't - most of us don't accept that, we would like to try and change it. But we don't know what to do to change it, and we haven't got the drive and the energy and the ability to change it. But it doesn't mean we should give up trying to work out something we can do to improve the lost of humanity.

Questioner 6: But this not accepting the negative or passive of our (?) is that the right, or wrong?

Bert Sharp: Well, you're talking about being a fatalist. And we try to do what we can for other people.

Questioner 7: Thanks, Bert. Do they talk about the transformation of the higher self... the correspondence of the high self with something that's dynamic and priceless?

Bert Sharp: Well, what we were generally saying was that the higher self already is fully functional, but that we are not aware of it.

Questioner 7: But when the kahunas speak (?) that it blatantly came (?) as something that has grown in itself and can change it's nature over time to become something different.

Bert Sharp: I don't think it has to grow and change its nature over time, I think we have to get in touch with it; to get in contact with it. This to my mind is perhaps a simple thing pointed to in the Norse myths of Odin, the Father God who guards the Bifrost Bridge which is the bridge that links the area of Earth with the abode of the gods in Heaven and this if you like can be symbolic of the individual's conscious mind and the individual's unconscious mind. You have to create a bridge between the two. That's the first stage. You don't have to worry about improving the Higher Mind which is already fully functional…

(End of tape side one)

I think you have to develop your own knowledge.

Questioner 7: You think so.

Bert Sharp: Your own knowledge. I mean, we're talking in words, aren't we. These words are describing knowledge, because the thing in itself we cannot describe. I mean, how do you describe consciousness? How do you describe love? How do you describe compassion? It means passionate together, passionate with one another. That is about as far as I get. But you can experience it. Yes?

Questioner 8: Did you find prayers are dangerous? With the Kahunas?

Bert Sharp: No.

Questioner 8: Do they also do any sitting, like we do?

Bert Sharp: I don't know. What I was interested in when I came across this book material was the description they had of the three levels, the three bodies and the way in which one has to pray verbally and also with the thought form clusters.

Questioner 9: In the demonstrations I saw there was a- I want to call them Trainer Magnus (?) yes it was a centering or a movement of quiet in before we begin, before they (inaudible)…

Bert Sharp: What I find interesting from what some of you are saying is there seems to have been a resurrection of this in Hawaii doesn't there? I mean a few years ago very few people knew anything about this.

There has been a movement there I guess 10, maybe 15 years of reviving of Hawaiian culture. Yes, and this is good, isn't it, yes.

Questioner 9: Something I am a little confused about, there's almost nothing known about kahunas unless their civilisation from the 20th century and you said that the Christian missionaries suppressed these practices (inaudible). So now these investigators you mentioned like Max Freedom Long and some other people all brought this information to the attention of people here who are interested here in the West…

Bert Sharp: With great difficulty.

All & Everything Conference 2002

Questioner 1: But let's suppose that the shoe was on the other foot. Let's suppose that nobody knew anything about Christianity and there was this group of people from some country that came to us for Christianity. Now why would we expect that they had come to us for what we see as esoteric Christianity, Gurdjieff's teaching? Why wouldn't it simply be exoteric, that is ordinary prayers and petitions as you said like God please send me a billion dollars or pounds or something. I mean, there seems to be this - are you saying that whatever they put down, the kahunas are entirely esoteric inner tradition or even the kids throwing the stuff - I mean you could have very good jugglers you see them in Las Vegas all the time, it doesn't mean they are doing the inner work, they're just playacting.

Bert Sharp: We don't know the origins of that. We don't know the origins of that; it may have just been developed and invented now, for the tourists. The main thing of the kahunas was that the whole teaching was based upon a secret language. They didn't use their ordinary language, they used a special language. That gave the big problem in uncovering it.

Questioner 1: Is this kahuna the primary...

Bert Sharp: Kahuna? The word itself means "keepers of the secret".

Questioner 1: Is there another indigenous...

Bert Sharp: It's not Polynesian, not the Polynesian language.

Questioner 1: Sorry, the question, as far as spiritual practice, people praying in the way I have described, is it kahuna, or is there like another spiritual tradition outside of that?

Questioner 10: No.

Questioner 1: I mean was that the predominant spiritual tradition?

Bert Sharp: No, it's not.

Questioner 1: It's not?

Bert Sharp: No, not as far as I know.

Questioner 1: Then is it Christianity that has taken over?

Questioner 11: Yes.

Questioner 1: But as far as indigenous spiritual practices, there's no other than that.

(tape inaudible)

The Kahunas and Gurdjieff's Three Brain Beings - Questions & Answers

Questioner 10: It was kept secret for many hundreds of years till some time after Cook was there. But there was only one king, it was united...

Bert Sharp: Some years ago on television there was what I thought was a very interesting and very good film, not wishing to change the subject but I think it illustrates this very well, and it was called Childhood's End. Now I have since been searching for a text of this, and I have come across a book with that title but it's not the same story. The film starts and you wonder where you are sort of thing and then you begin to realise because of the scenery around you that you must be on board a ship because you can see the rivets in the sides of the walls and things of this sort, and then you are shown to the main congregational area, where all the people are coming together and then these uniformed organisers bring out the picture of the tree. They worship the tree on the basis that in the last days we will worship the tree itself and not the picture - yes?

Questioner 12: Yes, I know nothing about the kahunas. I know a great deal about the Native American traditions not too different in some ways... I wanted to explain something that sounds like...

Bert Sharp: Can I just finish what I was saying then, I thought it was relevant to that. As this film develops you find that in fact we're on a space ship and they've been on it for generations and the ship is automatically looking for a planet similar to Earth on which they could survive and create a new society because Earth has been destroyed and the greatest sin that anyone could commit for which they are immediately exterminated is to learn to read. Then there is this grandfather teaching the little boy to read, in secret because there's also this tradition that tells them that in the last days, when there is the shaking and the noise, and the lightening, somebody must be able to read. And it unfolds in the end that the little boy can read, and then when the shaking does start, this is the retro rockets firing because its found the right planet, and then somebody has to be able to go up to the bridge, to the higher levels which is prohibited, and open the door and read the instruction manual for landing the spaceship. And the kahunas and their teaching I think is somehow something like that. It's kept in secret, but it survives.

Questioner 12: (inaudible) What I am concerned with, I saw a film the other day about performances of the Sun Dance photographed by Eddie Kirk which I found very interesting on television - except the original Sun Dance, it was banned, and the last man to know anything about it was Dr. James Walker. After he died the secret was no longer transmitted so it had to be reinvented when finally the American Indians were given the right to have religious practices again, because you know their ancestors were prevented from practising from the late 1870s till the 1920s. Everyone thought, how do you transmit; you transmit secrets through designated intermediaries. Designated very carefully. So once Christianity comes with the missionaries at the end of the 18th and early 19th century to Honolulu - Hawaii if you like, it's very difficult to keep something transmitted secretly, in fact the point is, problem is, the anthropologist comes, he speaks to the natives, and he gets their stories. He gets their stories, he thinks he's got their secrets, but the problem is half the time the anthropologist is getting a lie, because these things will not be revealed to him. And so on, and then in the 20th century you'll find Pueblo Indians putting Sioux head-dresses at a Cherokee village in South Carolina for a rain dance they never did because they are living the white man's expectations; not only for money, they are living the white man's idea of the romanticism of the noble savage, but also in a sense they have to reinvent an indigenous tribe, an indigenous tradition This parallel; I don't know with the kahuna, but with the American Indians you have to have classes teaching the Indians what they should know about themselves, half those classes are taught by a white man. For a language, a people have a language, they have to have a language in order to say that they have a tribal identity in order to operate (inaudible) at the time the biggest casino in the East. They had to get the white anthropologists, the white linguists to teach them to speak a language which their ancestors did. Now you go through this transmission of indigenous tribe to anthropologist to writer back to teacher, back to tribal entity, what in the world is legitimate? Where is the secret?

Bert Sharp: Are you familiar with the sand paintings of the Navaho Indians?

Questioner 12: I am very familiar with the sand paintings of...

Bert Sharp: Yes well, how do you explain the significance and the structure of the sand paintings, and the way in which it relates directly to what Gurdjieff taught?

Questioner 12: The sand paintings as you know are part of a Blessing Way or (inaudible) ceremonies. They are secret, and the only way the secret is kept is that they are destroyed, but of course now they are frozen into things and...

Bert Sharp: Yes but how do you explain the fact that in some of the sand paintings there is an identical structure to what Gurdjieff taught, where did that come from, how did the Indians get it?

Questioner 12: This is (inaudible) Jung had an easy answer, it's in the genetics and stuff, ah, unconscious, and....

Bert Sharp: What's your answer? But what's your answer? Or don't you know?

Questioner 12: (talking at once - inaudible) identical to Gurdjieff but that's the pollen - which sand painting - what exactly is distinctive in which sand paintings?

Bert Sharp: The pollen path.

Questioner 12: Hmm?

Bert Sharp: The pollen path.

Questioner 12: The pollen path?

Bert Sharp: Yes.

The Kahunas and Gurdjieff's Three Brain Beings - Questions & Answers

Questioner 12: Yes, there are a lot of pollen paths in almost all of the Blessing Way ceremonies. But where is Gurdjieff in this pollen path?

Bert Sharp: Well because it gives you the three lowers leading to the two higher.

Questioner 12: Well, excuse me Bert, that is YOUR meaning. If I go to Tony Beneha (?) now on the Navaho reservation who does these things and ask him, he'll not say that; he'll say "the significance of the secret". See, so here we go with a catch-22. I mean he would not answer what you just answered. You might be right, but he wouldn't answer. And I know a lot of them would answer, "That's Tupee (?) business". I'm just raising these questions because you have tourists watching these things, and you are told of a revival of a lost cultural artefact, or a lost cultural practice, you have to be sceptical about everything. And that's the problem, what is real and what is not real.

Bert Sharp: How do you decide?

Questioner 10: Regarding the Hawaiian culture, it cannot be revived with any kind of authenticity because it was too totally destroyed.

Questioner 12: Not necessarily - some American Indian has, and I think… (inaudible)

Bert Sharp: Incidentally, Joseph Campbell gives the explanation which I gave relating to Gurdjieff in his book...

Questioner 12: Joseph Campbell, oh he's marvellous.

Bert Sharp: So it's not just coming from me.

Questioner 12: NO, no, I didn't say that. You gave an explanation that may be Campbell's explanation, but there are many others. No, that's a good point you (J) raised, and the person I talked to in Honolulu in the National Native Cultural Centre had other ideas too. The problem is, they say to me, as the Native Americans say to me everywhere I go - we cannot go back; we must make new. And we cannot make new with what the white man gives us, we must recycle what the white man throws away. And so we recycle it into the development of our own past traditions and many rituals have indeed been irrevocably lost, the Sun Dance which is irrevocably lost...

Questioner 1: Perhaps it's like this: Gurdjieff gives Nicoll an independent key to esoteric Christianity. So Nicoll goes and looks at the New Testament and he says "Oh, this passage really means this" because he has the independent key. So maybe when Steve (?) and Marlena go and they see these kids doing what appears to be an attention exercise, that is really there, whether or not they know. It could be something like that, just like the three levels you're talking about....
Bert Sharp: That's right, that's right.

All & Everything Conference 2002

Questioner 1: ... if you have the independent key, we don't know that the individual practitioners or congregants of the kahuna in Hawaii, at least most of them may have none.

Bert Sharp: Which brings me to the Hermetic Code, which brings through so many things...

Questioner 1: It's like the parables...

Bert Sharp: That's right. What we are all here for, as I understand it, simply is to exchange ideas and models of mentation, etc., and if the model seems to have meaning for any one of us as an individual, then we can use that model in order to explore our interior mentation, and begin to work on ourselves, and to change (inaudible). That's what this gathering is all about, isn't it?

An Accursed Mirage

Keith Buzzell

"How will it all end? Is there really no way out at all?

"Must these unfortunate souls who were formed on that unfortunate planet really remain eternally unperfected and be endlessly coated into various planetary forms and everlastingly toil and moil on account of the consequences of the properties of that accursed organ Kundabuffer, which, owing to the reasons extraneous to them themselves, was attached to the planetary bodies of the first three-centered beings of that ill-fated planet?

"Where, then, is that pillar upon which, as it were, our whole Megalocosmos rests, and which is called Justice?!!!!

"No! This cannot be! Something is wrong here, because during the whole time of my existence, not once has a single doubt ever crept into me as to the existence of objective Justice.

"All I have to do is just to clarify and understand... why! ... why!

"At any rate, from this present moment, the aim of my existence shall be to understand clearly why the souls arising in these terrestrial three-centered beings are in such an unprecedented, terrifying situation...." (*Words of Hassein, pp 1117, Beelzebub's Tales*)

As the chain of horrific events stretches out from its onset on September 11 questions like, "What is a *just* action?" Or, "Where is Justice in this kind of situation?" have been raised by many. As Gurdjieff devoted an entire chapter to the subject it seemed appropriate at this Conference to raise a number of questions that are related to events in this chapter, point out several of the paradoxes that Gurdjieff appears to present, outline a tentative understanding of a concept of Objective Justice, and engage this audience in an exploratory dialogue on this 'burning question of the day'.

First - how does Gurdjieff set the stage?

The opening quotation, from the next to the last page of the chapter 'Beelzebub's opinion of War', has Hassein speaking out his dilemma regarding the fate of the higher being bodies formed on the planet Earth. That fate, to be eternally unperfected, drives him to ask, "Where, then is that pillar upon which, as it were, our whole Megalocosmos rests, and which is called Justice?..." He insists that it must be his own lack of understanding that is the problem and not that Justice is non-existent. Hassein then dedicates himself to the pursuit of understanding "why the souls .... are in such an unprecedented, terrifying situation..." Beelzebub, we are told, is very glad that his grandson was experiencing such a depression. Hassein's dedication and the gladness of Beelzebub - each of these events creates its own lineage of questions.

On the final page of the chapter on War Beelzebub reiterates that it would appear that the only way in which they could be saved is with "time alone...", with the caveat that it would also require "the guidance of a certain Being with very high Reason or to certain exceptional cosmic events".

Thus is the stage set for the chapter "In the Opinion of Beelzebub, Man's Understanding of Justice is for him in the Objective Sense an Accursed Mirage"

The Content

In his consideration of "Objective Justice" Gurdjieff's myth has incorporated proportioned 'images' - images that have a cosmic level of resonance. The two stories, or series of images that comprise the bulk of this chapter, take up the issue of Justice from two seemingly different viewpoints; the first being Beelzebub's detailed presentation of his first, or partial, pardon; the second being the convoluted events on both Purgatory and Earth surrounding the life of Makary Kronbernkzion. From our readings and study of these 'cosmic-levelled' events have flowed a number of impressions and, more importantly, many questions. The first group of questions concerned the original Russian meaning of words that play a singular role in this chapter. For his etymologic help I am indebted to Nick Tereshchenko. I asked him, in particular, about the words Justice, substitute and Makary Kronbernkzion In answer Nick first reminded me that, by theosophical addition, Chapter 44 becomes the number '8' which, in the Tarot is the symbol for Justice. Further he wrote:

"There are in Russian two words both correctly translatable as JUSTICE: pravosoodie, literally meaning "right judgement" and used for "Justice" mainly in a legal sense, and spravedlivost, the word used by MG and meaning, as well as "justice (in the abstract), also righteousness, right mindedness, veracity". We found the additional meanings of the Russian word of singular importance."

And…

"As to your other queries: for the word translated (correctly) as "substitute", MG uses zamestitel, basically meaning "one who takes the place of ". The word translated (correctly) as "direct" is neposredstvennomoo literally meaning "without anything in between", which I would have translated as "immediate".

About the name Makary Kronbernkzion he wrote:

"Note that in Russian the 4th letter is an H as in Holy, NOT an N, and that it is not a simple Z sound after the second K but is usually represented in English as TZ or CZ, as in TZar or CZar; same sound as the Hebrew TSADDI letter. The name "Makar" is used in a couple of popular sayings, but otherwise has no special meanings in Russian, while Krohbernktzion is certainly NOT a Russian surname. The word KROH is the plural of a word meaning "crumb", "grain" and as a root of other words means "small". None of the other letter combinations make any sense in Russian".

Gurdjieff's use of the word itself - of 'justice' - is also of interest. While he includes it in the title of the chapter the word itself never appears in the text. One wonders why? The word 'injustice' does appear once, on page 1124 and the word 'justice' is used on 21 other occasions in the *Tales*. For us it seems that Gurdjieff is pointing to the necessity of whole, completed *events - not words of abstraction* - as a primary consideration in the concept of Justice. We'll return to this point later. In contrast to the word justice the word 'substitute' appears twice in this chapter (once as 'direct' and once as 'future') but appears nowhere else in the *Tales*.

Another circumstance that begs a question is contained in the first petition of the fifty righteous souls. This petition states: "First of all to lay a petition at the feet of our Maker Creator that He in His Providence should send to the 3 Brained Beings of the planet Earth a Messenger from Above with data corresponding to such a Reason as could on the spot find a possibility of uprooting this maleficent idea".

No direct mention of this 'Messenger' is made in the remainder of the chapter. Why? Is it possible that Gurdjieff is pointing to a circumstance that is already underway on the planet Earth?

This first petition also includes the request that the higher being body of the terrestrial 3 Brained Being who was the cause of this maleficent idea not be taken onto the planet Purgatory but rather be doomed to exist eternally on the planet Remorse-of-Conscience. Our question is 'What is the difference between the states of Purgatory and 'Remorse-of-Conscience'?? Does it relate, perhaps, to possibilities?

Mention of these two states (Purgatory and Remorse of Conscience) associatively raises the question of the many 'twos' in this chapter. There are the two forces - Good and Evil, Involution and Evolution; two pieces of the Boolmarshano; two sons of Beelzebub; the duo-Beelzebub and his substitute, Hassein; the two pardons of Beelzebub; the two petitions by the righteous souls of Purgatory to Endlessness; and the overriding two stories - of Beelzebub's exile (an involutional motion) and his return (an evolutional motion) and - of Makary's effort (the Boolmarshano-an evolutional motion) and the 'righteous judgement' of him by the souls on Purgatory and his 'suspension' at the very point where he has become one of the "first candidates to be taken onto the Most Holy Sun Absolute".

The many 'twos' in this chapter was, for us, the first indication that the absence of a 'third' - the third force, perhaps, - played an essential role in determining why man's conception of Justice is an 'accursed mirage'. Note, for instance, that the title of the Boolmarshano is 'The Affirming and Denying Influences on Man' and that while Makary carefully qualifies the *'Good'* - (the involutional, 'passive' flow away from the Source) and the *'Evil'* - (the evolutional, 'active' striving to return to the Source), a similar single word expression does not identify the "third independent World force". It is "only the result of the clash everywhere and in everything of these two fundamental descending and ascending independent forces". That 'clash' between the Affirming and Denying influences, as properly identified by Makary, takes place within Man and, as such, it is from within Man that the 3rd Force, the Holy Reconciling, must manifest itself. In reading the title of the Boolmarshano as we usually do it is easy to miss this critical reference to Man as the carrier of the Third Force.

Seeing the above we came to the tentative conclusion that the absence of a Third Force in man's conception of Justice contributed significantly to the 'mirage'. So deep seated is this lack of a balanced inclusion of the Third Force that it seems that even the '50 righteous souls' on Purgatory made the same error with respect to Makary. It is Beelzebub, not this group of higher being bodies, who roots out the interstices of the 'clash' by looking deeply into the life of Makary, discovering the 'two' pieces of the Boolmarshano and, in the end, maintaining that, "although the idea of 'external Good and Evil' first arose there thanks to the individuality of the Makary Kronbernkzion, yet he was, in my opinion, not to blame for it having taken such a maleficent form". The form Makary gave to it identified cosmic (external) origins to the forces that lawfully 'clash' within man. These forces are called 'Good and Evil' only in their contextual relation to whether they flow *down* from the Source, or strive *upward* toward the Source. Subsequent to Makary a superficial and *literal* interpretation was given to the *externality* of the two forces, thus leading to the maleficent idea that Good and Evil (taken literally) exist in the world *external* to Man.

A Concept of Objective Justice

Regardless of Beelzebub's opinion regarding Makary's essential innocence we must try to fathom why Endlessness, *after only thinking a little*, consented to restrict Makary's Higher Being Body to existence on Purgatory "until the future results of his *evil* deed should be revealed". A notion of profound significance seems hidden in these words, especially if we understand 'evil' in the contextual way that Makary used the word. Evil, as he used it, is then 'a striving to return to the Source'.

As Beelzebub points out Makary, regardless of his essential innocence concerning the maleficent result, is "the *fundamental cause* of the impossibility for all the higher being bodies which arise in the presences of certain three-brained beings of this planet to perfect themselves completely". Endlessness, having the *Hope* that ultimately we three-brained beings will cognize our errors and begin to exist as is becoming for us to exist, would not need to punish Makary so terribly. In this act (of Endlessness) a balance is struck, - a balance between the laws of Involution (the 'Good') and Evolution (the 'Evil'). Makary, as a terrestrial 3 Brained Being is a product of the Involutional flow of the laws-as are we all. In spite of his conscious labors he was not a perfected being in all his manifestations. His lack of perfection shows itself in the lack of a comprehensive explanation of the Law of Three, an explanation that led eventually to a gross misinterpretation by others. Nonetheless it is Makary who is the '*fundamental* cause'. A real paradox seems presented here.

An Accursed Mirage

Great effort is made by Makary, a great 'help' is shared with other three-brained beings via his insight into the Law of Three. This sounds very much like an example of the cosmic process of the sacred Antkooano, that process of sharing knowledge of cosmic truths on which Ashiata Shiemash also counted. Unfortunately, Makary's insight is shared with, and misinterpreted by, non-conscious three-brained beings and the results are disastrous. Here, in an unbalanced 'clash' between Involution and Evolution it is Involution that wins out. The *words* of Makary inadvertently feed the involutional flow under which other three-brained beings live. Things become worse, for Man, and consequently it will take a very long time to show whether man will 'wake up' sufficiently to live more becomingly. Makary's individual effort is not seen in all this as primary - rather it is his 'words' - *the abstraction* - that are taken as truth by the less conscious three-brained beings.

Another aspect of this situation is related to the cosmic *insignificance* of Makary (as an individual). It is *all of mankind* that lies under the sway of Involutional law and Makary's fate, as with all of us, is bound up with the possible future of many other beings, - ultimately all of mankind. Perhaps Gurdjieff is underlining our 'nothingness' as individual, involutionally derived beings and simultaneously pointing to the reality that Man (collectively) has the possibility of becoming a prime focus for the manifestation of the Third Force in the Great Ray of Creation. This would be a Great Work (a great 'clash' and reconciliation) involving all of mankind, not just a solitary individual. Makary, then, must *wait*, on Purgatory, until this 'evil' (this evolutionary thrust) works its way through Time. That he must wait out that long, indeterminate process is *Just*. Now let's turn briefly to the story of Beelzebub's partial pardon and look for evidences of the Involutional and Evolutional 'thrusts', for the somewhat enigmatic Third Force, and for a balance of these forces that could provide a clearer representation of Objective Justice.

Three paragraphs into the opening of the chapter Beelzebub tells Hassein that he must "say something about certain of those long-past events which at *first glance* have nothing in common with this idea" (the idea being that of 'Good' and 'Evil'). He then speaks at length about the partial pardon, that which applies to his posterity (one's *descendants* - his sons etc.).

Beelzebub, because of a youthful but *lawful* 'personal transgression' (itself a paradoxical circumstance) is exiled - sent 'down' (an *involutional* motion) - from the level of World 3 (Holy Sun Absolute) all the way to Worlds 24-48 (Mars-Earth) (We understand that Beelzebub, during his Descents, is *in* World 48 but *not of it*). Involution is a lawful and required motion by everything that moves away from the Source. Once in this solar system Beelzebub must *labor*, through an exceptionally long life of "conscious labors and intentional sufferings", to 'pay for his arising'. When he has paid that price (via his influence on the practice of Sacrificial Offerings) his *results* (his 'sons' -perhaps to be understood as *two* aspects of his Holy Affirming - a 'passive' *witness* (Tooilan) - and an active server or Zirlikner (Tooloof)) can then be released from his restriction and can ascend (evolve) to those levels where it is appropriate for them to serve.

For us this represents one level or *order* of Justice. The Involutional and Evolutional flow of the laws has been balanced by Beelzebub's individual, life long-effort. In that circumstance he himself is the carrier of the Holy Reconciling force as it is within him that the 'clash' of the 'Good' and 'Evil' forces takes place.

It is notable that at the point of the partial pardon Beelzebub *himself* (however we understand that Individuality) is not permitted to return. A further *evolutionary* thrust/effort is necessary before the Individuality itself can return to the Source of its arising. That evolutionary effort is related to the further perfecting of Reason, a task Beelzebub undertakes in the 6th Descent when he strives to get to the bottom of the cause(s) of War. During this pursuit he "fulfilled a certain need in connection with the mission" of Ashiata Shiemash. We are told that as a result Ashiata intercedes with His Endlessness and Beelzebub is granted his full pardon. Ashiata's 'need' can only have been a need for Reason, for a Cosmic level of understanding - (What else could Ashiata 'need'?). Here we must also remember that Ashiata is described as having reached the level of Reason of the Sacred Podkoolad, a level of Reason which qualifies him as "one of the first assistants of our Endlessness in the government of the World" (pp 1118) and "Now one of our seven Most Very Saintly Omni-cosmic Individuals without whose participation even our Uni-Being Common Father does not allow himself to actualize anything." (pp 405)

Can we rightly infer a similar circumstance in regard to Beelzebub, who also attains, *at least*, to the level of the Sacred Podkoolad?

The final pardon represents a second, and, presumptively, a higher level of Justice - a further balance or equilibration of involution/evolution. For there to be Justice, both sides must be *fulfilled* and *balanced*. No one, no thing' can escape these requirements.

The Accursed Mirage

The 'accursed mirage' becomes Man's Understanding of Justice because we fail to see the cosmic requirements (1) of the reality and the role of the Third Holy Force and (2) of balance between the Involutional and Evolutional flow of the laws. For the right working of the Megalocosmos both are necessary. They *appear* to be opposed to each other when in actuality they are essential to each other in the working out of the Universe. As such, an action is objectively just when it fulfils the lawful requirement of both Involutional and Evolutional flows or currents and when they are balanced via the action of the *3rd force, the clash <u>within</u> of the first two independent forces*. These forces are neither 'Good' nor 'Evil' in the moral sense, but are the lawful and required expressions of Involution and Evolution. The 'mirage' appears when we neglect the role of the Third, reconciling force and impose a subjective moral interpretation on Involution and Evolution, identifying them as *external to ourselves*. There is a perspective that relates man's self-creation of this mirage or illusion to a particular misuse of Sexual Energy, a theme that can also be applied to the other 'opinion' chapters (War and Electricity).

An Accursed Mirage

Summary

Objective Justice requires that equal attention and significance be given to Involutional and Evolutional processes, always relative to the circumstance being looked at. From the two myths, or sets of 'images' in the lives of Beelzebub and Makary, we can recognize certain requirements that a concept of Objective Justice must have. First, an evaluation of an action, or of a series of related events, must resonantly include the action of the Third, or Neutralizing Force. It must be seen as a force equal to, and independent of, the Active and Passive Forces. Second - that the 'arena of action' of all three Forces is *within* the individual.

It might be useful at this point to review our common understanding (via dictionary and symbol) of the words 'just' and 'Justice':

1. The rendering of what is due or merited - Conformity to the law; Equity, fairness, impartiality, even-handed, also a strict rendering of deserts;

2. Righteous in the sight of God.

3. Behavior to oneself or to another which is strictly in accord with law, showing full appreciation of the worth or importance of oneself or another.

For at least 4,000 years Justice has been pictured or imaged in many different ways - one of the most common elements being the presence of a scale or balance.

Figure 1 is a composite of elements drawn from this chapter and given a triadic, scalar representation:

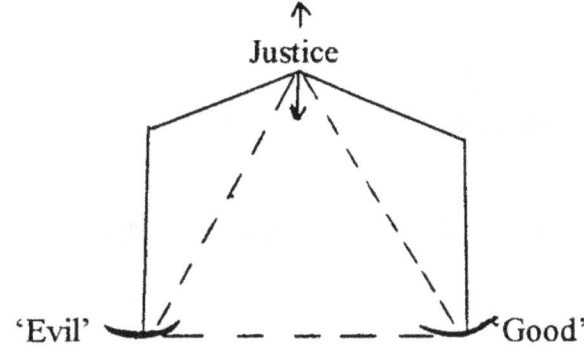

The principles could be rendered thus:

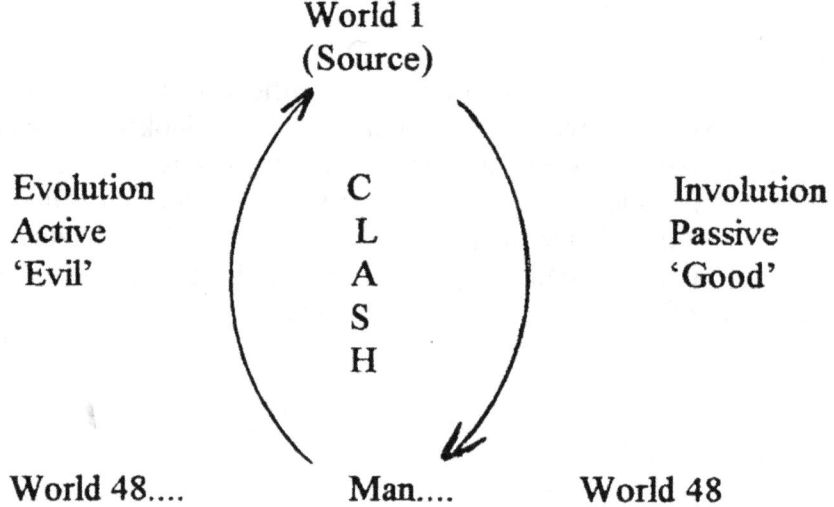

Objective Justice refers to the impartial balancing of the equally essential flow of Involutional (downward) and Evolutional (upward) law. The 'clash' of these two lawful flows -'away from' and 'toward' the Source - takes place *within* the carriers of the Third force.

These two World forces enter *into* every World formation and "Although the third independent force is only the result of both first fundamental forces, it is nevertheless the spiritualizing and reconciling source of every World formation... because it arises and must exist in them as a presence all the time while the given results exist..."

If we understand Makary's description of the 'Good'-Evil-and Third Force to *include* a reference to their *placement* in a triad of law, then the following form unfolds. If we understand 'passive' to refer to the 2nd position in a triad of law, and 'active' to refer to the 1st position in the same triad, then:

2	1	3	
'Evil'	'Good'	'Clash'	2-1-3
Active	Passive	Reconciliation	the Law of Transformation.

The implications of this form of law, in regard to Makary and Beelzebub and, inferentially, to each of us, are useful to ponder.

© Copyright 2002 - Dr. Keith Buzzell - All Rights Reserved

An Accursed Mirage - Questions & Answers

Keith Buzzell: What I would like to do now is to engage you in a discussion of your impressions and in particular take up this issue of *Objective* Justice, not 'little' justice, and why for us this is an accursed mirage. The concept that I have tried to develop here is that it has a very high, a cosmic level of requirement. The Laws must work themselves out and they must be balanced. They can only be balanced by the clash producing the results. Makary defines the third force as the *results* of the clash - and only this can balance the lawful requirements that we are all stuck with. We are all under Involutional law. In order even to consider the concept of Objective Justice we have to see that that has to play itself out. Makary has to stay on the planet Purgatory while all the "results of his evil deed" work themselves out. He is just an individual - it is all of mankind that is involved in becoming this carrier of the Third Force.

Questioner 1: One problem we have with the word Justice as used is that it is a translated word from the Russian or Armenian. In all Indo-European languages, where justice means pretty much what you said, it means a 'balancing of accounts'. In English we 'pay back' literally. We pay our debt. We forget that, but it becomes important here because evil (which comes from the Gothic and means 'excess' of something) and 'good' means the balancing of accounts. The reason why we have the scale or balance is because Justice is a commercial term. Also, your use of the word law (which is a Norwegian word from 'leggia') which means to lay down. The use of the word 'law' in this chapter and elsewhere comes from the 18th Century when lay people were prescribing a *cosmic equilibrium* (what we call now a scientific equilibrium). The term law as Gurdjieff uses it does that, but it also does the other thing, which is that which is laid down, prescribed by a higher authority. It seems to work out very well. But I just wanted to emphasize that in all Indo European languages all the terms you use have to do with commercial balance (which associatively brings up 'The Material Question'). All Anglo-Saxon law, all civil codes, have to do with balance of accounts, property and goods protection. This is where the word 'good' comes from. It doesn't have a moral tone until modern times. The native English term for law is right or right. All these things work together very well in this chapter, but what I'm trying to highlight is the fact that we have an enormous 'poly theme' going on in this chapter and in any discussion of justice. We don't know really what Gurdjieff, in an original sense, was thinking of; but all these terms were negotiated during the translations by Orage and many others, who knew very well what all these terms meant.

Keith Buzzell: That's why it was helpful to me to go to Nick (Tereshchenko) and ask him, 'How do you understand the original Russian?'

Questioner 1: Oh, by the way that first term means *true*. I think Nick said 'good'. But the Russian means *true*.

All & Everything Conference 2002

Keith Buzzell: (Referring to Nick's quoted letter) You are referring to pravosodie?

Questioner 1: Yes.

Keith Buzzell: He says, "literally means right judgement and used for justice mainly in the legal sense".

Questioner 1: Yes, that's why it's true.

Keith Buzzell: It is the other one that is chosen by Gurdjieff. And in the Russian, which I presume has something to do with why this was selected, it also includes righteousness, right mindedness and veracity - which gets us away from only a legalistic definition.

Questioner 1: Yes, we really do go round and round in definitions.

Questioner 2: This reminds me very much of man as having two natures and it seems there is a very dynamic problem in the relationship between these two natures. He speaks in 'Meetings' about holding this inner protection between the Wolf and the Lamb. It strikes me that we are all 'Makary's' - waiting to understand these relationships between what is going up in us and what is going down in us.

Keith Buzzell: As a definer of what is just, in terms of Makary, I think that is why Gurdjieff creates this marvellous mythic image. We can certainly take this image inside and say "yes, this applies to me - it is not an abstract kind of thing".

Questioner 3: At the beginning of the presentation you read some material from the *Tales* that seemed to imply the necessity of an external Being, a very high level Being, to support this inner work. Is this so? How do you see that?

Keith Buzzell: Oh! Lots of impressions - that's why I kind of buried them there. Because he talks about a messenger, he talks about - in one place - this is part of the petition, the first petition of the 50 righteous souls. They ask, *first*, for a messenger. And then they get vindictive in the second part! - to banish whomever it was that was responsible for it. We have all had that experience inside when you suddenly, in total embarrassment, realize that exactly what you blamed is *yours*! We get so self-righteous about something and really want to whip it and then realize that it's something inside of us that has set this whole thing in motion. In any case - a special person, of high order, with Time alone, plus the caveat that I mentioned, that unless there is help from some higher being and so forth. That's one reference. The second reference is in the petition of the fifty souls for a messenger. *Then* one can ask the question, 'Who is the messenger? Who is this Higher Being? Is it possible that Gurdjieff is planting something here, because clearly we're approaching that point of absolute dedication by Hassein? It is contained in the quotation that Chris read at the beginning, "From this moment on..." Hassein is dedicated to understanding the sources for this dilemma. He is spoken of as 'the direct substitute' as 'my future substitute', 'this is *your* planet' 'when you perchance, live on this planet' etc. etc. - lots of pointers in this direction that build up through the *Tales*. Starting with interest, like we were talking about before in the opening to the early chapter we were studying (Chapter 8) - where Hassein says 'talk about anything' and Beelzebub says, 'No! What are *you* interested in'. So we start from that interest, curiosity - and if you follow the use of those terms it is initially 'those three-brained beings who interest you' and then it becomes 'your favorites' - then later it is 'your planet' and then it is 'your people'. He becomes more and more defining of the role as we move through the *Tales*. So I think it is possible to consider the question, 'Is it Hassein - however we understand that word - who is to take on this responsibility?

Questioner 3: Well, that's one interpretation. But the thing that's troubling me is, I mean, - in exoteric spirituality there's always been this need for an external messenger, a very high being, whether it's Jesus Christ or the Messiah that the Orthodox Jews are waiting for, and Gurdjieff does mention this in there. Now, should we take it allegorically - is it Hassein-in-us or - it's going on right now, it's going on with us.

Keith Buzzell: I offer a capsule version, - there is a big difference between Modiktheo where Angels, Archangels and Sacred Individuals closest to Endlessness are *made*; they are made perfect. Karatas, on the other hand, - they are different, and the most important difference is that they have an independent will. What characterizes the planet Karatas and the beings who are, like Beelzebub, who are sent away from there, is that they can say *no* - to Endlessness. This is what gets Beelzebub in trouble. He sees something and he goes after it, 'and he's youthful and inexperienced and so on - so he gets hammered with the consequences. That would never happen to an Angel or an Archangel. They would never say no or come up against Endlessness. And Gurdjieff characterizes this several times in the *Tales* - that never would an angel understand etc. - unless he can enter into etc. And, for me, the most important characterization there is relative to the Will. So - Karatas, for me, is the independently 'willed' Higher Beings and they can say *no*. That's why it's Beelzebub - that's why he is a 'devil' - he says 'no' and gets sent away. He's exiled, but Hassein is not! He selects himself; he chooses to dedicate himself: That's very, very different. We were talking about Messengers being 'sent from above'. That's one thing - that order of perfected beings that derives from Modiktheo. They cannot do otherwise because they serve the cosmic order. They cannot say no. That's why I see Ashiata's "need" as a need for Reason. Because he can't say no, he can't understand how in the world these crazy three-brained beings can say no. That final 'no' of the Will is something that Beelzebub does understand. He can go to the bottom of that because that is also inside of him. It's also inside of Hassein, as part of his nature. But he (Hassein) has decided himself - he makes this decision to Be *that* and he is the future and direct substitute. So I see Hassein in the context; possibly, as being the self-selected Messenger, different from being sent from Above. That may seem totally daffy to many people, but it has a consistency to it for me.

Questioner 4: I have a question about the drawing over there. I understand Evolution as the arrow going up, and Involution as the arrow going down. I understand Evolution and Involution being in a clash. I understand active and passive being in a clash. I understand evil and good being in a clash. I don't think I understand why Involution - Passive - and Good are on one side, the three of them together - and Evolution - Active - and Evil being on the other side, the three of them together.

Keith Buzzell: Oh, OK - you mean the use of the terms? Only because that's how Makary defined them.

Questioner 4: How - what!

Keith Buzzell: Good means anything that moves from The Source, because its origin is from the Source. He calls that 'good'. All the consequences, - considering that they flow *from* the Source - those are considered good. But they are also involutional because they are moving away from the Source. They are also passive, because they have the thrust of Holy Affirming behind them - so he characterizes those as passive. So that's why those end up Involutional - passive - good. Whereas - and this comes back to what we were talking about last night - about Kundalini, Kundabuffer...

Questioner 4: Yes, yes I just wanted...

Keith Buzzell: Because buried in the 'evil' is, by Makary's definition, the striving to return. And here at the base of the spine, the bottom of the spinal cord, the source of Kundalini, that which must rise.

Questioner 4: Now, my next question. Since Beelzebub was sent away he is somehow 'good' and 'passive'.

Keith Buzzell: In his exile - under the lawful exile that carries him from Holy Sun Absolute....

Questioner 4: In what sense is he good?

Keith Buzzell: Only in the sense that he has gone from a higher world and moved down and that's moving away from the Source.

Questioner 4: So who is the recipient of this 'good'? Does this imply that somehow the presence of Beelzebub is good for the beings that he meets at the lower levels? Who is it good for? I'm just trying to understand it.

Keith Buzzell: I don't think that it has that kind of subjective intent, the way it's spoken out by Makary. Gurdjieff is clever here because he simply says 'anything that moves from the Source has to be good - coming from the Source it could not be evil. So we get caught in a paradox - it's coming from the Source, so that makes it 'good', but it's moving away from the Source, downhill, and that means that it gets further and further away from the Source of the good - so what do you call that? I would ask the same question, but I don't think that's what Gurdjieff is up to here. He's catching us in the middle of *our* abstract definitions - that's why I think he avoids 'Justice', doesn't use the word itself in the chapter. What he does do is tell us two stories - one where Makary appears by Involution and must strive to return. And the other story - at a different level because it's a *one*-natured being rather than Makary as two-natured. Beelzebub starts, already conscious at a high level, and is exiled, thrust away from the Source of good, and now he must strive to return. So we've got these two stories, and it seems to me that in the balancing out of those is the question of Justice. That's where Objective Justice is going to enter - only when those two have been brought into balance through the results of the 'clash'. Until that has been completely balanced Makary is stuck on Holy Planet Purgatory and...

Questioner 4: where does this balance occur? Is it on the highest level, my level, an intermediate level?

Keith Buzzell: It would appear, to me, that in the end Objective Justice would be a judgement by Endlessness - because Endlessness intervenes here and rules, with Hope, that in time the Three Brained Beings of Earth may wake up. So in that instance, if they finally come to work out all the "results of his evil deed" - and if we take 'evil' in the sense of the striving to return, then Makary, rather than being sent to Remorse of Conscience, will go on to Holy Sun Absolute - because of the balance. That's the Justice. But until that happens he is on Purgatory. He must wait that out - like all of us. The implication here to Individuality is one I wanted to make sure I put in the paper. That individually, this Work, is not for you, me as individuals. We are involved in this enterprise that involves the whole of humanity.

Questioner 5: It's very obvious that the overlying thing is that we don't have the ability to judge between good and evil - at all. We're still far from being able to do that. So, if we go through this balancing of things then we have Hope.

Questioner 6: When you talk about, and this picture is brought to me (in reference to the Tibetan book again, it refers to the Bodhisattva ideal which you people are very familiar with) - the aspect of the voluntary taking on something. When Tibetan teachers bring their teaching to the West they have tremendous difficulty putting across 'compassion'. Also, in my experience, to come to some understanding of what this means to work for the Work and for Others is a long search and it seems to me that this process you're describing (to try to 'fathom the gist') is moving in that direction. Perhaps Justice only is meaningful in terms of something based upon compassion, and not just balancing out in this mechanical way.

Keith Buzzell: The decision of Endlessness here, to allow Makary to remain on Purgatory - this shows great compassion. He doesn't go along with the recommendation regarding the planet Remorse of Conscience - which brings up the question - not commented on so far - of what the difference is between the planet Remorse-of-Conscience and the planet Purgatory? The *state* of. What is Gurdjieff trying to tell us here? Or is he going to tell us anything specific? Let me re-emphasize one point - in case there is some disagreement - remember I spoke of the 'twos' and among the twos are the two sons of Beelzebub. In the same sentence that he speaks about his sons he speaks about them as 'results'. Throughout the *Tales* we have to be very careful that we don't over-anthropomorphize. This is often one of the things that can trick us. He anthropomorphizes the Angels, the Archangels etc. - maybe he is doing the same thing with respect to the sons of Beelzebub. They are 'results of his labors'. So if we see them, not as the biological sons - forget that! Take it only as 'results of his labors'. One of them is active (Holy Affirming) and one of them passive (yet Holy Affirming). One a Zerlikner, one a 'witness'. They are results of the efforts of that Individuality and they move on, they evolve and move up to that level within the Cosmos where they can best serve. The Individuality of Beelzebub is still responsible for the fundamental error in judgement that he made. It is that error that has to be equilibrated (that's Justice) in order for the Individuality to return. If we take the 'results' of Beelzebub as 'results' and not as biological, anthropomorphic 'sons' - then what do we do with Hassein? Think about it.

Questioner 6: Makary is a Greek word - it means the 'blessed one' who is very happy, who goes to heaven. In the New Testament, in the Sermon on the Mount, with 'blessed be' etc. - the Greek word is Makary.

Keith Buzzell: Is that referring to the poor or to the blessed?

Questioner 6: To the blessed.

Keith Buzzell: When I talked to Nick (Tereshchenko) he said it had a Russian meaning.

Questioner 6: Yes, but I think it's clearly a Greek word.

Keith Buzzell: Well (laughs) - I can't argue with Nick about Russian. He says the word exists. But the interesting thing is that he says it enters into a number of common sayings - a kind of expression of 'Joe Doe'.

Questioner 4: So perhaps it has *both* meanings.

Keith Buzzell: Yes.

Questioner 6: In Greek the name is very common.

Keith Buzzell: Now, is there anything in Greek about Kronbernkzion?

Questioner 7: Is the difference between Purgatory and Remorse of Conscience that the suffering on 'Remorse' is more intense?

Keith Buzzell: I just threw it out there, just wanting to get impressions. What is yours?

Questioner 3: What struck me is - Purgatory is a transitory place, a place you can move from. Whereas on 'Remorse' you are stuck. Once on Remorse you can't get off.

Keith Buzzell: That's how it strikes me. Does this have to do with possibilities? On Purgatory you still have possibilities. Being sent to Remorse of Conscience you're just in remorse. And where is the hope?

Questioner 1: God's power of salvation extends only to Purgatory. He cannot go below. God has no 'touch-control' over Hell. Church doctrine makes this clear. Whereas on Purgatory, as you say, there is always the possibility. You may stay there forever, but you may move on. You cannot move from Purgatory down. Gurdjieff says as much.

Questioner 8: How about the old prophets?

Questioner 1: That's true. He had to bring them up. No one that Christ brought up was damned - no one! He didn't bring up the damned. He brought up the Prophets, John the Baptist.

Keith Buzzell: Those who have served.

Questioner 1: Hell as a place is a moral designation. This is in the Apostolic Creed but not in the Bible.

Questioner 8: I thought that you said that His Endlessness could not go beyond...

Questioner 1: No! No! In organized Christianity God touches nothing in Hell, nothing below Purgatory. The Church Fathers set that up. No one has come out of Hell since Christ gave man the possibility not to go down. The moment that Christ delivered those who were not to be damned - that moment is in eternity.

Questioner 9: A place in history that signifies something that has always been. It is - the Word. But it is a representation of something that is outside of Time. It enters *into* time and becomes concrete.

Questioner 1: Yes, but no man went to heaven before Christ delivered...

Keith Buzzell: I think we have to...

Questioner 9: This is not about bad and good...

Questioner 1: No...

Questioner 9: This is about the influence of His Endlessness...

Questioner 1: Excuse me, I'm not talking about that - I'm talking about Christian doctrine of the Fathers, that's all.

All & Everything Conference 2002

Keith Buzzell: We can look at the Christian symbology, but its symbology may have nothing to do with this chapter.

Questioner 10: Forgive me for coming in late on this, but on a technicality - in the *Tales*, in Purgatory, they could leave and go to Holy Sun Absolute, but not after the Choot God Litanical period. I've always felt this had something to do with - the conditions change. After Christ everyone went down - The souls have to wait there until the end of time. And, as far as the planet Remorse goes, there are three of them that the Hasnamuss go to, and only the eternal Hasnamuss, like Lentrohamsanin, can never leave - or be redeemed. With the other two degrees they can.

Questioner 5: You mean they can get off the planet Remorse?

Questioner 10: Yes, they can. From two of the three planets.

Questioner 11: There are 3 degrees of Hasnamuss?

Keith Buzzell: Yes, it is only the planet of Eternal Retribution that is beyond - beyond. I was wrong before. It is good to do this - I fall into this thing - it is a trap. We've got to stay inside of the symbology that Gurdjieff has created. When we begin to say, 'This is like' what we find is this. This is tough enough to plumb. If we stay inside his symbology and the images he has created - because they have so much to do with us in our inner world now, then it's much more useful. I'm convinced that Gurdjieff, as Master, had this palette. And on this palette was all of his verbal knowledge and knowledge of symbology of the Great Traditions - and he uses the palette to paint with - so he uses these. Does that mean that it means the same thing? No - maybe it means exactly the opposite or whatever.

Questioner 1: I was not saying it is the same. I was saying that in Orthodox Christianity Purgatory has a very fixed meaning. In fact if you go back and look at Church history there is no Purgatory - it is an invention of the 10th Century. Then, you're either in Hell, in Heaven or on Earth. That was clearly the way it worked. Aquinas, later, said what do you do with a certain body of people who were neither here nor there. So Aquinas picks up on this - and they invent Purgatory as a place where you could move up.

Keith Buzzell: That's my point. Purgatory would create useful images, from Gurdjieff's perspective.

Questioner 12: Would you read that section about the three planets.

Questioner 11: Yes -

"One of these four disharmonized planets called 'Eternal-Retribution' is specially prepared for the 'Eternal-Hasnamuss-individuals' and the other three for those 'Higher being-bodies' of

Hasnamusses in whose common presences there is still the possibility of 'at some time or other' eliminating from themselves the mentioned maleficent something.

"The three small planets exist under the names of

(1) 'Remorse-of-Conscience'
(2) 'Repentance'
(3) 'Self-Reproach.'

"Here it is interesting to notice that from among all the 'highest being-bodies' which have been coated and perfected in every kind of exterior form of three-brained being there have, so far, reached the planet 'Retribution' from the whole Universe, only three hundred and thirteen, two of whom had their arising on your planet and one of these is the 'highest being-body' of this Lentrohamsanin.

"On that planet Retribution, these Eternal-Hasnamuss-individuals must constantly endure those incredible sufferings called 'Inkiranoodel' which are like the sufferings called Remorse-of-Conscience but only much more painful.

"The chief torture of the state of these 'highest being-bodies' is that they must always experience these terrifying sufferings fully conscious of the utter hopelessness of their cessation."

So there are actually four planets - one only is eternal. The other three are possible to leave.

Keith Buzzell: I was wrong, then, in what I said about Remorse of Conscience. Even on this planet there is a chance…

Questioner 11: As pointed out, Purgatory is a late-comer in terms of theology - and it is a late-comer in the Book (the *Tales*). Purgatory was created later, after things went wrong and, due to absolutely no fault of the three brained beings themselves, they could no longer go to the Sun Absolute. In the misfortunate, which produced Purgatory, there is a kind of parallel - they were stuck there.

Keith Buzzell: In terms of Objective Justice (just to ground us in what the paper concerns) it raises so many questions that remove a too-ready reaction to events of the recent past (9/11). In other words we tend to demand Justice or look for it in this kind of situation and I would suggest, on the basis of what we find in this chapter, that we are asking the wrong question.

Seminar 2 - Chapters 11, 12 & 13 of Beelzebub's Tales to His Grandson

Facilitator: John Scullion

Facilitator: What I would like to try and begin with at least a simple and personal impression of this chapter 11, if there is something you could say about that and it may seem very obvious or it may seem simple.

Very simply, (and I'm reading the notes we made when we had a small group we had several years ago) this chapter seems to be referring to the established church and its tendency to deal with unimportant things in an impractical way totally unrelated to what they should be giving their attention to.

It is just that chapters ten, eleven and twelve are very progressive and it's too bad if we are leaving out ten because we have three different instances of Justice in those don't we? We have the High Commissioners who are applying a sort of Court of Justice in ten. Then we have the problem of Earthly Courts, whatever they are, that are going to exact judgement because of the language of Hassein and then in twelve we have the power-possessors who are using their (influence) word about money. In fact we go into different things. We are worried about language in eleven; we are worried about money in twelve. Judgements are made on these items. So that is one link I am suggesting between the chapters.

Participant: There is this impression of him setting out a set of things, not developing them yet, but just establishing somewhere to build upon later.

Participant: Yes just after that, because in ten too, we end ten with an instance of Objective Language. The Ravens have an Objective Language so there is a sequence of evolution or devolution; I don't know whether it is going down or up, that seems to me to be very important since language becomes the problem of Hassein using the words slugs.

Participant: I looked at chapters 11, 12, and 13 and came up with a question that was related to the three chapters together. The question specifically relates to chapter 13. Beelzebub advises Hassein that only by the realisation of being-Partkdolg-duty can a being become aware of genuine reality. What advice does he give Hassein regarding the practice of being-Partkdolg-duty?

Participant: Along that line of the reality and unreality. One of the interesting threats Hassein has to face is to lose his horns, right? Beelzebub gets his back at the end of the book. In that same

Seminar 2 - Chapters 11, 12 & 13 of Beelzebub's Tales to His Grandson

chapter, if I remember correctly we have that lovely expression - "Struth! What might not happen in this world. A flea might swallow an elephant." Now since Gurdjieff knew Greek very well the Greeks have always had this pun between ivory and horn. I don't know if you know this, this is an old, old thing. Gurdjieff knew it because is a story-telling thing.

There are two gates; the gate of ivory and the gate of horn. Now the gate of ivory is the gate into which you go. It looks more valuable but it is the gate into dreams and fantasy, unreality. The gate of horn looks much less interesting, but because horn is like a Greek word for truth, it is the gate of truth, that is reality and distinguishing from unreality. So to remove someone's horns, as Gurdjieff knew very well, in a sense, is to remove their problem of reality. Then when you mention an elephant out of a fly we are playing with something Orage and Gurdjieff knew very well, you are playing with the game of what is real and what is not. That which looks real, of value, ivory is deemed unreality. That which looks less valuable, horn, is truth. And because he poses that in the chapter, he begins the horn and elephant and ends up with the elephant and the fly he had to be setting up that, as you say, because we have this unreality and reality as the issue here.

Participant: Something in chapter 11 that caught my attention on page 95. Beelzebub was concerned at first because he felt anxious that his grandson should use this name towards the Man on Earth and more so here the second (concern) because he had laid up a menace for himself in the future. And I'm not sure I understand that because I look at someone unknowingly insulting someone just out of ignorance, not really knowing...

Participant: A faux pas.

Participant: And yet he refers to the fact that Hassein may have set him (self) up in the future for something that may be a menace to him. It sounds like such a big deal for such a... faux pas.

Participant: Yes that crossed my mind too and just looking at it on the surface. I thought that maybe, because we are in chapter 11 now and Beelzebub has been talking to Hassein for two or three chapters, that he is getting a little information and he thinks he sees Beelzebub being critical of the beings on Earth. So he leaps in impulsively to criticize already without real knowledge of beings on earth and he calls them slugs because of a certain description that Beelzebub gave in a previous chapter that they were slimy. So he leaps to the conclusion that these are slugs, which is an insulting term.

I think to me it would seem like this that I get a little knowledge about esoteric subjects and I start to assume that I understand something. I could therefore have the privilege of insulting somebody else who doesn't know and that would, if it's not cracked on the head, lay up consequences for the future, if I am unable to curb them.

Participant: When I first read this material on anathematizing it was several years after I was introduced to these ideas. And without peeling the onion too much, just superficially I am inclined to take this as fitting in with the main title of the book 'An Objectively Impartial Criticism of the Life of Man'. And what I saw here when I read this a few years after reading In Search of The Miraculous was this is exactly what is in 'In Search of The Miraculous'. I do not have the book here or the reference to the pages but Ouspensky presumably quoting Gurdjieff, (although I question that), comes down very hard saying, (and it has to do with groups) that if one person leaves the group then they are cut off. Its there, or if one person married and leaves then they both have to leave (the group) and it has always bothered me. And I am inclined to, maybe incorrectly, to attribute that stuff which I did not like in 'In Search' to Ouspensky, even though he is quoting Gurdjieff. That was reaction when I read this material and it is still feel today that it is something along the lines that there is something not quite right in 'In Search' given what is in this chapter here.

Participant: This reaction of The Church seems to be out of proportion, out of scale. It even seems to be a preposterous reaction but in countries, in actual countries where there is a lot of Fundamentalism going on, like Greece at the moment, there is always a very real possibility of having such an explosion at any moment, in real life, a real anathema. I think this is a very different and if you will excuse the term 'educative' chapter in the sense that it what a little thing could produce such an incredible reaction. How silly the process is and how easy it is, because he smiles at the end, to be rid of the fear and even the consequences of such a thing. Just be careful about it.

Participant: Yes that is why there seems to me to be the flavour that already Beelzebub is, by warning or however we want to see that aspect of it, that he is teaching. He is saying 'this is how to hide, pay attention'.

Participant: Hide?

Participant: Hide, that is presumptive on my part, he is still looking at the future. If and when Hassein has to go to Earth ... around that notion already there is laying out the foils, the difficulties you may get into and so forth and so these are simultaneously a warning and also as Dimitri says, it is an instruction. If you don't want to get into trouble remember this. It's not a big deal if you just don't do this you are not going to create this sudden explosion of negativity and so on.

Participant: Which will go on for a long time and become more and more important and from such a trifling cause.

Participant: This is the flea and the elephant. Out of all proportion.

Participant: But I have found that whether someone needs it or not, if I am insulted this is exactly how I feel. This is it.

Participant: This is what I want to begin to talk about. What does this mean about us?

Seminar 2 - Chapters 11, 12 & 13 of Beelzebub's Tales to His Grandson

Participant: I think it is advice to Hassein but I also think it is also very accurate. This is how we are; this is how I am, especially if it is true! If it is true you would do anything to get rid of it. And I think this is exactly at the heart of it all. I really think, this is deep down, you know if we could anathematize anyone who inadvertently insulted us and even have the audacity to mistakenly be accurate!

Participant: Maybe especially if they are accurate this is such an offence to our false picture of ourselves, our vanity, our self importance. The upside-down-ness and backwardness of this is that it is from such a trifling cause and eventually it will actually define that person in relation to the whole of the rest of humanity. 'Oh, he is the guy we anathematized because of this.' So this anathema is quite important, it is the sort of sanction... in groups.

Participant: Well I mean really, exactly one thing our teacher Mrs Staveley used to say, 'We live in a one-man Universe'. And you know more and more that is absolutely true. I mean basically and to some degree everyone is anathematized. You know, I am me at the centre and there are these kind of annoying satellites. So I think that is deep down, you know when we were speaking yesterday, about (how) deep down we all feel deeply that we are right and to me that is what I am up against. That is the involutionary force.

Participant: That is our identity, we identify with that and so that becomes our identity which from another point of view is not our identity, not necessarily our ultimate nature nor ultimately who we are. Yet as we are we have everything staked on this.

Participant: Everything, all the marbles in that illusion.

Participant: I was just going to follow on a point that was made about feeling worried for Hassein because he has called men slugs and at first I was worried for him because Beelzebub makes it quite a dramatic thing when he said it. But then at the beginning of the next chapter he says that it might not be such a bad thing if they found out about it. Then the next chapter is about, he doesn't name the individual that wrote down the modern version of the Gospels, and about how the individuals (unclear) it actually made it great. Everything turns out roses, roses for him. So he actually says it might not be so very bad for you if the humans do that. Obviously Gurdjieff was anathematized totally himself so it may be a beneficial after all.

Participant: Would you like you say what the difference is between Hassein's remark and how it turned out for the writer of the 'gospel'? Well, with Hassein it is just a mistake almost, a small thing, but one might also use this same characteristic intentionally.

Participant: Publicity, it creates publicity.

Participant: Yes, do this, go through this, suffer this process consciously or initiate all of these inevitable reactions as inevitable parts of a strategy. You can do this consciously or you can do this unconsciously and Beelzebub is saying to Hassein this will happen and then in the next chapter he is saying that you might employ this deliberately for a consciousness purpose. You might use this mechanical inevitability for a better reason. It might be used against, or, not against mankind but for mankind but against on another level. They will react and anathematize this person who will become famous because people will come down on side or another and will become identified for or against whoever has 'written the gospel'. So it can either be a catastrophe where Hassein suffers needlessly and for no reason or it can be something creative, you can engage human nature in two different ways.

Participant: Isn't this a bit though like a fear of a repetition of what happened to Beelzebub himself. To anathematize someone is to isolate them; it is to 'send them to Coventry' isn't it? We don't know exactly what Beelzebub did but it may have been a speech problem too. So then the threat in chapter thirteen that he will have his horns taken away is warning Hassein about doing what he himself (Beelzebub) did but in a completely different context and level.

Participant: It is more of a caricature in this one.

Participant: That is what I mean, a completely different level, it becomes comic, ridiculous in a sense.

Participant: 'That the food in your stomach turns to coffin nails or that you wife's tongue become three times its size!'

Participant: That's the worst one!

Participant: The retribution towards whoever insults these men-beings is physical. I was just wondering why it was always only physical. Is there a deeper meaning to these physical things?

Participant: There is no consideration and we react, that is the physical level of our way into the world. It is the most mechanical level of taking things in and reacting there is nothing gets processing. It is just in-out. That's step one, if we can't get beyond that then we are not getting any further.

Participant: Like a slug. That reminds me of a slug.

Participant: The point about the physical punishments is that they all are metaphorically physical. The images are physical but it is possible to see behind them several layers of meaning. 'May your wife's tongue become three times its size!' 'May you lose you horns!' Here we have sex and diet the things that are going to destroy...

Participant: What about 'picking one to pieces' that could be very psychological.

Participant: Just to connect the physical with everything else, this is part of the sensation-picturings. This is Gurdjieff saying 'I will speak to the waking consciousness and the sub-

Seminar 2 - Chapters 11, 12 & 13 of Beelzebub's Tales to His Grandson

consciousness simultaneously.' So by creating these sensations or pictures it has its superficial meaning, its meaning in the world but then it also has these other levels of meaning and somehow we feel those. We take these in whether we realise it or not on the first reading or the second reading but hopefully at some point it begins to speak in a way that connects the sub-consciousness with the waking consciousness and we sub-begin to see 'Ah yes - this is what is going on.'

Participant: I think that he is talking about criticising my ability to be critical, to discern. And with this first one here I felt that this was such a precise description of how I am and of course at the same time I am sure he is using real material. He knows the judge as well and so he is precise there as well. But you know this is how things happen inside me, I have this meeting, this synod if necessary and the self is always the same, I'm sorry to say. This seems to carry on and then he really gets on a high here in chapter thirteen where he says it is not actually Kundabuffer and the consequences it is they themselves. So he is clearly making me face something about myself; something quite terrifying.

Participant: There is also the incongruity about being judged by secular authorities as being innocent but that doesn't end things because there is this higher authority which can find you guilty. He puts that township or town hall in there, which is very interesting, which can nevertheless find you guilty, but guilt in the two instances have nothing to do with one another. In other words we have got the problem again of intent and result if you like. But what are you judging? Intent? That is the higher authorities, that is the Catholic Church or any church but the secular authorities are supposed to be judging results or effects of acts, is that not so? A criminal act is that which has a particular effect it means nothing to the church authorities in this chapter. They are judging something else altogether. I assume that you all know that in the Catholic Church you can be innocent of committing any act whatsoever and be excommunicated and even sent to the electric chair because you intended doing something.

Do you remember that marvellous story in *A Place in the Sun* with Elizabeth Taylor and Montgomery Cliff where Montgomery Cliff is going to take Shelley Winters out and because he is in love with Elizabeth Taylor he is going to drown Shelley Winters. He takes Shelley Winters out in a boat and he is going to throw her overboard but he gets frightened and he can't do it but she falls overboard and she drowns. He is sentenced to death. The priest comes in and sees him and Montgomery Cliff says 'I didn't do it' and the priest says, 'It doesn't matter, you intended to do it'. So we have got this seemingly illogical here. In other words - What is innocence?

Participant: It seems important to remember that this is very early in the *Tales* and that these are the first instructions to Hassein around his interests. In other words when we come to, say, Form and Sequence and Beelzebub explains why he has done it this way it is built, all of Hassein's Oskiano, around his interest in the three brained beings of Earth. Going back through each of chapters through here has this feeling for me of being built on the interests of Hassein. Because this is early on he is not yet into feeling about these three-brained beings of Earth. He is not identified with them. It is not 'your favourites', by no means yet. It is not 'your planet' etc, that comes much later

It is just the feeling of that that is important to pick up on. In chapters 11, 12 and 13 Beelzebub is saying something like 'Now, it's like this, whatever you do; don't do this'. In other words it is a beginning kind of circumstance. The errors that are really going to get you into trouble in the external sense, which is why (the retributions) are always physical. It is just in this external sense you will be in big trouble if you stick your foot into things. So he takes the superficial and those more obvious aspects of our reactivity to help us see that if we fall into these traps we are not going to go anywhere. Unless we this, see what he is pointing out that we should see inside of ourselves then we are caught in fantasy. We get to chapter 44 and we are still stuck in fantasy. This is important, essential, and fundamental because if you don't get this there is a whole bunch of things down the road that are not going to work out right.

Participant: I think that chapter 13 as far as I know is the first introduction of the idea of work to Hassein. This is the first time Being-partkdolg-duty is mentioned. I think that ideas of that kind have appeared under a veil in previous chapters but not directly to him. Here in chapter 13 he definitely mentions this idea in the first couple of pages, this idea of the possibility of work being the antidote to this kind of condition. And work begins with the physical.

Participant: About the physical thing he begins by saying that these, especially contemporary three brained beings do not discriminate on such fine points. We take everything at face value. We begin by taking the tactile and connotative aspect of something as the whole thing, that is as far as we can go. And so then we imagine then that the consequences when we meet out justice are at the same level, all of this is fantasy.

Participant: I would like to add something to what you said because you said 'we'. I think that all of this book puts a pressure; the question is where do we place the 'we'? Are we on the part of Beelzebub's tribe or are 'we' the people? This pressure exists throughout the book and it places a demand on us to choose somehow. There is a division there. Are we going to 'be informed about' these things or 'are you' these things? Are we (the readers) part of the solution or are we part of the problem?

Participant: A very curious thing is being said here, "just this particularity arose in them only because their predominant part (which I take to be formatory apparatus), which was formed in them as in all three-brained beings, gradually allowed them to perceive every new impression without what is called 'being-Partkdolg-duty". So what is he saying here? Something allowed mechanical working without the first or second conscious shock not being as is proper to three-centered beings is somehow giving us the blame, that there is some kind of volition... why is he putting it this way.

Participant: That is the beginning of him getting tough, on the top of page 105 he says but they themselves are to blame for it.

Seminar 2 - Chapters 11, 12 & 13 of Beelzebub's Tales to His Grandson

Participant: I don't remember my childhood very well so I can't remember how this process of falling asleep and failing to maintain an inner openness occurred. Some people seem to be able to remember. They have very vivid memories of sometimes how it was inner compromises arose when they knew the truth and yet let it be submerged in some way. I do not have those memories. I do believe that as each of us grew up there was an increasingly consensual compliance with a 'caned in' centre of gravity consciousness. I do believe that. It is very hard for us to undo, because as he says it has to be done by fraudulent means. We can no longer go directly back to innocence because it's too late; the inner structures have been changed. You said is it the formatory apparatus? I think not. I think it is the sense to which we can return of true I am-ness which has when it is pure, an amazing authority. Why does that go to sleep?

Participant: I think it is a tremendously important to get this as clear as you can.

We are born as three brained beings on the earth with a whole range of unchangeables. We are really under the law. These are the involutional mechanical laws that hold us down. So then the question becomes when and where is the road to responsible behaviour. I believe that he is trying to point to that here. He is saying 'this we are responsible for because *we could pay attention!*' We do have a modicum of attention and *if we don't use that* we are responsible. So we must use whatever little attention we have to begin this process. If we don't, nobody else is to blame, Kundabuffer is not to blame, biology is not to blame because we were given that attention.

End of Session

Remembering Gurdjieff

Professor Paul Beekman Taylor

What I remember best of my brief association with Gurdjieff are the children, of who very little has been written and said in other reminiscences. I knew three distinct overlapping groups of children. First were the children about Gurdjieff and his brother Dmitri in the Caucasus. Lonia, the son of the Mme. Ouspensky's daughter, Lenochka, and Valentin Anastavseff ("Valia"), son of Gurdjieff s sister Anna, were the eldest, each born about 1911. Svetlana Hinzenberg, Natalie Salzmann ("Boussique"), Luba Gurdjieff and Nikolai Stjernval were born around 1918 or 1919. I knew all of these with the exception of Svetlana, who was in the United States from 1924 on. It is amazing that all of these children were involved in the exodus of Gurdjieff's group to Western Europe. They shared the trials so often written about their parents. (I apologize for my inexact dating; I assume ages.)

Some of these joined a second group of children born during the Paris and Prieuré days. Dmitri's daughters Genia (b. 1920?) and Lydia ("Lida," b. 1921) were born in the Caucuses after Gurdjieff and his entourage had left, but before Dmitri, his sister Sophie, his mother Evdokia ("Eva"), and his daughters reached France in 1923. At the Prieuré in 1924 and later were Fritz and Tom Peters. Michel Salzmann (b. 1923), Sergei Chaverdian (b. 1926) who left for the Soviet Union with his mother Lily shortly after his birth, Anatole ("Toly") Mercourov, my sister Eve, and myself. Tania (b. 1929) and Lonia Savitsky lived in Paris, but did not frequent the Prieuré.

In New York City in 1948 and 1949, there were Dushka Howarth (b. 1924 in the United States), Mary Sinclair, Lord and Lady Pentland's daughter, Marthe ("Patty") and Richard Welch, Eric and Carolla Nyland, Marian Sutta, and Iovanna Lloyd Wright, all of us in our teens or early twenties. In London were Richard and Ann Orage, and Adam and Jimmy Nott, but I am not sure any of these had a direct association with Gurdjieff, with the possible exception of Jimmy in the summer of 1949.

Gurdjieff enjoyed the company of children. He treated them with both affection and respect. The children, as a rule, admired Gurdjieff, but were in awe of him. We called him "Monsieur" in almost every context, though to our adult parents he was either "the old man," "Georgiivanich" or, simply, "G." I recall that in New York as well as in Paris, a child invited to lunch for the first time would be seated at the long table set up in the largest bedroom of his suite on the 11th floor of the Wellington Hotel on 55th Street and 7th Avenue. Often, a child (I saw only male children there) was placed at Gurdjieff's right, and throughout the meal was expected to drink a male adult portion of vodka for each toast. Inevitably, that child would be given a choice morsel of food, often a sheep's eye. For meals afterwards, children were seated at smaller tables set up in the salon, where they were supervised strictly not to disturb the adults (I recall Louise Welch and Dorothy Wolfe as guardians of the children while I was there). For the only time in my life I was served bear meat (tough and stringy) and camel sausage, which I found difficult to chew or swallow. Its color was the color of what I imagine comes out of the nether end of a camel.

While I was there, I was given tasks to perform, and I imagine most of the children were given similar tasks. One was going to markets downtown to fetch sheep heads. Another time I was sent to get five hundred silver dollars from the Federal Reserve Bank downtown. Later, Gurdjieff gathered the children together (I was not there on this occasion) before sacks of silver dollars and a pile of five dollar bills. He offered to each child a choice between a five dollar bill and a one dollar coin. I am told that all the boys chose the bills, while three-fourths of the girls chose silver.

For readings and music in late afternoons and after supper late at night, children would be seated on the floor, cross-legged, in the salon, while adults occupied chairs behind them and along the east and west walls. Before the north wall - behind which was a bathroom and Gurdjieff's bedroom - was a couch upon which Gurdjieff sat during readings by an adult on his right, and where he played his harmonium. More often than not, he played "noo moosik," that is, improvisations. After a session he would often take from his pockets handfuls of hard candies and ask some child to distribute them. I once started to pass them out one by one, but Gurdjieff interrupted me, took the candies and said, "No, like this!" and threw them out over the children.

Two or three times Gurdjieff would gather the children in front of him after lunch, while adults were cleaning and re-ordering the dining area, and give them advice. The children, whom he called during meals "unformed idiots," or "aspirants for ordinary idiot," sat quietly on the floor. I do not recall any one of us asking him questions, though we responded to questions he asked us. I remember him talking about sleep. He said that children slept too long, that six hours should be enough for us if we learned to sleep efficiently. He said that one could sleep even during the day, and mentioned that there were ways of measuring efficiency of sleep. One means was to hold a pencil between the fingers, doze off, and when the pencil dropped, that was enough of a nap.

He spoke also of breathing, telling us to be conscious of the rhythm of breath, particularly while talking, because the force of speech is related to the ability to breathe correctly. Breath, he said, is related to bodily rhythms like pulses. He said that self-conscious breathing concentrates thought and, more importantly, the absence of thought. It is important to know how to think of nothing, so that other bodily centers could function independently. He told us about the bandit on the steppes who could sit without thought on a rock so still, that the caravan he was waiting to rob, could not tell he was not a rock himself until it was within meters of him.

This shifting of force from one center to another is important in putting oneself soundly to sleep. One must relax the body part by part, but it is better to start with the head in order to diffuse its energy throughout the rest of the body; and then relax downward the rest of the body until concentration exits through the toes.

He spoke of eating, or diet. Eat everything, he told us, and drink everything. (I remember many of the children saying later that they had not gotten drunk drinking Gurdjieff's vodka. The only instance I can recall of something getting absolutely drunk from the toasts is Lincoln Kirstein at the Prieuré in 1927.) Gurdjieff said that he could read personality from eating habits and comportment at the table. His meals were tests. I recall being given the task of bottling pink vodka made in his bathtub. On a tray over the sink I filled bottles. As a reward, I was given a bottle for myself. A few days later, on the train back to Providence, R I. where I was studying, I opened my bottle and took a sip. It was horrible! I hadn't realized that the pink color came from peppers!

The routine in Paris was much the same, except that only the lunches were grand affairs, although the table there could only serve a dozen or so guests. After a first lunch at that table I was assigned to the small kitchen to help in preparation of the food. The kitchen was miniscule, but in it operated Alfred Etievan, Luba Gurdjieff; Lise Tracol and Gabo when I was there. I cannot now imagine how we were able to move about. One of my chores there was to take leftovers in the afternoon around the corner to a Catholic hospital, St. Ferdinand, to give to the sisters.

© Copyright 2002 - Professor Paul Beekman Taylor - All Rights Reserved

Remembering Gurdjieff - Questions & Answers

Question: After New York, did you go back to Gurdjieff voluntarily, with a sense of wanting more of his teaching.

Paul Beekman Taylor: I don't know. I went because going to Paris was an occasion to see something of a world I wished to see as a young adult. I was there to have a good time, and I did do many things outside of the life of Rue des Colonels Renard. Perhaps what appealed to me most as the difficulty of life associated with Gurdjieff? I was living in a student residence near the Places des Nations, and the last metro ran about half an hour after midnight. Taxis charged "double tariff" at that hour which was beyond my means. Since evening with Gurdjieff rarely ended before that hour, I face walking a long way, and I was often ordered to return to Gurdjieff's at 7 or 8 in the morning to help preparations for the day. In the early morning I always walked, because I enjoyed going past the Austerlitz gardens and across to the Louvre before going up the Champs-Elysées to the Avenue Carnot. So, at night I often slept on the floor at Mme Dupré's where many of the girls lived. Those with money, like Marian Sutta, stayed in the Hotel Belfast on Avenue Carnot, those with less in one of the small dingy hotels like the Rena near Gurdjieff's, while some - Iovanna, Tania and my sister - stayed off the Avenue Foch in François Dupré's grand villa overlooking the Bois du Boulogne. Iovanna, curiously, always slept on the floor. She was the most outwardly serious of all. When we were travelling together she seemed always to sing to herself which was a bit bothersome. Dushka Howarth told me that this was the result of a comment Alfred Etievan had made to her during a movements class. He had approached her and said in his thick French Accent "Think." She heard "sing," and so she sang throughout the rest of her stay.

Question: Would you repeat the story of Lida's watch.

Paul Beekman Taylor: Well, one day when Gurdjieff was having his coffee or tea on the terrace at the Prieuré, his favorite niece, Lida, came up to him and showed him her play watch, a sort of mickey-mouse watch on a rubber-like wrist band. He looked at it, pulled it off her wrist, threw it on the ground and stepped on it, smashing it. Lida was appalled, ran to her father Dmitri to tell him what had happened. Dmitri knew his older brother well, and said nothing. The next day, as the children played on the lawn in front of the terrace, Gurdjieff called Lida to him. She went cautiously. When she stood in front of him, he pulled a real watch from his pocket and put it on her wrist, saying something to the effect that "time must be accurately measured."

Question: You have talked about Gurdjieff's story-telling. When did he have occasion to tell stories.

All & Everything Conference 2002

Paul Beekman Taylor: First, in the baths. The Saturday night baths at the Prieuré were story-telling sessions. They seemed too many to be obscene story competitions, but Gurdjieff said he could tell much about a man by the manner and matter of his stories. I remember in the hot room of the Luxor baths in New York with the thermometer at °160 F. Gurdjieff told stories while we sat and sweated. He told stories to Philip Lasell who lay pinned beneath the wreck of his car in August 1948, though Gurdjieff was hurt far more than Lasell. He wanted Lasell to take his mind off his injuries until help arrived.

Question: What was Valia's relation to Gurdjieff?

Paul Beekman Taylor: Valia was Feodor Anastasieff's son. Feodor and his wife Anna were killed by the Turks when they invaded Armenia in 1918, and Valia walked some 40 miles (someone has written 400 miles) to Dmitri's to join the Gurdjieff family. In Paris in the thirties he served as Gurdjieff's "factotum," managing the kitchen, shopping and so forth. He was with Gurdjieff when he died. At the time he had a restaurant with his wife Sylvie on the Left Bank, and later in the south of France. He had served in the Resistance during the war and was given French citizenship. Webb mistakenly (I believe) says that he was Sophie's son.

Question: Fritz Peters says that he was assigned to clean Gurdjieff's room at the Prieuré and always found it in disgusting condition. Is this true, or was this a test?

Paul Beekman Taylor: I do not know. Gurdjieff could be equally slovenly or immaculate, and I could not guess why on some occasions he was the one or the other. He certainly seemed to know what he was public, though he was not always neat and mindful of manners in restaurants or hotels.

Question: Did you have a sense of Gurdjieff's "mission."

Paul Beekman Taylor: It was obvious to me during the war, when people close to Gurdjieff in the past visited us in Connecticut, that they associated the "work" with a mission. They spent most of the time swapping stories about the "old Man," how he lifted automobiles out of ditches, and how he almost killed burglars who entered his apartment, but at the same time they seemed to have enormous respect for him. I thought certainly that it would be a fine thing to join a sort of Gurdjieffian mission, but I knew too little about his teachings at the time to undertake it.

Question: Of his family, what of his mother and wife do you know?

Paul Beekman Taylor: Very little. I have been told that Gurdjieff adored Julia, protected her, and spoiled her. She spoke very little, but moved with great dignity. I am told she spoke no French, English or Armenian, and that her Russian was heavily polish-accented. It was assumed by many I talked with that there had never been a formal marriage. She was always Madame Ostrowska, never Madam Gurdjieff to any one. His mother was also quiet, but was strong-willed, I am told by

Luba, her granddaughter. Her name was Evdokia (pronounced "Yevdokeeya"), but that is a Byzantine name whose Armenian cognate I do not know.

Question: In the records at Avon her name is given as "Eva."

Paul Beekman Taylor: Of course, since names in France often had to be transcribed in official records in an accepted French form (saint's names, classical names, etc). "Eva" and "Eve" are forms used for Evdokia in France, as far as I know.

Question: Do you know of any of Gurdjieff's restaurants, whether they still survive?

Paul Beekman Taylor: I believe the "Charlot" on Rue de Pic, off the Bd. Montmartre in the 9ème arrondissement was the "Ecrevisse" that Gurdjieff once managed and which was his favorite seafood restaurant. At any rate, the "Charlot" has, I believe, the best seafood in Paris.

Question: Gurdjieff seemed to know everything that was going on, and yet was not known as a reader.

Paul Beekman Taylor: He seemed to know everything, that is my impression, and I never saw him read a newspaper. I find it extraordinary that he alludes to the Scopes "Monkey Trial" in *Tales*, and yet that took place in Tennessee in 1925. Who told him the details or where he read it I cannot imagine. He read little English at the time, but he was aware of the latest scientific and technological developments.

Question: There is a photo of him somewhere reading a comic book.

Paul Beekman Taylor: Why not? He also wrote constantly, jotting notes while sitting in cafes if he wasn't in conversation. I remember him in New York at Childs writing, but I have no idea about what or in what language.

Question: Perhaps it was the fourth book!?

The High Commission and Other Sacred Individuals: What Do They Represent?

Moderator: Sy Ginsburg

I would like to say a few words about this morning's topic, "The High Commission and Other Sacred Individuals: What Do They Represent?

The history of the discussion of topics by email actually began after A&E2000, because we took names and email addresses then and circulated them to the participants. Several people started to email each other and a rather interesting discussion developed informally over several months on the topic of Higher Being Bodies.

So last year at A&E 2001, we specifically stated that if anybody wanted to be in an email discussion group during the year, they should put their name and email address down on a list and the planning committee would be in touch with them. Several people did and the result was that the planning committee, especially in the person of Marlena Buzzell, received these email addresses and sent out an email to them suggesting five proposed topics for discussion. The result of this expression of interest was that there were two topics that seemed to be of interest to those who wished to participate. One of them was this topic, "The High Commission and Other Sacred Individuals: What Do They Represent?" The Other Topic Was, "What is the Role of the Moon and Anulios in Gurdjieff's Psychocosmology?"

The six people who had expressed interest were divided into two groups of three each, and it was left up to them to initiate these discussions. I'm not sure who initiated the discussion group on the Moon and Anulios, but eventually that discussion just died down.

The other group continued their discussions and some of the people who had participated in the Moon and Anulios discussion began to join in on this topic, "The High Commission and Other Sacred Individuals: What Do They Represent?" This discussion group was actually initiated by Ana Fragomeni, I think in July of 2001, with an email proposing her ideas on this topic. Several people entered this discussion, and some left the discussion. Over a period of time three papers were produced by those people who were interested in producing papers; that is, a more formal presentation of their personal views on this topic.

The reading panel that reviews papers for the conference thought that these papers would be good to present here, followed by a discussion period to elicit the views of all of you who are present here, on this topic. This is the background of how this happened and the result is the three papers that are going to be presented this morning followed by a discussion.

As it turns out, the three papers that were written and are to be presented are by Nicolas Tereshchenko, Ana Fragomeni, and myself, Sy Ginsburg. Nick, as you all know, is not well and he could not attend. But we decided to go ahead and present his paper in any event, and I will read it. So, we are going to read these three papers before the coffee break. To the extent that we have time, we can have some questions and answers about each paper, but the time periods for this cannot be as long as they have been in the previous two days because we are going to deal with three papers instead of two this morning. After the coffee break, we will put the chairs in a circle and, for those who are interested, you can participate and give your views on this topic: what it is, what it means, what you think about it.

I am going to go ahead now and read Nick's paper. It is a very Gurdjieffian paper, but Nick begins it with some terms which some of us might not be familiar with, because they are really from Rosicrucian and related traditions. So, in an email, I asked Nick, because this is not my paper, if he would explain some of these terms. I am just going to read his explanations now, so that when I read them in the paper, you will understand what they mean if you are not familiar with them. What Nick said in response to my queries about these terms is as follows:

The "Fourth Way" is, in fact, a Gnostic and Rosicrucian manifestation even though neither of these terms is ever used. Then Nick talks about the "Invisible College," which is a symbol for reality and which can only be entered in states of self-remembering and higher.

I asked Nick about the "Rosy Cross." Nicks replied that to be a brother of the "Rosy Cross" is to know how to achieve these states of consciousness which the average man does not even know exists.

As to the "Mason Word," Nick said that to have the "Mason Word" means to know the whole truth about something which to others is a mystery.

I asked Nick about "Second Sight." About that he said it is a symbolic description of reading between the lines and pondering on the hidden meanings of words and expressions. Perhaps there are some other terms which we can also talk about later.

Here is Nick's paper.

How to "Read" Beelzebub's Tales, with Particular Reference to the "High Commission", other "Sacred Individuals" and Beelzebub's "Saturnian" Connection

Nicolas Tereshchenko

Narrow is the gate and straight is the way that leadeth unto life, and few be they that find it. (Matthew 7:14)

I form the light and create darkness; I make peace and create evil: I the LORD do all these things. (Isaiah 45:7)

Few readers of *Beelzebub's Tales to His Grandson* would disagree with the statement that it is a cleverly coded Legomonism[1] with many hidden meanings.

We know right from the start, from the author's own "Friendly[2] Advice" that it *must* and therefore *can* be read in three different ways, that is: (1) rapidly, as a work of fiction; (2) aloud, **as if** to a listener, that is, carefully vibrating its words, especially the *Hapax Legomena*[3], and, finally, (3) with full attention and the intention to **understand** everything the author wishes to transmit, overtly and covertly, that is, by "pondering" each word and phrase, and reading also "between the lines".

It is much easier to do this with the original text, many Russian words carefully chosen by the ingenious linguist,

---

[1] Легомонизм = Legomonism, NOT Legominism, as in the first (1950) English version, NOR LégAmonism as in the 1956 French one.
[2] The Russian word is actually Доброжелательный (Dobrojelatel'ny^Y) = Benevolent. Friendly is Дружеский (Droojeski^Y) in Russian.
[3] All Esoteric Schools affirm that Objective Truths can be transmitted ONLY directly from the Master's mouth to the pupil's ear. MG circumvented this limitation by advising to read his *Hapax Legomena* aloud; but the desired psychosomatic and spiritual effects can be obtained only when they are vibrated correctly and exactly as written.

The High Commission - Nicholas Tereshchenko

Mister George Gurdjieff (MG), having inner meanings either quite <u>UN</u>translatable into English or French (I do not know about other languages) or conveying these inner meanings only approximately by the nearest English or French word or phrase.

Even when read the three times, as the "Benevolent Advice" asks, few unawake readers can "see" the real veiled meanings, just as the average "man" (in quotation marks) can never find the right way to enter the omnipresent flying "Invisible College" of the Brethren of the **ROSY + CROSS**, who "have the Mason Word and second sight".

Let us also note that MG had originally called this "First Series" *An Objectively Impartial Criticism of the Life of Man* (now used as the "sub-title") and left the reader in no doubt whatever about his grim purpose, that is: ***"to destroy, mercilessly, without any compunction whatsoever, in the mentation and feelings of the reader, the beliefs and views, by centuries rooted in him, about everything existing in the world"***.

So we must at all times bear this strictly in mind when reading for the third time and subsequently the very dense and often deliberately complicated sentences in the *Tales*.

In chapters 8 and 9 we are told about a collision between Earth and a comet and the "High Commission" sent from the "Sun Absolute" to our Solar System to investigate and remedy this. It was made up of "Sacred Individuals" such as "Angels" and "Archangels", some of whose somewhat strange "names" are mentioned. But the true "name" of the "Creator" of our Megalocosmos is not revealed by Beelzebub; reference to "HIM", always in the masculine tense, being made only by a qualifying description.

As MG deals in the *Tales* with subjects referring to "God", "Angels", "Devils", "Saints", etc. and mentions other galaxies, solar systems and planets in addition to our planet, solar system and galaxy, we must accordingly, especially when "reading between the lines", examine **ALL** that in his writings relates to the "Divinity" (however called or characterised), the "Higher Individuals" (also whatever names, titles and attributes they may be given) and indeed **EVERYTHING** and **EVERYONE** dealt with in this monumental cipher document with its prime purpose, as quoted above, strictly and constantly in mind.

English is not my mother tongue, but I love and admire some of its pithy and witty expressions such as "damning with faint praise". In the case of HE and some of HE's myrmidons, the "praise" is fulsome rather than just faint! This makes the damning even more pointed in my reading of its covert meanings.

Accordingly, let us start at the "top", with "God", most frequently referred to as "HIS (or OUR) ENDLESSNESS", whom MG presents in the *Tales* as a rather gormless and vain, easily influenced, slow thinking Personage with immense powers that HE is just as likely to misuse as to use wisely. Except in the case of *"our all-common Master, the Merciless Geropas[4]/Геропас"*, that is, *"the flow of Time"* (p. 35), whom HE cannot control, HE is undoubtedly the Big Boss as well as the Creator of the Universe and, though mostly indirectly, of all its "three-brained" Tetartocosmoses, including the "Sacred Individuals". As apparently the latter are all born on the same planet Модикθео = Modiktheo (pp. 771-3) and created on the one basic model, perhaps that of HE it/her/himself, HE then can be considered as no more than just the first and greatest "Sacred Individual". That is all that can be said about HE, who is not even given a "personal name" in the *Tales*, but seems to be the spitting image of the "IALDABAOTH" of the Gnostics.

Next, let's have a look at the named "angels and archangels", members of the "High Commission". Question: are their names "significant" in themselves?

Thus for example, the name of the Commission's Director, the "Most Great Archangel[5]" **Саккакий** = SAKKAKI, in the Russian original is spelt with **TWO KK**, not with just one, as wrongly transliterated in the English and French versions, and so can be divided into two: SAK and KAKI. "Kaki" in Russian is the genitive of the word KAKA[6] originally meaning "ugly and repulsive", but nowadays used for "fæces", and SAK sounds like the French word *sac* = bag; thus the name could well be interpreted as "Bag of shit".

Similarly, for the Angel **Луизос** = Looizos, by anagram we can get two words: **ЗЛО**, Russian for "evil", and **СУИ** which sounds like the French "*suis*", that is, "AM". So perhaps this name is meant to hint: "(I) AM EVIL", very appropriately because, almost certainly, it is he, LOOIZOS, who, in his capacity as the great *"Chief-Common-Universal-Arch-Chemist-Physicist"* is the *"certain Sacred Individual concerned with the matters of World-creation and World-maintenance"* (p. 88), whose *"erroneous calculations"* were the cause of the collision between a comet and our Earth (p. 82). He is also the 'inventor and installer of the maleficent organ Koondaboofer/**Кундабуфер** which, with his help, was *"caused to grow in the three-brained beings"* living on Earth (p. 88). Further, after his promotion from Angel to "Archangel", this "Most High Sacred Individual", now "His Conformity", acting apparently on his own initiative, asked the exiled "Right Reverence" Beelzebub *"to undertake the task"* of stopping the practice of animal sacrifices (pp. 181-2). By using several wily, hypocritical and shameless "religious" inventions[7] and immoral lies,

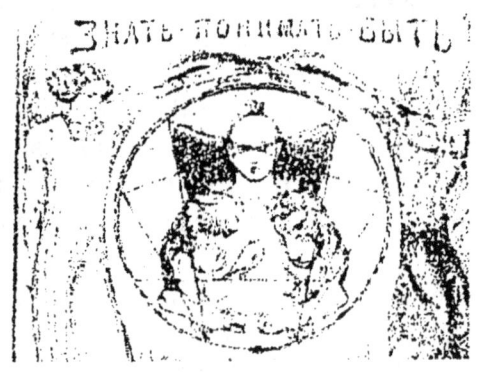

---

[4] In Russian this word begins with Г, a <u>hard G</u> (as in God) letter, NOT a letter sounding like an H.
[5] Later promoted to: *"Divine Individual"*, one of the four *"Quarter-Maintainers"* of the whole Universe (p. 90).
[6] From the Greek **κακος** (kakos), meaning: stink.
[7] As did before him (p.342) the great "TZar" (NOT "King") **Конюцион** = KONUTZION, later promoted to "Saint" (p. 700).

Grandfather Beelzebub performed this job quite successfully, but the final result of suppressing the "*Sacrificial-Offerings*" was the first (1914-18) World War (p. 1104), with its millions of human deaths and much misery, and most probably the second (1939-45) one also, with even more deaths and suffering, not to mention the present global on-going military strife.

In accordance with the Sacred Law Triamazikamno and the French saying: "*jamais deux sans trois*" (= never two without a third), let us try once more with the name of the third member of the "High Commission", the Arch-Engineer, His Pantameasurability Archangel Algematant = **АЛГЕМАТАНТ** who "*was good enough to explain*" to Beelzebub (p. 83) that "*Glory to Chance (...) the harmonious general-system movement was not destroyed by all this,* (the collision between the comet Kondoor and Earth), *and the peaceful existence of that system 'Ors'*[8] (our Solar System) *was soon re-established*".

This name also can be divided into two: "ALG" and "ematant". There is no Russian word made up of the three letters A, G & L in any combination, but in Hebrew there is the word גאל = GAL (GIMEL-ALEF-LAMED) meaning "to redeem, to deliver, to free", thus seemingly indicating that this Archangel is a sort of "Redeemer"; but the rest of his name: **ematant** sounds exactly like the French idiom "*et ma tante*" (= and my aunt) which in my childhood in France in the 1920s, just when MG was writing the *Tales*, had the same meaning as the American "*tell it to the marines!*". I do not know whether this idiom is still used nowadays or not.

Perhaps, with enough knowledge of all the languages MG spoke more or less fluently, appropriate meanings would be found for all the other names of the "Sacred Individuals" of various hierarchic statures.

If my innermost feelings and analyses are right, then many of the "Sacred Individuals", especially those nearest to the "*All-Loving All-Merciful and Absolutely Just Creator Endlessness*", are nothing more than glorified "whitened sepulchres".

Before leaving the Sacred Individuals we must note also that, though Beelzebub expresses his distaste and amusement at the grandiose titles humans give to their rulers and other "greats", he himself applies to various angelic Entities similar honorific terms! And do note well that the spaceship's captain, and others, including his own body servant, always address Beelzebub as "Right Reverence".

Of course I fully realise that all the above could very well be nothing more than sheer wiseacring, which the colourful French idiom characterises as "*chercher midi à quatorze heures*" (= to look for noon at 2 p.m.).

---

[8] ORS is **OPC** in Russian, and its anagram gives **COP**, Russian for dirt, dust, filth, litter or rubbish. But in Hebrew ORS = ערס (AYIN-RESH-SAMECH) means "crib" = "Barred receptacle for fodder" (Concise Oxford Dictionary).

All & Everything Conference 2002

Now, let us leave the angels and have a look at Beelzebub's Saturnian connection.

To begin with, he tells us (p. 92) first that the Saturnians' "*exterior (...) resembles that of the being-bird raven*", then that "*their utterance is the most beautiful I have ever heard. (...) It can be compared to the singing of our best singers when with all their Being they sing in a minor key*" and finally that "*these bird-beings have hearts exactly like those of the angels nearest our ENDLESS MAKER AND CREATOR*".

Before going any further, let us not forget that in all old and new "astrological" systems Saturn is always said to be the most **maleficent** of all the planets. And also, remember that all ravens are **black**, the colour traditionally and "symbolically" associated with **evil**.

We are given in chapters 18, 23 & 45 fourteen (14) Saturnian words as a sample of their language:

Горнахур	**Крхррхихирхи**	**Кхрх**	**РхахарахрРхи**	**ХарахрахрухриХархринхрарх**
Gornah<u>oo</u>r	Krhrrhihirhi	Khrh	Rhaharahr Rhi	Harahrahr<u>oo</u>hri Harhrinhrarh
Хархурхи	**Хир-хир**	**Храпрхальнихрохный**	**Хре-хри-хра**	**Хри-храхри**
Harh<u>oo</u>rhi	Hir-hir	Hraprhal'nihrohnŷ^Y	Hre-hri-hra	Hri-hrahri
		Хрхахархцаха	**Хрх-хр-ху**	
		Hrhaharh<u>tz</u>aha	Hrh-hr-h<u>oo</u>	

Just try and sing melodiously, whether in a minor or a major or any other fancy key, any of or all these fourteen words in Saturnian! May be this is a covert criticism of the voices of the "best singers" of Beelzebub's tribe, whose dialect is perhaps akin to the Saturnian language. And what Beelzebub means to suggest about the "*hearts*" of "*the angels nearest our ENDLESS MAKER AND CREATOR*" I shudder to think! Especially when one knows that the Russian for raven - **ВОРОН** (voron) - can be divided into two words: **ВОР** and **ОН**, which together say: ОН ВОР, meaning: he (ОН) is a thief (ВОР)! Note also what, referring to his actual and potential detractors and enemies, MG writes about "ravens" in his first published (1933) work: "The Herald of Coming Good" (p. 79.): "(they are the) *type of people who, though resembling us in outward formation, have yet become in their responsible age as a result of their abnormal education in childhood, as well as, of course, of their degenerate heredity, the possessors of the nature and heredity of real and rapacious **ravens***". See also p. 722 of the *Tales*.

We are also given the name of the Saturnian being who, says Beelzebub, became "*one of my real friends during the whole period of my exile in that solar system*" (p. 93). The name is **Хархарх** = **HARHARH**, not at all a euphonious or beautiful sounding name, which should have alerted us at once, as it sounds, to Russian ears at least, in a manner similar to that of the word ХАРКАТЬ (HARKAT') meaning "to hawk and spit in a revolting manner". Moreover (p. 151) he adds to the name Harharh the word **Горнахур** = **Gornah<u>oo</u>r**, Saturnian for Mister, which seems obviously to derive from **GORNAH**, used in "*Meetings with Remarkable Men*" (p. 70) as the Tartars' name of "*an evil spirit which used the bodies of people who had recently died and appeared in their shape* *to do all sorts of villainies"*. Could these terrestrial "Gornahs" be Saturnian "souls" exiled to Earth after the death of their bodies?

It is thus evident that the praise of the Saturnians' voice; *inter alia*, is meant mockingly, "with tongue in cheek", and must be understood as a hint to take everything in chapter 18 at least, and most probably also in many preceding and following chapters, in the way exactly opposite to what appears to be a positive statement. See particularly chapter 36; perhaps the joke and the "problem to solve" in it are related to the above? And a final question: does comparing the highest and/or HE's favourite "angels" to a bird-like being suggest that they are all "bird-brained"?

On the other hand, it is also quite clearly stated by Beelzebub in his *Tales* that beings of his tribe, and so, by extension, all "Higher Individuals", are strictly forbidden to tell three-centred beings on Earth the truth[9] about anything in the "Real World" (p. 901).

In most of his writings, sayings and actions, **Господин** (Gospodin) or **Пан** (Pan) **Жорживаныч ГЮРДЖИЕВ**, Mister or Monsieur **Georgivanŷch GURDJIEFF**, the Teacher of Dances, Artist and supreme Master-Joker, as great as the Olympian God **HERMES/MERCURY**[10] or even Lord **SHIVA** himself, merrily plays games with us, poor deluded threebrained tetartocosmic suckers, born every minute with all the crystallised properties of the accursed organ Koondaboofer ready and raring to do their appointed task.

© Copyright 2002 - Nicolas Tereshchenko - All Rights Reserved

---

[9] See chapter 11 in Seymour B. Ginsburg's *In Search of the Unitive Vision* (New Paradigm Books, Boca Raton, 2001).
[10] The versatile HERMES/MERCURY, son of ZEUS/JUPITER and MAÏA/CYBELE, Messenger, Herald and Spokesman of the Gods, the Psychopompos who leads Souls to the Kingdom of the Dead and back to life again, was the God of athletes, eloquence, gamblers, merchants, milestones, orators, shepherds, thieves and travelers; he invented the lyre, prestidigitation, boxing, games of hazard and racing; and was the father, amongst many other children, of Ithyphallic PRIAPOS and of the Great God PAN. Later, under the "semi-pseudonym" of HERMES TRISMEGISTUS, he left us the enigmatic "Emerald Tablet" and a series of informative writings, now known as the *"Corpus Hermeticus"*.

All & Everything Conference 2002

How to "Read" Beelzebub's Tales - Questions & Answers

Questioner 1: This is not a comment for or against the paper. I just want to add my idea on the names of these animals on Saturn, these ravens. It was very funny, the way you recited those names. But there is also something very funny about it in the Greek language. There is a whole category of words that start with "kh."

(A guttural sound is indicated by the questioner, something like the clearing of one's throat of mucus).

I have just made a small list here, and you will be surprised:
(The Greek words following are transliterated into phonetic English by the transcriber.)
"Khrama" which is "color."
"Khreema" which is "money."
"Khreosos" which is "gold."
"Khronis" which is "time."
"Khristos" which is "Christ."
And even -
"Khristol" which is "crystal."

So these are everyday backbone words to convey meaning. They are not just little words that mean small things. They are big basic words: color, money, gold, time, which come from the same root.

Bert Sharp: I think this is an important contribution.

Questioner 2: Also sound! When you said those words in the talk and when Questioner #1 pronounced those words which is for him easy to make in the Greek language, and for us is easy to make in our language which is Dutch, but when you said Gornahoor Harharkh, referring to that bird in the Dutch version of *Beelzebub*, I am very interested in what the sounds of those words do to peoples' psyche. In various different languages those sounds cannot be made.

Bert Sharp: This is really interesting to me because I had no idea that a "kh" or "hr" sound as it is shown in the English translation of *Beelzebub's Tales*, would be pronounced with a guttural "kh" sound. I have some knowledge of Hebrew and am very familiar with the pronunciation of words like "Chutzpah" and "Chanukah" which I know how to pronounce, but I did not know to do that until just this minute if that, indeed, is how these words are to be pronounced.

Questioner 3: Years ago I ran into a very interesting book on Indian yoga. This man combined the sounds of the various internal organs, and most of the sounds related to the organs are exactly like that. It comes from Sanskrit according to him. I mean they are not exactly the same, but are so close that you could really make the connection. It is like this sound belongs to this particular organ and the pronunciation of that sound belongs to another organ. So they each have a different sound but they are all very similar to those phrases in Saturnian.

Bert Sharp: Nick Tereshchenko called Mr. Gurdjieff a master linguist in his paper, so perhaps he was getting at something that requires those sounds.

Questioner 4; I don't know if it's relevant, but in my conversations with Nicolas, he reckons that he is tone deaf. Therefore, music and sound means nothing to him.

Questioner 5: It is interesting to elaborate a little further on what Questioner #1 said. It seems that a great deal of emphasis was placed on the discipline of pronunciations especially in the legomenistic creations of Gurdjieff. I think it is possible to infer that in the proper sounding there may be an influence that Gurdjieff wants to put into our subconscious, because it is speaking in the resonance of the organ system or the charkas or whatever. Then this would be a direct and for us a totally subconscious influence. But it would only come through and only have its appropriate effect if it were pronounced, sounded out, in the right way. The emphasis on this in some quarters of work is on being very, very precise about how all of these words should be sounded, because they have influences that are beyond the literal or even the allegorical mythic meaning.

Bert Sharp: That's certainly related to how to pronounce all the special words in the *Tales* in addition to these particular words.

Questioner 6: Two things. One is that in Rosicrucian meditations they have some mantras, and "pa" is the male force as "ma" is female. And the second is that I think that Gurdjieff said in the book that Gornahoor Harharkh had the exterior body of a raven.

Questioner 7: Just a little point. It is true that "caca" in almost any Indo-European language means "merde," "shit," whatever you like, but that root means disorder. "Cacophony," for example, is disordered music.

Sy Ginsburg: Let us go on now with the second paper that was produced. So may I call upon Ana Fragomeni who is going to present her paper on this topic.

The High Commission and Other Sacred Individuals - What Do They Represent?

Ana Fragomeni

I didn't prepare this as a paper for the conference. These are some excerpts from the discussion group during the year. It was written for four people, not for so many. It's very personal.

If this Discussion Group did not substantially increase our knowledge of the Sacred Individuals, nevertheless, it opened doors for our search. The way will be long: questions and more questions.

1. Some fundamentals

From *Tales*, it becomes evident that there is a HIERARCHY OF BEINGS between God and us. In my opinion, Gurdjieff is a Sacred Individual who came here with a special mission, as part of a High Commission.

In "The Holy Planet Purgatory"[1] Gurdjieff talks about the planet Modiktheo, where "all our now existing angels, archangels, and most of the Sacred Individuals nearest to our COMMON FATHER ENDLESSNESS arise". They begin as individuals belonging to three different sexes and further they blend in one higher Individual, with all THREE BODIES already completed.

By the way, Asimov wrote a science fiction book, *The Gods Themselves*, where in a different dimension there is an alien race with three sexes - physical, intellectual and emotional.

2. How to know Them?

We ought to study the Sacred Individuals analysing everything Gurdjieff said in *Tales* and at the same time looking INTO ourselves.

Well, we don't have the hardware nor the software to understand them. However, Christ said: "by the FRUITS you shall know the tree".

I know a Sacred Individual and I talk with him continuously - well, not so continuously. He usually helps me. But he sometimes wants to interfere with my aims. I wonder: What aims are "mine"? Who else can be interested in "my" aims?

---

[1] *Beelzebub's Tales*, Chapter 39 -The Holy Planet "Purgatory", p771-2.

The High Commission - Ana Fragomeni

It seems there is an Angel, when I enter in certain blessed states of conscience and I feel the Peace. But when I think about the aims - and whether there is enough union in myself for "us" to agree with all the aims "I" intend - then, it seems there is also a Devil.

This "Angel" has no visible body. Sometimes I feel him like a big balloon of energy; sometimes I know he is around because of the incredible coincidences that occur.

Once I was searching to know more about the communication with them, and I found this in Bennett's *Dramatic Universe*:

"A complete philosophical language is created only when those who intend to use it have established a context of EXPERIENCES in which all the necessary meanings can be recognized."
- *"... a recurrent process of TRIAL AND ERROR..."*[2]

It has been an exercise of communication. They could have been teaching me how to understand them. Some coincidences were amazing: I found strange texts in my computer, gathered and shuffled with parts of texts that were already there. They usually had meaning for my current situation, or for the situation of someone I know. There are periods of different kind of communication. A few times later, there "appeared" suddenly some drawings in the screen, some of them I could save on the HD, others I could not.

If I speak about the "Angel", he disappears for a good while, perhaps along with my level of identification.

From another point of view, I remember Flatland, where two-dimensional beings can only see flat projections of three-dimensional beings. They see them as several "individuals". For instance, the two legs of a man when they intersect the surface of the lake appear like two individuals; the five fingers, when a man dips the tip of his hand in the water, appear like five separated individuals.

"I am the true vine, and my Father is the gardener.
He cuts off every branch in me that bears no fruit,
while every branch that does bear fruit he prunes
so that it will be even more fruitful.
I am the vine; you are the branches.
If a man remains in me and I in him,
he will bear much fruit;
apart from me you can do nothing." (John 15)

I think that, without noticing, we can be living together with at least one Sacred Individual that appears like ten or twenty individuals, maybe ten or twenty different "persons" like us? Like the branches of a tree.

---

[2] *Dramatic Universe*, Vol.1, p. 81-82 - Sign Language.

All & Everything Conference 2002

I decided not to try anymore to explain who is my Guide, my Angel or my Master. I call them "HE". These things don't fit in my head.

It only remains to me the behaviour of a sunflower, that turns itself towards the light and the heat. I orientate myself for the happy coincidences that lead me towards my aims and my values. If everything that happens seems to help, I conclude that I am in the right direction "according to the law"; and that there is probably "somebody" sharing my activities.

Nevertheless, I don't know if HE helps me or I am the one who serves HIM.

3. Help - Why should Sacred Individuals be interested on us?

With everything that has been said in this discussion group, about animal sacrifices and wars, Ilnosoparnian process, etc, I lost a little more of my naïveté about the High Commissions. I still had the tendency to worship saints and angels. The group made me realize that they also can commit big mistakes.

The relation between a Higher Individual and ordinary man may be similar to that I have with a bird, a dog, a gecko, the flowers or the lettuces of my vegetable garden. I did not cage the bird, so I don't take care of it - I just appreciate his beauty and his song.

I only help inferior beings who are in some way under my responsibility: then I give them food and well-being. But in this case I have some INTEREST, something I can earn from this. The whole nature lives from interest - a healthy reciprocal maintenance.

I won't "help" the dog in his personal interests. I don't have any concern for the lettuce, unless it grows very chubby for me to eat.

Initially, I would not help a lettuce to increase its level of being. On the contrary, I would make everything to hinder the lettuce of being anything but a lettuce. The idea of implanting a kundabuffer in the kitchen garden is very good, and man has been doing genetic experiences for that - quite like the angels do.

To implant a kundabuffer in the kitchen garden may make the plants grow and reproduce themselves more, in order to provide us more food - like it was once made by Sacred individuals to feed the Moon.

The implantation of the kundabuffer was a genetic experiment, and we must remember this when we see today scientists choosing to "make people" - artificial insemination, cloning, etc. (what is always, in some instance, food for the moon) - instead of "making food for people" (agriculture and ecologic experiments).

But there is another side of the question. If I eventually saw that a certain lettuce, almost by a miracle, was in some way helping ME to take care of the other ones, or helping me in some of MY business, then I would not eat it (not for the while) and I would supply it with the best fertilizer I could. That's what I think Sacred individuals do.

As for the flowers, it is probable that I am helping them without conscious intention, maybe irradiating some energy, because it is amazing: the plants that are closest to the place where I work or to the room where I sleep, they grow much more than the others in the rest of the garden. I say that they give me flowers because I "appreciate". When somebody uses or appreciates our work, we work better.

The little birds, by their turn, "guess" my presence and come to peck my window. They are usually the same ones, and I give them names. I could be those bird's "angel", a being that they don't see, but they can sense.

The dogs also sense us, and it is probable that we have one more dimension to them, everything on an instinctive level. A dog can "see" me in my shoes.

Could we put ourselves in His Endlessness' place? Can I put myself in the place of the little BIRD at my window?

Once I said "my birds" and my sister corrected me: "Maybe you don't own them, but they own you, for you are in the cage of your house and they are free." If they are more free than me, maybe they are higher beings. Could birds be Sacred Individuals? Could they be disguised Angels spying or supervising us? Was Gornahoor Harharkh a RAVEN?

Could They be only a special kind of free intelligence? An Intelligence that sometimes we can touch and feel, but has no owner, simply "is"? It would be the "I am" without the "I".

Could they be SOUND?

There are some "savage Indians" who dance and sing all day "to hold the sun up in the sky". I wonder if birds sing to hold nature alive - like a phonon, the unknown vibration that holds the atoms of matter in a solid-state, as we can see in Hans Jenny's videotapes showing sound organizing matter.

4. The place of High Commissions and Sacred Individuals in the Ray of Creation

Why in this Discussion Group we often stray from the main subject? - Because it is ALL-EMBRACING.

Material things are limited and separated, so it is easy to talk about a chair or about our physical bodies without falling out of the subject. However, when the subject is less material, things begin to be confused.

When we have dinner together, we eat on separate plates and we drink from different glasses. Nevertheless, we share the air we breathe, whose molecules leave one's lungs and enter the lungs of others nearby, without us having any notice. Thoughts and feelings are shared, not only with people that are near, but also with others who are in tune with our ideas and emotions. At this level, "I AM YOU": ideas have no owner and feelings are mutual.

We are not separated at the highest levels of being and in higher bodies. We are part of the higher worlds that permeate each other. The same as we, human beings, share our higher energies, those higher energies/bodies are probably also matter of Higher Entities, with which we are naturally in touch through higher levels of conscience.

As well as there are worlds inside worlds; there can be Entities inside Entities. We are LATERAL OCTAVES inside higher octaves. We may be an octave inside a note of some Higher Individual.

Kepler thought that behind each PLANET there was an Angel to push it along the orbit. A planet is a being, for us a higher being. We belong to a Lateral Octave. It is important not to mix the scales, so, to what OCTAVE do Sacred Individuals belong?

I remember some interesting things from Bennett's *Witness*:

1. Once the group asked Gurdjieff what would become of them when he died. He answered: "I am Gurdjieff, I NOT will die."
2. In another occasion, Gurdjieff said: "One day *Beelzebub's Tales* will be read in the Vatican for the Pope, and maybe I will be there".
3. Bennett also told that after his mother's death, Gurdjieff made his own mother help Bennett's mother and taught him a technique to make the two mothers meet (and he saw them).

In another book, Gurdjieff said to a woman whose father had died that she could help her father by working on herself.

All this seems to confirm that not only we communicate through higher bodies, but also we really INTERACT and SHARE LIFE through them.

5. My reason of Living

When I had my third son, due to an internal haemorrhage, I entered in coma and had a fantastic "Near Death Experience" (NDE). I was assisted on time and "decided" to stay because of my children, although to stay "there" was much better. I said I decided, because I felt it was up to me to choose.

My values changed. Soon after that, I found the Fourth Way. And here comes the connection with the SACRED INDIVIDUALS: they are my reason of living.

It has always seemed strange to me that the most important decisions of a man's life (career, marriage and occupation) need to be taken very early, when he does not know yet himself. We pass the whole life trying to know ourselves, trying to perfect ourselves, and when we are "ready", we DIE. The only explanation is that this life is THE SCHOOL, and TRUE LIFE will begin later. After that experience, of course, one side of me prefers to die, because "there" is better. However, I love to work and I don't like to be doing nothing, being useless. What would I do "there"? I think I must prepare myself for "then". Therefore, I asked the Sacred Individuals for a job and decided that in the next stage I would appreciate to work with them in the administration of the universe (Gurdjieff opens this perspective for us, and says they need help).

I know that they would not accept someone that doesn't know how to deal even with the simplest things of this planet Earth, and so I need to continue living the more I can to learn so much that I could be accepted for the new job I apply for.

6. Here and Now

It is possible that there is a High Commission at the planet exactly this moment. Last August I received the 4th R+C Worldly Manifesto, which says:

"R+C Brotherhood breaks almost 400 year-old silence and brings light to the THREATS that weigh about the Humanity on this third millennium. The objective was to transmit R+C Brotherhood's position for THE STATE OF THE WORLD and to put in evidence what seemed preoccupying for the future."[3]

Is it a coincidence that a World tragedy occurred just a month later?

© Copyright 2002 - Ana Fragomeni - All Rights Reserved

Moderator: Are there any questions about this paper?

Participant: We haven't got much time.

Moderator: Then we'll go on with the next paper and take questions later.

---

[3] The Rosicrucian Order A.M.O.R.C. http://www.rosicrucian.org/downloads/manifesto.pdf

The High Commission and Other Sacred Individuals, What Do They Represent?

Sy Ginsburg

In reading through *Beelzebub's Tales to His Grandson* over many years, I have often speculated about just what Gurdjieff intended when he wrote about the High Commission and the Sacred Individuals. The email discussion group on this subject that emanated from All and Everything 2001, has helped me to organize my thinking on this matter and I wish to propose the following ideas about what Gurdjieff intended.

Throughout *Beelzebub's Tales* Gurdjieff exaggerates the nature of Endlessness with pompous and superfluous titles and adjectives. "All-Most-Gracious Endlessness" (BT1128), and "All-Loving, Endlessly-Merciful and Absolutely-Just Creator-Endlessness" (BT745), are but two examples of more than sixty such appellations throughout the book. In a similar vein, in writing of the High Commission and the Sacred Individuals, Gurdjieff uses the same tactic. "Universal-Arch-Chemist-Physicist Angel Looisos" (BT88), and "Most-Great-Arch-Seraph Sevohtartra" (BT89)[1], are just two examples of many used throughout the book to describe these supposed beings. These overly gushing descriptions ought to put us on our guard.

Gurdjieff goes even further in mockingly calling Looisos "His Conformity" (BT182-183). Let us remember that Gurdjieff was keen to follow his grandmother's advice when she said to him: "Eldest of my grandsons! Listen and always remember my strict injunction to you: In life never do as others do." (BT27)

And we can just picture the buffoonery of Looisos who, with his colleagues on the Most High Commission, not only messed things up for the three-brained beings by implanting the organ Kundabuffer in them, but then had to return to Earth to beseech Beelzebub to help stop the animal sacrifices resulting from the unintended consequences of that implanting. Picture the ridiculous pomposity in this quotation from *Beelzebub's Tales* as Looisos shouts down to Beelzebub: "His Conformity ascended and when He was fairly high up, added in aloud voice, 'By this your Reverence you will be rendering a great service to our Uni-Being All-Embracing Endlessness'." (BT183).

---

[1] "BT" followed by page numbers refers to Gurdjieff G. I. *All and Everything, First Series: An Objectively Impartial Criticism of the Life of Man, or Beelzebub's Tales to His Grandson* (London: Routledge & Kegan Paul, 1950).

The High Commission - Sy Ginsburg

What is going on here? Gurdjieff is clearly making fun of these so-called Sacred Individuals. Are Gurdjieff's overly obsequious descriptions of Endlessness as well as of the High Commission and the Sacred Individuals really serious? Obviously not!

Are they examples of the primary title of the First Series: An Objectively Impartial Criticism of the Life of Man? My short answer is "yes!"

In my view, there is no reality to either a hierarchy of angels and other Sacred Individuals or to an Endlessness that is separate from each of us. There is no separate Mr. God as Gurdjieff makes abundantly clear to us in chapter XX of *Beelzebub's Tales*. (BT217). Mr. God was invented by clever leaders such as King Konuzion as an ingenious religious-doctrine for a specific purpose (BT219) in the *Beelzebub's Tales* allegory. Similarly, Gurdjieff has invented a separate Endlessness, a rather bumbling one at that, and separate inept Sacred Individuals who throughout the *Tales* are encumbered by the scores of pompously descriptive titles with which he weighs Endlessness and the Sacred Individuals down. This is a prime example of Gurdjieff's objectively impartial criticism of the life of man, who imagines that he experiences such external beings as separate from himself because he/she cannot see reality.

I am going to ask you to explore with me, at least by way of hypothesis, the idea that there is no reality to any apparently separate sacred individuals, no matter whom, no matter how they appear, no matter that they are Endlessness itself.

All of the hierarchy of angels and all our imaginings of God are projections of our mind in which we erroneously create God and his supposed assistants in our image. Because of our improper oskiano, our improper education, we have become convinced of the truth of a lie. That lie is that our persona is real and important. We believe this lie even in the face of the history of our planet which demonstrates the temporariness and insignificance of all the personas of the three-brained beings that have inhabited it since the time of their first arising. Because we erroneously believe that we as personas are real, we are then able to separate ourselves from other so-called entities like angels or God, however we perceive them.

Because we have become convinced of the reality of the personas of mankind, we anthropomorphize everything, seeing everything in terms of the anthropomorphic state, and we do this based upon our respective conditionings. So, while someone from the Judeo-Christian background may think in terms of angels that look like men and even converse with them, someone else from the indigenous Hawaiian background of the Kahunas, for example, may think in completely different terms and see completely different images. The wrathful deities experienced by the Tibetans as described in the *Tibetan Book of the Dead*[2], is another example of this anthropomorphizing, with still different images such as the blood-drinking deities Ratna-Heruka and Karma-Heruka.

---

[2] Evans-Wentz, W. Y. *The Tibetan Book of the Dead* (London: Oxford University Press, 1927) 131-152.

Well then, if there is no separate Endlessness, no separate Mr. or Ms. God, is there no divinity at all? I must answer that question with a "yes", a very firm "yes there is." Yes, there really is a divinity of which each of us are the three-brained tetartocosmic projections on planet earth. Enjoying a bit of levity in the contemporary language of today, we may say that "God R Us." Or to use Gurdjieff's word for the divinity, "Endlessness R us" as are all the rather soupy group of angels, arch-angels and the rest of the so-called hierarchy with which Gurdjieff presents us.

Gurdjieff helps us to see this when, in the *Third Series*, he explains his great discovery in terms of scale. He writes: "For He is God and therefore I also have within myself all the possibilities and impossibilities that He has. The difference between Him and myself must lie only in scale. For he is God of all the presences in the universe! It follows that I also have to be God of some kind of presence on my scale."[3]

This idea, that we in the form of tetartocosmoses, the three-brained beings that have evolved on Earth, are the most conscious expressions of the divinity on this planet, is an idea that has been largely lost to most human beings because of our inability to see reality. But it is this very idea that is at the basis of all religious doctrines because it is the vision of truth, the unitive vision, that was seen by the founders of every religion, and subsequently distorted by their less perceptive followers.

This game of finding the true Self, of finding out who we really are, requires what Gurdjieff has called metanoia, a change of outlook. To take an example from another tradition, the Advaitic philosophers of esoteric Hinduism have long insisted on this change of outlook. Two well known contemporary exponents of Advaita, Ramana Maharshi (d. 1946) and Nisarga Datta (d. 1981) have expressed the idea in modern terms. Nisarga Datta explains it in this way:

"The world is but a show, glittering and empty. It is, and yet is not. It is there as long as I want to see it and take part in it. ... Only the onlooker is real, call him Self or Atma. To the Self the world is but a colourful show."[4]

Nisarga Datta in agreement with other Advaitic philosophers goes on to express this idea even more directly and more forcefully. To a questioner who asked, "If I am the sole creator of all this, then I am God indeed! But if I am God, why do I appear so small and helpless to myself" Nisarga Datta replied, "You are God, but you do not know it. (The world) is true in essence, but not in appearance. Be free of desires and fears and at once your vision will clear and you shall see all things as they are."[5]

---

[3] Gurdjieff, G. I. *All and Everything, Third Series: Life is Real Only Then When I am* (New York: Triangle Editions, 1975) 22-23.
[4] Sri Nisargadatta Maharaj. *I Am That* (Durham, N.C. Acorn Press, 1973) 178-179.
[5] Sri Nisargadatta Maharaj. 533.

These are dramatic words, but they raise several questions for students of Gurdjieff's teaching because his teaching presents us with an apparently hierarchical structure and an apparent path to get from our belief that we are real as personas in the second state of consciousness, so-called waking consciousness, to the fourth state of consciousness, that which Gurdjieff called objective consciousness or enlightenment[6], in which we can see things as they are.[7] In that state we stand in the unitive vision by which "the identity of the individual with the universal is experienced."[8]

But what about the hierarchical structure of orders of laws from ninety-six to one, with their increasing degrees of freedom that Gurdjieff teaches?[9] What about the intermediate higher being-body kesdjan that Gurdjieff suggests must be crystallized prior to the crystallization of the spiritual body (BT 765-768). It is one thing for the advaitic philosopher to say "you are God, but you do not know it" but quite another to realize the truth of this statement in more than an intellectual way. Gurdjieff, in the *Third Series*, acknowledges this difficulty in his great discovery that even though he has to be God, it is in terms of scale and at the moment of his discovery he recognizes his limited state of the awareness of his divinity: "He is God of all the world, and also of my outer world. I am God also, although only of my inner world."[10]

The uniqueness and great value of Gurdjieff's teaching is that to overcome our limited state of awareness, he gives us specific methods designed to help us discover the nature of reality by helping us to change our outlook. His methods are intended to correct our improper oskiano through the techniques that we know as the Work. To do this Gurdjieff builds an interesting though illusory hierarchical structure so that we can struggle our way "up" as we are accustomed to struggle in our incarnated experience.

Gurdjieff suggests, for example, that there is an intermediate state between the sleeping self that regards the persona as real, and the awakened Self or big "I" that experiences the identity of the individual with the universal spirit or Endlessness. I equate this intermediate state in which he says that the body kesdjan is crystallized with the practitioner who has balanced his/her centers, is almost continuously aware of being aware, and so exists in the third state of consciousness, self-consciousness, with perhaps glimpses of objective consciousness.

I mention the hypothesized intermediate, interpenetrating body kesdjan here only as an example of the sort of hierarchical structure Gurdjieff builds for us to appeal to our accustomed struggle to attain, whereas there is nothing to attain, there is only that to discover. Many interesting questions derive from a hypothesized intermediate interpenetrating body. For example, how does the body kesdjan in the three body structure of *Beelzebub's Tales* fit in with Gurdjieff's four body scheme

---

[6] Ouspensky, P. D. *In Search of the Miraculous* (London: Routledge & Kegan Paul, 1950) 141.
[7] Ouspensky, 141.
[8] Ginsburg, Seymour B. *In Search of the Unitive Vision* (Boca Raton: New Paradigm Books) 165.
[9] Ouspensky. 83-89.
[10] Gurdjieff, *Third Series*. 23.

put forward in *In Search of the Miraculous*?[11] How does it square with the seven body scheme of theosophical teachings? How is it that hypnotic powers may be a characteristic of the being with a crystallized kesdjan body, and yet many accomplished hypnotists may not be seen to have any such crystallized interpenetrating body at all? These and similar questions are beyond the scope of this paper. We should note, however, that ultimately the body kesdjan, just as the planetary body, must decompose (BT766), and in that sense is no more real than the planetary body.

Gurdjieff gives us numerous practical exercises to help us enter the two higher states of consciousness that he says are possible for a human being, self-consciousness and objective consciousness. These exercises, of which I would like to mention six, are familiar to pupils of Gurdjieff's teaching. These include first, exercises to help us exist in the third state of consciousness. Three of these exercises are:

1. **Self observation over a long period of time** to discover the things about ourselves, the identifications that keep us from realizing the truth. These identifications are mostly with the so called negative emotions of which Gurdjieff speaks, but these identifications also include those that can be classified as desires. These identifications fool us into believing that our persona is real.

2. **Self-remembering, the discipline of being aware of being aware** by which we enter into self-consciousness. This state is the gateway to objective-consciousness in which we realize that we are Endlessness as is everything existing. Gurdjieff taught body sensing exercises in which we direct the tool of attention to help us enter into this state.

3. **Sacred dance, known as the Gurdjieff movements.** Practice of the movements are another method of making use of the body to overcome the intellect so that we are seated in the observer in the third state of consciousness. Many years ago, I participated in regular weekly movements classes over a six year period as part of a Gurdjieff study group, and afterward I participated in occasional movements classes as part of another Gurdjieff study group. I can attest to the efficacy of the movements to carry one into a state of profound self-awareness. But I do not claim to be an accomplished practitioner of the movements and consequently, I cannot speak with authority about whether adequate practice of the movements will carry one into the fourth state of consciousness, the objective consciousness that I have characterized as the unitive vision. We know, however, that Gurdjieff placed great importance on the movements and signed his great literary work, *All and Everything*, as written by "simply a 'Teacher of Dancing'." We know further that sacred dance is a suggested exercise in other esoteric traditions from the dervish whirling of Sufism, to the ecstatic states induced by dance that are characteristic of esoteric forms of orthodox Judaism. The dance of Shiva in Hinduism is another suggesting the importance of sacred dance.

---

[11] Ouspensky, 40-44

Gurdjieff then gave additional exercises that are clearly designed to help us into the fourth state of consciousness assuming that we already reside in the third state of consciousness. Three of these exercises are:

4. **Using the "as if" technique,** in order to function as if we already stand in objective-consciousness. Gurdjieff's "I am" exercise is an example of this technique using constructive imagination to imagine a vibratory reverberation in the solar plexus when "I am" is pronounced[12]. An actual vibratory reverberation is characteristic of the person who already stands in objective-consciousness. It can be described as the life force that vivifies us. By repetition the practitioner actually experiences the vibration because the vibration is real even though it formerly had been unnoticed. In quiet meditation the vibratory life force is readily experienced.

5. **Conscious laboring and intentional suffering** to develop the will which is a characteristic of the unitive state. As we learn to like what "it" (the persona) does not like, we come to realize more and more that we are not the persona, that temporary collection of tissues and memories, but that we are essence, "the truth in man."[13]

6. **Putting ourself in the other person's place.** In the *Beelzebub Tales* allegory, Gurdjieff tells us that "only he may enter here (the Holy Planet Purgatory), who puts himself in the position of the other results of my labors" (BT1164). He tells us further that it is the dwelling place of the higher-being-bodies (BT745). We know, therefore, that existence on the Holy Planet Purgatory is a characteristic of those individuals who have crystallized the higher-being-body. As we practice putting ourself in the position of others, we begin to realize that this is more than mere empathy. We realize that we are the other person. In this state we realize that we are Endlessness manifesting through all other persons.

To enter into this ultimate state of consciousness, objective-consciousness, is where metanoia is required. The direction is inward, whether in meditation or simple introspection in which we ask, "who is aware of all this?"

Given that we can enter the third state of consciousness using the body sensing exercises proposed by Gurdjieff and other techniques in other traditions, we need then to look further inward, benefiting from the additional exercises given, not only to realize who in us is doing the observing, but then to realize who is observing the observer. It is like an infinite regression inward until one stands firmly in the unity of all being. To remember this from moment to moment, to remember who we really are, to be aware of being aware, is self-remembering taken to its deepest level. At that level in which we are aware that we are all other persons, in which pattern blends with pattern in a vast and wondrous whole, we enter into the unitive vision.

---

[12] Gurdjieff, Third Series. 132-136.
[13] Ouspensky. 162

All & Everything Conference 2002

This is not to maintain that people do not have the experiences of meeting angels, guardian angels, spirit guides, all the messengers from above, and even Endlessness as Ezekiel did in the recounting of his story in the Old Testament. However, we eventually come to recognize that all these experiences are projections of our mind based on the anthropomorphic conditioning with which we have been inculcated.

It is a mystery that many individuals who have entered into objective consciousness continue to guide others to the same goal long after their physical deaths. They are Endlessness in full and they are the projection of Endlessness in individuality (not persona) tempered by a series of human lifetimes in which essence has grown through experience. These lights of awareness as, for example, the energy we know as Gurdjieff do indeed come to us in dream, in meditation, through channelled communication, or sometimes simply as intuitive understanding. Their appearances to us are similarly projections of mind by which the one power that is really us all along can communicate with each of us who are not sufficiently awakened to realize our true nature. As the extent of our awareness becomes greater, and is less limited to the lower intellectual center - the mind of our persona, that awareness of mind in higher intellectual center begins to include other minds. It is akin to C. G. Jung's idea of a collective consciousness. In this way the projections of so-called entities not limited to the mind of our persona are possible.

Whatever the phenomena experienced, we must then always go more deeply inward and ask the question: Who is aware of all this? When we fully enter into that state in which we are aware of being aware, we move toward objective consciousness, toward enlightenment.

It is a very great work, a metanoia, to remember from moment to moment that we really are Endlessness, and to give up, in these moments, our identification with the persona. In my case, for example, I need to give up the importance of being Sy.

We each need to give up the importance of being "me" so that we begin to see our persona as transient, ephemeral and in that sense unreal. When we stand in the real world, that which Gurdjieff has called objective consciousness or enlightenment, we realize that we stand in the unity. We are that which is indescribable, and which Gurdjieff has called Endlessness including all our projections of High Commissions and Sacred Individuals.

Metanoia, the change of outlook described here, when it is complete, is a breakthrough in which the individual in whom it takes place is no longer a separate individual. The light of universal awareness shines, unobstructed by the persona, through the vehicle of its own form. In this great spiritual journey we ultimately come to discover who we really are. In that sense it is a journey of discovery, not of attainment.

We ultimately discover that "Thou art thy Self (capital S), the object of thy search."[14]

© Copyright 2002 - Sy Ginsburg - All Rights Reserved

---

[14] Blavatsky, H P. *The Voice of the Silence* (Wheaton: Quest, 1973 facsimile of 1889 edition) 34.

Discussion about how the procedures for the email discussion groups worked

Sy Ginsburg: There is just one thing before we begin the comments, questions and answers, but it is related to this. It is our idea as a planning committee, assuming that there is sufficient interest for this forthcoming year, to come up again with a list of proposed topics and put that list out by email to whoever has signed up for the email discussion lists. So for any of you who are interested, please respond back to that email telling us that you want to participate and indicating your preference as to topics listed. Then we will simply group together those people who are interested in each topic and send each of those groups an email showing the names and email addresses of those people who wish to participate. Then it will be up to those people to initiate and to carry on their discussion. In order for this discussion then to happen, some person from each of those email groups will have to contact by email those other people and say something like, "this is what I think about the subject, etc." This is exactly what Ana did on the topic that we are discussing this morning. She was the first one to send out an email to John Scullion and to me (Sy Ginsburg), and that was in July. Nick Tereshchenko was not initially in our discussion.

Dorothy Usiskin: Nick was in our group with me and Steve Wheeler. But then Steve quit and it was just me and Nick, David and Goliath.

Sy Ginsburg: Then you two joined our discussion. There were also some different people that came and went, and it resulted in this (this morning's papers and discussion). So if you think it is of value then participate. It is just like this entire conference which is self initiating. Even though there is a planning committee, it is based upon the interest, participation and energy of the people in it. So, we'll begin it and see what happens. That's what we did last time.

Toddy Smyth: It sounds like it is of great value to discuss ideas in that way and to stay in contact that way, but I must admit that the thing that scares me a little is this vision of pages and pages of email, responding to each one, and it scares me. How does it actually work out?

Dorothy Usiskin: Some people have more family and work affairs than others, so they were not able to participate as much as others or as often as others, or some didn't care to write such long emails as others.

Ana Fragomeni: It was a bit difficult sometimes, because sometimes I received from others very interesting things, but I am so busy. And I have to print and read in a very special state. But the others have the same problem, so sometimes someone writes more and the other writes less, but that is no problem. We do what we can.

Email Discussion Group

Marlena Buzzell: That's what we found. We participated the year before, but not last year. Sometimes there would be a lot of emails when we came in, and maybe there would be three or four days when we just didn't get to it. So on Sunday afternoon or on Friday evening we would sit down and read them. Then we would have dinner and discuss it and think about it. I think the sense of urgency gives us an opportunity to just work with it, or even noticing that I am not doing it.

Ana Fragomeni: It is a new thing for everybody. We must learn. Oftentimes I received very good things, so good that I sit there and read it, and I mark it, and I work a lot. But then when I came back to the discussion everybody was ahead of me so I didn't send my email. But I think we must learn because it is a new way of communication and we will reach new positions sometimes.

Sy Ginsburg: There is no obligation to write a paper. Some of us were disposed to do so. In fact, there was a fourth paper written by Kevin Roberts who eventually withdrew the paper, so that's why it wasn't presented. It seems like what happened was due to the energy and interest of those of us here and even possibly to others who did not participate in the conference. In the case of Kevin, for example, I don't think he was at last year's conference. He found out about the discussion group and participated. He was going to participate in the conference this year, but then did not.

Bert Sharp: I would have thought that when we get to tomorrow and the "Where do we go from here session," obviously we are going to continue, and that would be the appropriate time to decide on a short list of topics for email discussions.

Sy Ginsburg: We can continue this tomorrow. I just wanted to call to your attention how this arose and how it resulted in these papers.

The High Commission and Other Sacred Individuals: What Do They Represent? - Questions & Answers

Moderator: Now you have heard three personal view papers on this topic which I will read the exact title of again as Marlena and Keith originally put it out:

The High Commission and Other Sacred Individuals: What Do They Represent?

Participant 1: We had this morning in the papers, a number of references to the raven. In the Mithraic cult, of course, the raven is the messenger of the Gods. Also, the raven in the Mithraic cult is considered to be symbolic of the alembic in which the transformation takes place. I had a lucid dream some years ago in which I was sitting on the edge of a golden sandy clearing. In the center of this was a very large, very beautiful diamond. I was watching this diamond, the way it sparkled and how beautiful it was. The bird went to the center and swallowed the diamond. I wondered what that was all about. I concluded, finally that the raven, being the alembic, then transformed the beauty of the diamond inside, into something which was alive and living.

Participant 2: This raven story is so patently a takeoff. In fact, no one says the raven is black. The raven is white of course. It always was white and it has the greatest song in the world. It's the sun bird. And it's only when the raven told the truth which hurt, that he was struck black by Apollo and lost his power of song. So, when you give the speech of the raven, what you are giving is of course our understanding of the most beautiful song bird, the song of creation. This is the music of the spheres. It was Apollo's bird and it was white. We don't know what color the bird is on Saturn. We're not told. Gurdjieff keeps that out. So the raven is white. We hear it as if it were a fallen bird struck by Apollo.

Participant 3: To me the raven has a beautiful song. Music is a very important part of what Gurdjieff is bringing us.

Participant 1: The raven doesn't have a beautiful song. It squawks.

Participant 2: The raven did have a beautiful song.

Participant 3: There is also the idea that the raven has no words.

Participant 4: Gurdjieff is up to a great many things. It may be helpful to see that he is serving many of his aims in the way in which he speaks of the sacred individuals. There may be a helpful analogy in one of the diagrams that I made use of yesterday, so let me put it up on the screen (A diagram is projected.)

The High Commission - Questions & Answers

We are in world forty-eight and we are looking up. We look up at the world of angels and archangels and so forth. So we have our subjective experience of that. Gurdjieff obviously knew of the older traditions. The whole of the past 4500 years has almost endless reflections in how we are to look upon that. But remember too, that Gurdjieff is out to destroy our beliefs and our views. So there is going to be a great clash here that Gurdjieff is inducing in us. He is going to give us images that will assist in producing the clash. There is going to be an involutional thing seen from below. This is a very oppressive kind of place to be in. We are under more and more and more mechanical laws. We have less and less flexibility. When something is imposed from an involutional descending law, we suffer. After all, this is all of biology. This is all of what puts us under more and more constraints. So, when Kundabuffer is implanted, it's implanted by the arch chemist, physicist. This is involutional law. It is imposing some further restriction on us. But it's coming through law. So, there is that way of viewing it. But when we are here, looking at that, that's a very, very restrictive kind of thing.

At the same time there is the other side. Because if this is the ray of creation, there is this side that is coming down involutionarily and there is this side that is going up evolutionarily. Remember the clash between holy affirming and holy denying that Makary speaks of. It is the results of the clash that are the holy reconciling, not the clash, but the results of the clash

So, I believe one way of seeing all of this that has to do with sacred individuals, is that Gurdjieff is producing in us, images that will simultaneously evoke aspects of this, that are involutional, how we subjectively look at this oppressive thing, and also simultaneously evoking images of the other side, evolutional images. And we get caught in the middle. Here we are and that is where the clash is going to take place, inside of us.

What is going on here? Why is he seemingly, from Nick's perspective for instance, so insulting? Why does he put down, from Nick's perspective, because he also builds up? After all, there is meaning to "all merciful," to "all loving," to "all forgiving." This is not a put down. This is a very, very big thing. So, it is not all black. It is both sides here and we are the sufferers. We have to create the clash inside of ourselves by exploring. What does this mean, what does this mean to be under great restrictive law? But we have to use the laws in order to ascend, and that's the clash.

Participant 5: Is that where grace comes in? Because when I was reading your paper and reading the chapter on the train, I always wonder, because that is how I was raised up and its still in me, is there any grace around?

Participant 4: Yes, there is grace, but the preparation is always up to us. We have to be ready for that, we have to prepare ourselves. That's the clash. We have to be realistic about the up and down, about the involutional and evolutional.

Participant 5: I am being realistic. We have to work. In the beginning of Beelzebub, there was a major screw up somewhere and we had to suffer because of that. Later, I also understood it has something to do with us, and we have to work a lot to ascend toward objective reason, to live somewhere else, to live more consciously, or however you might name it. But what I never understood nor ever found, is that if there are higher beings, and they can make mistakes, are they also capable of doing us good?

Participant 4: Of course. Whenever we wake up, we never make ourselves wake up. Whenever we have moments when our attention is suddenly there, we didn't create that. We just struggle to hold on to it. That's a moment of grace. I should feel great gratitude in this moment and try to hold on to this that has been given to me. This is, for me, the image of Beelzebub. This really is the image of the great thrust to return, that waking up that happens to all of us. And that's what can initiate the clash. We have to do that. We have to see the oppressiveness, if you will, of great nature. Great nature's aim is not for us to come to consciousness. Great nature has its own aim and that is this great ray of creation that has this step by step by step restriction imposed on us by orders of laws. That's real. It's necessary, it's not negative. We see it as negative when we are down here subjectively looking up because we are under this great pile of laws.

Participant 3: You had a wonderful line, "however you may name it." I think that's very relevant to this discussion about the many titles of all these characters.

Participant 6: What about grace? We don't know how to do it, and we need help.

Participant 1: I find grace very difficult. I get to it by keeping it very simple. Grace is the intrusion of a higher power which will help us. Again, I think as to these papers with the greatest respect, we are all getting much too complicated. What Mr. Gurdjieff is saying, in painting a picture of these higher individuals, these angels and archangels who make mistakes and who have pretentious names, what he is really saying is that it is no good looking outside yourself to fantasies which you create of Gods and demi Gods and helping angels. You have to look within yourself and you have to do the work on yourself. There is nothing else that will do it for you. In working on yourself, you have to create a bridge to the unmanifest world.

Participant 7: I think it's time I challenge this thing about pretentious names, i.e. "his conformity." When one is in a state of grace, what is the overriding impression? It is that there is a real order, a real meaning, to which one is invited to relate. And if I may say so, as to "conformity," if all these ideas that we are toying with have any real meaning, then there is a hierarchy of conscious reality, and we have to admit at a certain point that we are under it. So "his conformity" is, in fact, a very high and proper title.

As to "his measurability or pantameasurability," I simply allude to the fact that members of the mesoteric circle contemplate, whereas members of the esoteric circle calculate. That is to say that they actually have objective knowledge of law. So "his measurability or pantameasurability" actually implies, I think something very profound.

Participant 8: Is it a matter of perspective? I agree with what you are saying. We begin in the ray of creation with world one, but world three and world six contain something of world one, all the way down to world 96. So, world one is contained within. If we were standing at the level of world twelve or world six, and we were from above looking down, we would have one way of viewing the cosmos and our world. But as we stand in our level of being looking up, it perhaps appears to be topsy-turvy. It appears to be that we are not being treated fairly, and that there are mistakes. Mistakes are being made. But, in fact, that's just because we see it topsy-turvy.

Participant 2: As was said, we look at those names in a topsy-turvy fashion, and to attribute qualities to the names is absurd.

Participant 9: When I read this text, part of the tension that is created in me and the questions that arise in me have to do with the fact that it presents not just one aspect of something. Even in terms such as "his conformity" or "his pantameasurability," there are two aspects simultaneously, because for me, Gurdjieff in this book is doing something that is not just here. There are several layers in the things that he is doing and not in sequence but interwoven into each other.

So, for myself, it isn't whether the raven is a good thing or a bad thing, or whether he represents a negative quality or a positive quality. And in the terminology even when he pokes fun at something, he is showing to me that there are many different ways of taking this. Here and here and here and here. So, he is using what I understand as symbolic language, and that it is not literal, and concrete and just logical. It's using pictures which give you many sides of something, because everything that is in me is not this way, or this other way only. It is multi-dimensional. So, any term or any image is carrying many meanings, and it's not about whether it is this way or that way. It is both ways.

Participant 10: I believe that the input is there in this image that Sy gave in his paper. It is not right to expect too many things such as that salvation will come just without anybody doing anything.

Participant 11: I do not have much confidence in what my intellect tells me about all this stuff. So, I am always looking for something practical. How can I bring this problem into my life? I clearly understand my situation, where I stand. So what can I do about it if I take this idea which is very well stated in the chapter on Justice on pages 1138 and 1139? So, if I can make myself transparent and receive something higher from above which perhaps even I might create myself. In other words, I can create my own hierarchy. If I make myself transparent enough and if the conditions are conducive, that micro-cosmic orbit can take place in me. The Chinese have an exercise called, "the running of the micro-cosmic orbit." They also have another exercise called, "the running of the macro-cosmic orbit." In other words, on these two pages he is telling me to do that in order to achieve what is required by my own transformation, because this material which descends from above is exactly the material I require to accomplish this. I can't really explain intellectually, what it means, but I can experience it if I put myself in the right conditions.

Participant 12: I would like to just read out the last four or five lines of the prayer (*Beelzebub's Tales*, p. 1174):

All & Everything Conference 2002

Extol thee MAKER-CREATOR
Thou, The Beginning Of All Ends,
Thou, Proceeding From Infinity,
Thou, Having The End Of All Things Within Thyself,
Thou, Our ENDLESS ENDLESSNESS.

Participant 4: This prayer is such an evocative counter to the perspective that we saw trying to be developed in Nick's paper. This is not a put down. This is an evocation. It is something that lifts us up.

Seminar 3 - Chapter 44 Beelzebub's Tales to His Grandson

Facilitator - Nick Bryce

Facilitator: I believe this session is the continuation of Keith's presentation of the other day in which he set the tone and the ideas for today's meeting. This is a very difficult subject as we would all agree. I was reminded at lunch that someone once said, "I am looking forward to the day when I don't want to change the world; I only want to change myself." The meeting is now open.

Participant 1: This good and evil thing interests me very, very much. In fact, it is one of the major reasons I was affected by 'Work' ideas when I was younger. In *Beelzebub's Tales* there is a structure in the universe which also interested me very much. When I first read it, the idea that somebody was looking at us through a 'Teskooano' from another planet and seeing all the beings on Earth was for me an eye-opener because there was a distance in looking at something which I never had. And at that time I had just seen a movie called The Time Bandits. The Time Bandits were dwarfs that were working for God and they got into conflict with him because they didn't agree with the work situation; they wanted more. The movie was very interesting because it placed God in a different perspective from the way I was raised to believe. Later I read *Beyond Good and Evil* by Nietzsche. A very good title for me that there is something beyond Good and Evil. Gurdjieff says, from Fritz Peters, when he talks about self-observation that you should not judge yourself because you cannot see yourself. I am doing this now for more than ten years in the group where you constantly meet people who try to do that. They judge; they judge themselves and they judge other people all the time. You have this commentator in your head constantly telling you about situations, it goes on all day. It comes from the way we were brought up, with a certain kind of religion which I later learned was no religion at all.

Participant 2: Does anybody have difficulty with his or her first impression when reading through the chapter? The way in which Good and Evil gets set up? Does it create any friction?

Participant 3: You mean how Makary sets it up?

Participant 2: Yes!

Participant 4: It struck me while reading the chapter, that in a sense it 'rubbishes' our own present idea of justice. He introduces Makary's idea which seems to be involution and evolution. What is he actually saying about justice? A whole chapter on justice, what is he actually saying? It seems very obscure to me.

Participant 3: OK, Just a reaction... When they saw something was wrong and they began to wonder why, they set up a committee and decided that whoever formulated this idea of good and evil was the source of all the abnormalities. I have a terrible reaction to the way the whole thing was set up, but the worst reaction is that it wasn't Makary but the organ Kundabuffer. How could His Endlessness accept that their decision the concept of Good and Evil wouldn't have come about without Kundabuffer? So that really wasn't the source of the abnormalities. And I am very righteously indignant about this.

Participant 4: In terms of the spreading of the idea of Good and Evil, the misinterpretation by the three-brained beings of the idea of Good and Evil, the spreading of the ideas by learned priests Armanatoora Beelzebub says that it was due to his action that the incorrect notion of Good and Evil came to be the predominant World View. And the term 'World View' was one of the important things I found in the chapter which speaks about "what is called 'various being-aspects of a world view', and instead of this a 'world view' is formed in them based exclusively on that maleficent idea about external Good and Evil" (*Beelzebub's Tales*, p.1141). And that is the world view that predominates, basically: the spreading of that religious teaching by Armanatoora.

Participant 3: But why was it spread so rapidly? Wasn't it due to the consequences of the property Kundabuffer? How the three-brained beings misunderstood the ideas was due to the lack of Being Parktdolg Duty? They swallowed it whole like we do. So the fact that this idea was misunderstood is still due to the consequences of the property Kundabuffer.

Participant 5: But he says about the global conditions that we are personally to blame for it, and maybe it becomes a kind of symbol for that. That it is separate from the organ Kundabuffer. And he makes it very clear that for the inner God 'Self-Calming' (which is indeed what this is all about) the idea of external Good and Evil is necessary.

Participant 4: Self-Calming is the result of the properties of the Organ Kundabuffer they themselves were personally to pay for it and just on account of the abnormal external ordinary being existence which they themselves had gradually established and perhaps this Kronbernkzion had a (finger) in that. And that is a very clever way a very efficient way of establishing those kinds of abnormal conditions to speak about Good and Evil

Participant 6: T. has a very good point when she asks, "Why should it be that they believe this thing?" There is a very interesting passage on page 1140 (of *Beelzebub's Tales*) which I would like to read out. It says, "The fundamental evil for all these unfortunates, from this fantastic idea resulted there chiefly because, even before this of course thanks always to the same conditions of ordinary being existence established by them themselves" and this is the important bit "data ceased to be crystallized in them for the engendering of what is called" and here I am going to go back to the Russian edition and tell you that that is a mistranslation "various being aspects of a World View" isn't in my opinion what it really says, which is (reads in Russian) which means in my opinion, "being-various-aspected World View" which I think is extraordinarily interesting because it is actually saying that data ceased to be crystallized in them for the engendering,

Seminar 3 - Chapter 44 of Beelzebub's Tales to His Grandson

basically, of a broad-based, or many-aspected World View. If you had it, you couldn't believe in Good and Evil because, as you already pointed out, you're not seeing the third factor. Unfortunately that point is sort of missed because "various being aspects of a World View" doesn't quite make it, does it? On page 1141 (of *Beelzebub's Tales*) at the top of the page this is the traditional wording "various being aspects of the World View". But I can show you the Russian texts, which I think would be translated literally as being poly-aspected or various-aspected World View, which to me has to do with the fact that if you see things broadly, the third force included, you couldn't believe in Good and Evil.

Facilitator: Can I ask a question? You mean ordinarily you couldn't see this, from an ordinary perspective?

Participant 6: Where does ordinary begin?

Facilitator: I mean from my own subjectivity.

Participant 6: Subjectivity?

Facilitator: Because it's all interpreted.

Participant 6: Where do excuses begin? It's very difficult to say. I suppose what I'm trying to do is simply to enforce T.'s question, which I think is interesting: Why should this idea have taken hold in the first place gives an explanation which has to do with this narrowing of our psyche? Which I suppose is subjective. But that's a label.

Participant 5: Is that the same as being third force blind?

Participant 6: Don't care for that one either. As soon as it becomes a tag, a label, I run away from it. I like what K. sort of implied, not seeing interactions clash, not seeing another perspective, saying, "third force blind". We all say, Oh yes! Third force blind. Tick. I just don't care for it. Sorry!

Participant 3: You know, I think where my question is going it has just occurred to me this is a question of responsibility and maybe this is just another way to get out of my own responsibility because in the end we can't get out of that. That's my responsibility. I can be very angry that it's been dumped at Makary's feet, at humanity's feet. The fact is, this is the situation. It's our responsibility as individuals as if we did it ourselves. It has to be, so that's it.

Participant 7: I think there may be a linkage between these two here or at least there is for me in the elaboration, actually starting from the title. That's why I spoke as to the title which Makary gives this, the affirming and denying influences on man. We see the affirming and denying. We call it Good; we call it Evil; and we forget man. That's the third force. He must be the carrier. This is where the clash takes place. Out of this clash rises the third force. So when we don't do that we are not paying attention. To get back to the point that we are responsible, if we don't listen and look carefully at how Makary put this together, then we fall into the trap and suddenly Good and Evil are things out there. We're responsible.

Participant 8: Isn't it only that Good and Evil was because of the minister Armanatoora? That Armanatoora took the idea from Makary and he established a religion of good and evil. And he discovered the angels and the devils. That's on page 1142 (of *Beelzebub's Tales*). He (Armanatoora) took the Good/Evil, Affirming/Denying thing which was mostly I think from a scientific paper by Makary because he taught it also as a symbol. It was not a psychological this or that. It was an explanation in symbols of forces in nature, and later Armanatoora (my English is very bad in this) in the blossoming of the Tikliamish civilization, built up a whole religious teaching based on this maleficent idea. It was just in that same religious teaching that he, among other things, explained for the first time that certain invisible spirits existing among them spread external Good and Evil and compelled man to take in and Manifest this Good and Evil and these spirits Blah! Blah! Blah! And I think that's marvellous! Marvellous since then also the aspects of what C. was saying, which was that data by various being aspects totally left us and instead we had a World View based entirely and exclusively on the Good and Evil thing, where we are now. And everyone talks only about Evil and not going back to Makary about the forces, and not even before Makary about when there was justice maybe.

Participant 7: If we use our attention and evaluate our own experience, use what attention we have, then perhaps there is some intimation that we wouldn't get trapped. If we use our attention we see and say, now wait a minute, does that match with my experience? Is that really what I see going on inside of myself? Do I see I mean how can I put together this notion of Good and Evil and simply accept it as one of these "Jones says and Smith says", as something that gets repeated and accepted as if; but I don't try to verify. I don't use what I have appropriately. So the end result is that I buy this picture of external Good and Evil, as if they were outside sources, when this religious person comes along and performs around me. But I don't criticize that. I look at that and say, is that really my experience? And not doing that, we end up with external Good and Evil.

Participant S: This maybe implied in what's being said, but where the subject is introduced on page 1125 (of *Beelzebub's Tales*) where these 50 candidates have done their research. Let me read part of this paragraph: ". it became clear to them that the fundamental cause of the whole abnormality of the psyche of the three-brained beings arising on this planet was that a very definite notion arose and began to exist," and here's the important clause "that outside the essence of beings, as it were, there are two diametrically opposite factors the sources of 'Good' and the sources of 'Evil'." So what that's saying is that this whole Good and Evil thing all has to do with personality, or at least that's how I see it. And again it gets back to this unreality of personalities and all this stuff like devils and angels. It's all personality stuff, it's not real, and he tells us that here because it's all outside of essence.

Participant 10: If we had really done our Being-Partkdolg-Duty we would have, hopefully, a higher degree of objectivity to look at this. Then we would have clichéd word third force. And

Seminar 3 - Chapter 44 of Beelzebub's Tales to His Grandson

because we are too lazy to do it, we latched on to this, what this well-meaning man was trying to do. But he didn't get to the bottom of it. You can't be objective unless you've cleaned your own slate.

Participant 1: Gurdjieff pointed out in Fritz Peters the same story. It's the story about the acorns. You know the story? About the tree and the acorns. At the end of the story he says, "Fritz, look at Good and Evil as right hand, left hand, and they have to work together, and the third force is conscience", and he speaks about conscience. What you were saying, that you have to look not outside yourself but inside yourself; and the (tape inaudible) from Mrs. Staveley that untrammelled conscience is the best guide for man. It's amazing that you can meet somebody from the other side of the world who is also in the 'Work' you are from completely different cultures and different personalities but what you know is the same. You know it's from conscience. He speaks about conscience being the third force to Good and Evil and, subjectively, Good and Evil is different everywhere. Conscience has nothing to do with morality.

Participant 11: What I would like to offer is how I saw this applied Good and Evil and consciousness in 9/11. I was working at home and a tenant came in; we watched the news. I had to go downtown in a neighbourhood where young people who are very active in their church. When I arrived I found these young people crying and in shock. But within a couple of hours they had put together a prayer vigil and put together a leaflet which they distributed to the local residents inviting people of all faiths to come to the church at 7pm for a prayer vigil. It gave us hope. It gave us an opportunity to deal with the truth of what had happened. People of all faiths and all walks of life came, grateful for a place to be. The atmosphere was very quiet and sincere. It was a wonderful opportunity to deal with something in my life that was a shocking tragedy. And to see people come together like that is where I see hope.

Participant 8: On page 1144 (of *Beelzebub's Tales*), 3rd paragraph, he says, "Of course, none of them even suspects that if every kind of villainy proceeds among them in general, then they do these villainies exclusively only because, existing wrongly, they thus permit to be formed in them their inner 'evil-God', which I once called 'self-calming' and which has absolute dominion over the whole of their psyche and for which only this idea of 'external Good and Evil' is necessary." That is for me what this Good and Evil and conscience is about.

Participant 11: See it from this point of view in regard to justice, we always look to who is to blame, who is guilty. It's like Jesus Christ. From His guilt, His blame, we punish Him. This is a self-calming factor for everybody, finding the one who's guilty. The devil is Osama Bin Laden and everybody else is good!

Participant 5: Isn't there a danger in discussing this subject? We discuss it in terms of what is evil and what is good. It's going to be a complete mess because we get into subjective descriptions of what is evil.

Participant 11: We believe self-calming is good for us. It is good like comfort instead of effort, so we see it upside down.

Participant 7: This is why I asked if people had any kind of instantaneous difficulty the first time they ran across the description by Makary. That Good comes from the source that's OK but then it turns out to be passive and it turns out to be involution. And then you look at Evil and it's active and it's evolution. Doesn't this create any difficulties inside? I mean this first description? That should create some raking inside and say wait a minute! This doesn't sound right somehow.

Participant 6: Against nature, against God, remember? So God's point of view, this is not so healthy. On the other hand using his right brain he obviously welcomes the possibility of having evolved servants. And it brings to mind the Yin and Yang symbol. If you see Evil and Good as all the same colour in themselves, we are really in trouble. I know many friends in America for whom this dreadful business with the towers is a memorably shocking thing. But seeing it from a very broad perspective, like the fact that Makary has to wait a long time for the truth about his actions to work themselves out, we have to wait a very long time for the truth to work itself out. And you can say that what happened in A.'s community was living proof that with a really severe shock, people, for a few days, begin to be open to relatively normal relations.

Participant 3: He also said it was time for planetary events, and that I would consider a planetary event.

Participant 6: That's true, but one more small thing. That is that it would interest me to ask what were the steps of creation, of conditions of ordinary being-existence established by them themselves. Because there has been a gradual process of following what at the time seemed good, in my opinion this is one of the most interesting things that for centuries we have been doing things which are good. You name them every time something happens something is done in the name of Good and yet gradually we have been creating more and more seriously difficult conditions for ourselves. How is it possible that all this evil has come out of the trend of doing something Good?

Participant 12: The relativity flying around here is overwhelming. But reciprocal destruction is self-calming. That's what Mr. Bush is saying right now. As Francis Bacon said, "Vengeance is a wild kind of justice". But the kind of killing that 'G' talks about is all right in there, but it's all good, isn't it?

Participant 6: Locally speaking.

Participant 12: Yes, of course. One's crusade. It's bad enough that Eisenhower talked about a crusade in Europe, etc. But you realize what we have slipped into from a linguistic point of view what we have slipped into. To take a vacation we go on a 'cruise' that's a crusade; it's the same word. We have a ship that goes out to kill people and we call that a 'cruiser'. And all of this is 'Crux'. For destruction or for peace. Good! The Love Boat against the Warship.

Seminar 3 - Chapter 44 of Beelzebub's Tales to His Grandson

Participant 6: You've got the wheel. Is the wheel a good thing? Is the internal combustion engine a good thing? Is printing a good thing? It's really difficult to see how without a third view, a view on another level. So much of what is counted a progress and good. Even the idea of progress itself

Participant 12: Dynamite was invented to stop all evil, all wars. Mr. Nobel said that this would stop all wars.

Participant 6: How right he wasn't.

Participant 7: This is not to deny the suffering. The individual subjective suffering that's come out of all kinds of events. It is to subjectivize it and make it exclusive from our part to say that I suffer and therefore there should be a righting of this, right now! So we don't look into where the source is of the suffering. Where does this come from? How did it begin? We don't use the attention that we have, and we always get ourselves into difficulties because of that.

Participant 1: Isn't it always one-sidedness? We always identify with one part of the picture. There is no unity, there is dualism.

Participant 5: And sometimes where we look at something and we don't actually analyze it, we will see it upside down. We will see it the very opposite of what it really is.

Participant 13: This is reductionism as against processing.

Participant 10: You had the great line, we identify with what we think is good. I think the key word is 'identify.'

Participant 5: It isn't even thinking, like and dislike. In my small inner world this is what I do. I calm myself by making sure that the world is what I like it to be, and I put labels. I don't like it and this is how I live. I like something or I dislike something. I don't think you can say it is reductionist thinking.

Facilitator: It's partiality.

Participant 5: Yes! Partiality! Which isn't a volitional thing. I am not in contact with another level. And this is the interesting thing about this chapter. There is the level of the movement up and down, and that is turned into the level of something very small inside myself, which then becomes the guide for my life, and there is no contact.

Participant 9: I can't give you the reference, but it's in one of the Ouspensky books quoting 'G', where it says that the only real evil is that which keeps us asleep. The idea is not to be asleep. Being aware, remembering, we don't identify and then we are not so much asleep. And then we are moving away from evil.

All & Everything Conference 2002

Participant 3: I would like to ask about how to understand the third force in this proclamation by Makary. Quotation from page 1139, "And it is the spiritualizing source of every World formation because it arises and must exist in them as a presence all the time while the given results exist which arise from various unusual mutual resistances occurring between the said two fundamental forces flowing in entirely opposite directions." Can someone enlighten me please?

Participant 7: He does put it in a little simpler form a little bit earlier when he does finally get to the point of saying that the first and second forces enter into every world formation, and it is the clash between them which then takes place inside each individual formation that can produce the third force. That's a little simpler I think. Not quite so difficult.

(Barely audible discussion between A. and K. about triads, bread-making and conciliation)

Participant 2: Bread is the result of fire the true character of the third force, the reconciliation of the flour with the water. The reconciliation is brought about through fire which results in the third force, the manifestation of which will be the bread.

Participant 12: Which has more permanence than any of the things that go into it.

Participant 5: That part you just read Toddy. The image I have from that part, especially the image of the negative and the positive, is that they can't exist without each other, are always in some sort of relationship of force, and that will happen continuously until there is the third force of consciousness. They change places constantly; negative becomes positive, positive becomes negative.

Participant 13: There is another aspect of this if you go back to the example of flour/water/fire. The flour, if you like, is one; the water is two; the fire is three. And out of the three comes the fourth which is more than the sum of the three. The bread is more than the sum of the three.

Participant 6: In *Fragments*, the question of Good and Evil comes up. He talks about the fact that evil is very relative for people in general. What's good for one man is not good for another, etc. etc. Nobody does anything deliberately bad. They have their own subjective perception of what is good. And someone says, "But do not good and evil exist in themselves apart from man"? "They do", said Gurdjieff; "only this is very far away from us and it is not worth your while even to try to understand this at present. Simply remember one thing. The only possible permanent idea of good and evil for man is connected with the idea of evolution, not the mechanical evolution of course, but with the idea of man's development through conscious efforts, the change of his being, the creation of unity in him and the formation of a permanent 'I'. "A permanent idea of good and evil can be called in man only in connection with a permanent aim and a permanent understanding. The man understands that he is asleep and that he wishes to awake and everything that helps him to awake is good and everything that hinders him, everything that belongs to sleep, would be evil" and so on. "This contradicts generally accepted ideas. People are accustomed to think that good and evil must be the same for everyone, and above all, that good and evil exist for everyone. In reality, however, good and evil exist only for a few, for those who have an aim and who pursue that aim. Then what hinders the pursuit of that aim is evil and what helps is good. "But of course most sleeping people will say that they have an aim and that they are going somewhere. The realization of the fact that he has no aim and that he is not going anywhere is the first sign of the approaching awakening of a man or of awakening becoming really possible for him. Awakening begins when a man realizes that he is going nowhere and does not know where to go."

Participant 2: This is a different Good and Evil in Gurdjieff's terms, than the Good and Evil that is spoken of in the literal words in the text.

Participant 6: Of course. I'm looking here at the concepts. The fact that there is objective Good and Evil isn't there, in the terms of the Makary story.

Participant 2: All I'm saying is the quality the attributes of good and evil as defined by Makary Good is that which moves away from the source, is involutional, and Evil (at the cosmic level). Here we are talking about objective justice the whole chapter is about objective justice. In our little world there is no such thing.

Participant 8: The relation between the two of you is the trogoautoegocratic process. Being a part of the process is justice, and not being a part of it is not justice. That if you help or are a part of the process, that it is the Good, and if not, that is the Evil.

Participant 6: Can you opt out of the Trogoautoegocratic process?

Participant 8: Well, at lunchtime I was thinking of the food, of all the different kinds of food. It's a little bit like committing suicide. If you have all the time bad food you are unconsciously committing a kind of suicide, which you could say is evil.

Participant 10: A cheeseburger is self-calming.

(coffee break)

Participant 9: There is a question which I certainly have no answer to. It was touched upon in the reading from *In Search of the Miraculous*. We seem to be zeroing in on the idea that Good and Evil on this planet is something which we can become relatively free from, through the 'Work,' by being a little impartial or non-identified. I believe there is a statement in *In Search* where 'G' says there really is objective Good and Evil, but on our level we can't approach this. I don't know if that means we shouldn't talk about it, but it seems to be referring to what you are getting at. I wonder if you would talk about that a little bit.

Participant 2: Quite closely associated with this notion, at least in *In Search*, is the notion that it is possible to come to a real 'I.' He speaks about the wrong formation of real 'I' in Man No. 5. It is only when 'I,' when our egoism disappears completely that we are then free of the encumbrance of responsibility in lower worlds. What I mean by that is that even Man No. 6 can lose everything, and the only way that Man No. 6 could lose everything is the expression of a remaining egoism. That would be for a person developed to that degree, Man No. 5/Man No. 6, very far beyond us, but it would be in a higher world. And perhaps objective evil would be what a highly developed person who, from egoism, performs some act from his egoism because he has real power, a real 'I', and he knows the laws as Man No. 6. And acting from that would be one way of looking at objective evil.

Participant 12: You're really defining Lucifer. By the way, in *The Fourth Way*, Ouspensky says evil is that which is unnecessary. And to pursue that which is unnecessary is close to what you are saying about Man No. 6. In other words, if you act out or do that which is unnecessary because of ego...

Participant 2: Yes. It starts on many levels doing that what is unnecessary for your own well-being because some of those questions in *The Fourth Way* are not very deep and he starts at that level and moves up. What is sin? Sin is waste.

(There follows an unintelligible bit of tape. The remainder of this session was taken up with discussion of 9/11.)

End of Session

Seminar 4 - Where Do We Go From Here?

Facilitator: Nick Bryce

Participant 1: (tape inaudible) ... I would like to read the last words which were said by the priest at Mr Gurdjieff's funeral from *The Struggle of The Magicians* - "God and all his Angels keep us from doing evil by helping us always and everywhere to remember ourselves."

Facilitator: This session usually we call it, 'Where do we go from here?' and in previous meetings we have gone around the circle and we ask each of us do give our impressions of how he or she thought this session went. Perhaps while you are waiting on your turn to speak you might give some thought to: (reading) Do we want another meeting? Do we want it in Bognor-Regis? Or are there any other suggestions where it may be held in any other place? Also you might give an idea if you got a lot out of this meeting that you might have some friends or group members who might be interested in coming along to the next one if we have it. If we can have some commitment from people to the next meeting. These are just some general things, something to think about as we're going around and we can have some consideration for these kinds of questions. Sy has some approximate dates for the next meeting if we decide to have it here.

I may as well start with myself. My impression of this particular gathering is on the whole very good and a step in the right direction was for me two or three years ago when we selected chapters from the book and a major part of the sessions was devoted to discussing these chapters. That for me is always worthwhile and I got a lot out of it especially in the past couple of days. There is a lot to think about and I think I have learned a tremendous amount particularly for me as someone who is intellectually lazy so I can always pick somebody else's brains and ideas but that is always useful for me and I will go back to Canada and start reading the book again and try to apply some of the insights gained from everybody who has contributed. So for me it is a real plus and I would like personally another meeting to happen.

Participant 2: One of the important things for me has been discussing or being in the situation where the topic is establishing a being world-view where different things are taken into consideration and the ways to deal with the current situation. In the *Tales* Gurdjieff talks about the way beings are living and the ways that aren't fitting for them and the way to live which is, I guess, one of the things that I am learning here.

Participant 3: It has been a wonderful conference for me. One of the things I noted is that everyone has been able to participate and that was a very good sign and I also thought we had less rubbish presented as we had in some of the prior years. It was a wonderful experience. I did not think that this conference would be an ascending conference and fortunately I was wrong. I don't have a great or wonderful idea for next year.

Participant 4: I am a better person now than the one who I arrived here, I am more intelligent because, as N. says the things that many people have said, especially yesterday are really useful for me as I am sure they are for everyone with the questions that they have at this time because the world is becoming more chaotic and we all wonder what to do.

At one end of the spectrum P. was saying, (in response to the hypothetical question) 'How would Gurdjieff respond to the events of 911?' He wouldn't. Which is true. But from that fact we are on our level and we are in our lives and we all want to know what to do and I thought that yesterdays session was one of the best, most useful sessions that this conference has have ever had. I really appreciated some of the things that were said, especially by C., for example.

Another thing I would like to say is that I appreciate the letter that was read out to the conference from the Foundation which I think is very graceful really. That is encouraging to us. It has been great to meet new friends and to meet people who have come back to the conference after an absence of a few years. I just get a lot from that because I remember this all the time when I am back in my life. It helps me back in ordinary life to have these friends here and it never lets me down, I am really grateful for that. I hope we have another conference. I agree with D. that this was an ascending conference and I would just like to thank you for all that you have done for me in this time.

Participant 5: Being a wordy sort of person or an intellectual sort of person I think the best way I can summarise the conference for me this year is that I had spent some time putting together an article, it is in Stopinder and it is called. 'The Function of Emotion'. In that is an effort to consider from a thinking perspective the essentials of a normal emotional life and how the work makes that really possible but I think that what I have experienced this year here is, for me, just one of the clearest examples of the function of emotion that goes so far beyond the words in the article because it is real. It has been just a very, very helpful expression of that (inherency?). I think one of the additional characteristics that we saw played out so well this year is that in most groups there is always a reluctance to experiment, to try something different and I think this year we tried several things and some things didn't work and I think I was more impressed by the group responded to the fact that it didn't work. In other words there was certainly no negativity and very little mechanicalness it was just 'OK, try that. Did it go well?' So we've learned something from it and I think there was something of that experiential way of non-judgement but a willingness to be to some degree to be spontaneous and to experiment with new ways to trying to share things and to try and kind of (plumb?) into things and we learned. I certainly did I learned a great deal from that from that circumstance. So I hope we will, we will continue to get together.

The conference in terms of planning in terms of 'thinking about', in terms with staying in touch with people throughout the year has become a real centre of gravity, certainly not the only one, but within work it has become an important focus for ideas, for sharing, for connections, for new ways of looking at, for planning ahead,, for making some efforts for planning in regard to, and that has been important for me.

Participant 6: I think one of the most important things for me this year was that, and one of the happiest things for me this year is that almost half of the people who are here this year were not here last year, and yet every year we find that the seminars in which we mutually discuss Beelzebub are more and more participated in and more and more people join in and have impressions and I just think that is so positive. On a personal note, I learn so much from other people's perspectives and with people being here from many different countries, hearing other people's point of view it is important for expanding and deepening my understanding. We discussed a lot about 911 and yet, being here I had a sense of a separation that I hadn't felt all the time I was home. I guess, what I mean is, that being here I could have the feeling of how personal I had made that and there is something about finding yourself plumped in the middle of Europe with all it's history and a place where so much war and suffering has happened that it pretty much deepened … it is hard to describe.

It has been a wonderful conference and appreciate all of your relationships I hope that we do have it again next year. The one thing I missed was actually having something like what Wim shared last year and I had this idea that Dimitri share this beautiful thing that he has with his group. They have this theatre and they put on these plays and I just thought something like that would be wonderful. I don't know what that means; maybe we could convince Dimitri to bring his group here?

Participant 7: It is difficult you know but… (tape inaudible)

Participant 6: Well that's a great possibility. I also thought - well I suppose that we could go there.

Participant 7: I am really very grateful to have had the opportunity of participating in this and in all the aspects of it there were for me for me opportunities to glimpse perspectives that are other than the ones that are in me. In a sense, I suppose it has been for me kind of like acquiring new ingredients for a new meal because I think in terms of many things that I have stored about this for nourishment. I mean I am going to be ruminating over a lot of this, I already am and I don't know how specific I can be over the aspects of it, but that being said, I would very much enjoy participating if it were to take place again. Thank you.

Participant 8: This is my first year so I cannot judge what direction the conference is going. I know that in myself it is a hunger for understanding how to relate what is so important to me in the work to the world and also to have had this opportunity with you to submit to the power of the ideas coming from such different directions and traditions as they are now are beginning to be called, I can only say that I feel that it is necessary to meet in some form or another. This exchange is, from the point of view of the ideas, necessary. But I don't know - there is so much that I take away and keep in the heart and ponder... (unclear) wonderful meetings and the feeling of being allowed to be open. It is remarkable, how you have proceeded because you have been practising over all these years, able to enter into an opening towards the idea from any kind of angle and I certainly see of myself that I certainly do not have the capacity to, enough capacity for responding to all these different impulses. We talk about rubbish, someone said, well it is also a part of life. It is also a paradox for me. I want to submit to refined and fine influences. I don't want Mr Gurdjieff's ideas to be dissipated but how? I think it is great to come here and really not know some very basic things. I myself am asking myself 'why do I need ideas at all?' So I cannot say whether it should carry on or not except the exchange is very good. But whether this forum is the one or not, I am not able to judge. The only one little comment I have about the form is that it would be quite hard when coming to discuss a chapter or trying to exchange, or open to it is very, very helpful to read together. You have probably done this before, but it is such a different energy in that than when I sit in my room or prepare to read over again. To sit alone at home all that is important and fine but to actually to read together and it also happens to be what Mr Gurdjieff advises.

Participant 9: 1 haven't been here for a number of years. I was here for the first two years and then did not come for another four or five and the changes that I have found I thought are certainly in the right direction, a satisfying direction for me. The main thing is, as you said Nick, the introduction of these discussions on All and Everything. I found this to be good, great. The other thing I found very important is something very basic changed in the emotional part or make up of these sessions. There seemed to be almost no nasty at all here like we had in the past where people were ready to propound their own ideas with intensity and they were being a bit cranky and things like that. It is more realistically facing the Gurdjieff work and our problems the way they are. And talking about this emotional bit which makes us more equal in the right sense I have to say that the person who embodied that for me the most was Michael (Smyth) in the past. As a memory over the years his face had this kind of thing that has the experience that I am talking about.

I think we should have a few more presentations and I don't think it is so difficult to have more presentations. I could have made a presentation. If I had known there had been holes in the system, spaces to be filled. I think, you know we think we can manage things. I have done so little to manage or to contribute to these sessions here I think Sy and Bert and Nick has put together (unclear) and they are propagating it still. So I don't know what they say about the future and the only thing I can say is that I really want it to be to exist, even when I was not here I was very happy for it to exist.

I certainly sincerely hope I will be able to attend.

About meeting other people there is a question there. I do not think it would be difficult bringing a few people from Athens from Thessalonica from Greece and advertising in such a way that a lot of people come, that a large number of people come but there is a question,. You know, I mean some of the cranks who have showed up are people who are very marginally connected with the ideas and they can make a lot of noise, unnecessary noise. So I don't know about that aspect of trying to bring other people, no matter what? Or what do you, I don't know. But advertising to people whenever one has a chance... What has been happening so far seems to be working so far as I am concerned.

And there is a question of how useful is this? About these readings from Beelzebub I thought what a fantastic idea what a fantastic session idea and of course I had the thought could this be done or should it be done in the sessions in Athens? I don't know there was something very special about the meetings here like I said before people come from different directions putting their own opinion there and you know this is very creative. I think instead of having the same old people with the same old attitudes kind of, you know like, creating their own little, the atmosphere that you know about such ideas. It is much better if they come from different directions from entirely different directions in my mind so I don't know if I would like to see this thing happening in Greece. I know I have it in my mind here but people come from entirely different directions and they put in their ideas. But I think it is marvellous. The other thing I was thinking is how useful is this for the work in general? What do I mean by the work in general? There seems to be out of Mr Gurdjieff's efforts this wave of energy that is propagated and exists in various forms now. How important or how centred are these meetings, these yearly sessions for this thing? Are they at all important? Do they contribute in anything essential? It is a difficult question to answer I think. Everybody has his own answer because he sees things from his own perspective. It was strange the letter that was read the first night about 'well you can do you want, and we won't block anybody from coming because we know that what we are doing is what is done and that what you are doing is what you are talking about'. I should say a joke of this, you know, Nasrudin decides to go into a garden and steal some fruit. So he had this ladder and he put the ladder and he climbs to the top of the wall with it and places it in the garden to descend into it. As he was descending and on the last step suddenly the owner of the garden was in front of him. He says 'Why are you in here?' Nasrudin is taken aback he didn't know what to say he was embarrassed at getting caught so easily but he quickly finds words and says 'I found this ladder and it is for sale!' The owner just didn't know what to say he says 'But that is no place to sell a ladder!' to which Nasrudin relies 'Aha! But that is where you are wrong a ladder can be sold anywhere!' Things can be done no matter where.

So am I speaking more than I should? Do you have a clock?

Facilitator: No, I don't.

Participant 9: So I believe that this is a very important session and I consider it important in the overall flow of the energies that I talked about. Thank you.

Participant 10: Well for me it was always a very useful period in previous years. For me to come here is like nourishment, it is all the impressions I get here from different people whether they are from different organisations or work alone for me it is useful thing. For me it is very unique station or period of my work life over the years and I feel that the bond which is established here it is much more strong every year and this year is the strongest bond.

All & Everything Conference 2002

Participant 11: I've got a lot from the conference this year but I've got a lot from the others. I always enjoy reading *Beelzebub's Tales* because its something I really don't understand, I find it very difficult but yet the insight I get from everybody here is always so useful. Also this year on Saturday the discussion I also found was very useful and different and produced a whole different energy to me to what's produced in analysing the *Tales*. So I think it's possible that maybe we should continue. Also I agree with the other people, who said that we need something and I feel it could be music, but something just doesn't always deal with the intellectual centre, something like just music played, just something. It's hard to say, you have a general idea and yet you really don't know exactly what you want, just something that hits you like the Movements Demonstration did last year. And I guess the thing that really makes this conference great is the people, every one of them. It's not always the presentation it is just what one gets from being here and talking with one another.

Participant 13: I think for me one of the really interesting things is the difference between a forum in which the aim is to find answers, make points, present hypotheses and generally as was said was (tape inaudible) and probably by you, B., to give vent to ego-angles on things. That is very common among the (tape inaudible) and at the beginning of this series of conferences it was one of the overt aims. There were quite a lot of people with very strong agendas and they were trying to find a new forum or a new platform (tape inaudible). I think it is very interesting for me to see how over a seven year period we have got closer to the nature of a work group in the sense that I think people appreciate more the fact that the real interest is in finding more intense questions, things which are harder and harder to answer in a cheap way. That's my view, and also that the process itself is seen as energising, and the actual living interaction between people's opinions, the doubts, the moments of conflict, all these things build up a certain interactive process where something of quality can enter. And it is very interesting to me that the formation of; as it were, something of in the direction of a workgroup enquiry can happen without the overlay of specific work exercises, of specific movement sessions of specific techniques and I think this is because most if not all of the people here are in some way connected with a personal or a connected aim of following the teaching in an interior way. I think it is very interesting then is to have someone like P. present who though he has huge knowledge, great interest, extraordinary background and the capacity to tell many stories. I have always felt slightly uncertain given the balance that we have between these two sides as to how it played out. He is very tolerant and an extremely nice guy. I think it is fairly clear that the strictly academic side represented by people like that Professor Rawlings who came and just gave us a straight paper on Gurus because that was his field. We have had one or two others; we've had that Italian Professor who came, Massimo Introvigne. They were strictly from the world of academia and I think we have already practically, completely moved on from that. Haven't we? It seems like it. I think it's a matter of; we have to meditate on whether or not we wish to see that trend complete itself I mean how many years can he come and tell us these lovely stories? It is almost like there is something that can happen and then you can have exhausted that theme.

Participant 1: Can I make a comment without meaning to interrupt you? What you have been saying about the presentation of papers essentially as an ego-trip on the platform and this brings me back to Aristotle with his System of Ethics and what he began to worry about was that his star pupils would get up on the platform and spout the System of Ethics as an ego-trip and he said, 'No, no, no, that is not what they are for. They are to be applied in Society and used by Society'. So he called them by a Greek word 'Organon' which means a tool, and it is intriguing me that we use the same word for Organic Life which is a tool for the use of the Higher on Earth and we are part of it. Sorry for interrupting you.

Participant 13: No, thank you for the valued gap. It isn't that I am ever saying that an individual gets up to do an ego-trip because I know how hard it is to get up there and be as it were, the force plus in a vacuum (tape inaudible). It isn't easy. Whereas, when we have these interactive processes there is this constant interplay which we obviously all appreciate. When it is in the background of the weight and subtlety of the *Tales* it definitely brings something. Now I come from an environment in which meetings like that in groups of this size is common. You know these sessions we had, especially Saturday afternoon's was not much different from what I would expect from one of my groups. So from that point of view it's definitely getting close, as I say to the atmosphere of a work-group and the enquiry is, I think, the very active force amongst us.

Now, it puts so many questions like the papers question, I think it is a very real one. What kind of papers go on serving the process. You have got to have something to get you going. At the same time the focus is more and more to be the real essence of our being together as being these seminars. So I feel with B. quite a lot that you can't infinitely prolong any process successful or otherwise. Things have a way of seeping out. Just at the moment you think you have got something, you finally encapsulate a truth, or fix an understanding and (its goes?) I wonder whether it won't be necessary if these meetings are to continue to find some new shock. Looking around one of the things I realised was that five people resident in the UK in this room. I know that we have had some UK people in and out but it is actually remarkable that there are five people who live in the UK in this room. A lot of our brothers and sisters and from across the water, the waters, and I wonder if it isn't necessary to actually do another of the US based trips, I know its hard on Bert, ... and make the really special effort to actually reconnect to some of the other people in the States including I think, being willing to re-absorb some of the big egos again. It is very interesting to me that part of the quality that has appeared is because some of the big egos have sort of melted away. I have in my notes a list of some of the big egos ....there are a number of big egos. Now that would really put the cat among the pigeons. Is this thinkable? Or not?

So you've got the options, do you go for trying re-animating the academic side? Do you go for the big egos or do we rather simply try to become a rather intimate, intimate partly because we know one another, beginning to know one another, work study-group? And then although we still might respect to a considerable degree the fact that not having overt work processes we have become a little sort of annual or BI-annual, twice a year or something study-group. What did strike me as interesting is that maybe people sit on the beach or do their own thing but there were only ever eight people in there sitting in the morning. No comment but it just really did strike me.

Some people like to sit by themselves.

Participant 13: Sure I just was interested in the fact that one of the community things ... (tape break) ... participation in the collective act of sitting in the morning.

Participant 14: We need at least a couple of more people on the Planning Committee, people who have email, people who are willing to think about the issues that come up. So just give that some thought when we talk later, as I understand from Nick, that we will talk specifically about whether we want to have another conference and where and how and all that stuff. One other thing I want to mention that turned out to be extraordinary for me, and that is this email exchange which as you know resulted in at least three if not four of the papers which have been presented here. It wasn't the papers so much it was the work of the people who thought about these issues in the *Tales*. And of course speaking just for myself I work at thinking about it and it is not work in the work sense it's just intellectual and we know that. I derived insights I would not have had and perhaps would not have developed as well without that internet discussion group in which I participated. That is my experience for those of you might have the opportunity to do that over the next year. I think you will find that it can have great, great value. So I look forward to hearing the comments of others and seeing where we go from here.

Participant 15: Two things, one is gratitude for all the labours that people have spent to make this happen, a lot of gratitude. And second, working on the *Tales* or any of Mr Gurdjieff's writings, to work in any way and especially this way where we work together I dare to hope for the future and I wish to continue to work in this way. Thank you.

Participant 16: Well I would like to say I appreciate what T. and A. said about the gratitude. I very much feel it has taken a lot of very hard work to get this together. I can only say that I have found this by far, personally the best in a way the most rewarding I have been to. I hope we can continue because it is quite unique. I feel particularly this year it is like coming back to a family reunion. I have to thank the people who have come because I have had a great deal of energy from the people who are here. When J. and I are in the situation where we can't get a group going and are rather isolated it actually provides me, I'm sure J. as well, it serves to provide with an energy and a recharge to continue to foster the work in myself. I say that because at my age it is all rather easy to start coasting, you know, I think I have been coasting all me life, but it provides me with an impetus and fresh impulse not to stand still and rest on my laurels. This is a very great help, a very, very great help. It does last throughout year and each time I come back I have gone back with a golden nugget. This time with two or three, particularly Ana's work on the Triads and Keith's and I have got to work upon Sy's idea that actually the Spiritual Hierarchy doesn't exist. I'm going to have a look at my record I dare say that I shall get to grips with that! I do very much appreciate this in its context and I haven't got any ideas about how it could be improved. I hope continues more or less as it is with such improvements that those people who have got ideas put forward.

Participant 17: For me this conference has become a part of my work for the year. I look forward to it each year and I also dread it each year. There are both sides to coming into contact with so many knowledgeable people. I benefit from it and it frightens me at the same time but I wish it to

Where Do We Go From Here?

continue. It has been a wonderful meeting this year and I feel gratitude to those who have spent many hours in the planning of this, so thank you for doing that. Thank you for everyone's participation. I think we have all to some degree participated in this session more so than in the other sessions I have attended and I think this is my third session or fourth, I'm not sure. My suggestions for next year... I think we should continue and continue work on the *Tales* but also work in other of Gurdjieff's writings. Sophia brought this up last time and I think it would be useful to include *Meetings* and *Life is Real... and Herald of the Coming Good* all of which have many important ideas that will enhance the basic study of the *Tales*. I also think it would be important to include music. I thought Wim's music last year was an element that we have missed this year. We need that, we need this music here we need Gurdjieff's work music here. I feel that I can bring back to our group in Salt Lake so much and I will do that. I feel like we are a part of a worldly phenomenon in the work that it is working in a worldly way and to continue that, I think, is a responsibility that we share. So I thank you all very much.

Participant 18: I agree a lot with B. about the music. Yesterday the vigil, I appreciated a lot the music. The power, because music can tell us a lot of things. We should have at least a Gurdjieff reading at coffee-time. I realise how important these conferences are and this year especially because there are more new people here and I think the most prepared we are the better. So I think the more developed we are, the better. This year I saw myself suddenly as a cube with only six faces to answer reality through the world. I thought I am so limited and I would like to come back to an original form of an egg, round and smooth. Then I thought Gurdjieff must be like this, so infinitely faceted and I thought that Gurdjieff, seen by a ghost it seemed like a big diamond. Diamond like a big (tape inaudible) with a lot of faces and each one that was very close to him saw only one face. So I think the most major importance of these meetings, and this time I knew something about Mrs. Popoff and Bennett's groups, so nice this, how other people work so I think we must join our deviation because it is them that made a lot of deviations. We must share an average of the deviations and so I think this is accurately at this time the most important work in the direction of unity of entering the real teaching, we must average. Thank you.

Participant 19: I feel so privileged to have been here. In the beginning it was overwhelming and it still is. The quality of the papers, the presentations and the discussions and the quality of the people who are here... it has been remarkable. For me personally I have had my vision expanded on World Creation and World Maintenance and Triads and I have enough threads to last me at least a lifetime. I hope I will be able to come here next year, thank you.

(coffee break)

Participant M: I would like a little clarification on something because I'm not quite clear about what the intent of say, the big egos, and pursuing (some of those mentioned earlier) for the conference, but what would be the intent?

Participant C: Well when these conferences originally started they turned out to be a forum for cross-fertilisation between people with different sort of currents and affiliations and by their nature some of these people have strong agendas but they have also have got quite a lot of people, they have energy, they do things. I mean one of the problems here is that we have sort of almost run out of people with small egos willing to present egoists. You have got to have some ego otherwise you can't act obviously. So it is just for me question as to whether with all those people who are out there doing something being that they are not Foundation and even that they are a sort of independent group whether we shouldn't be re-opening an effort to connect with these people because they are part of a constituency to which we might be addressing ourselves. I tell you for free that it will not ever be the Foundations who come here en masse. They have their own life, they have their own agenda, they attend two or three meetings a week with their own groups, they have weekend sessions, they are all busy with something they are happy with, they are not going to come here en masse. They are busy, happy, but, the other people may be, you know it is just a question mark here as to whether you just form yet another form, another independent little thing which is separate.

Participant D: I want to add something to your questioning. Yes, I do appreciate the fact of virtue of interacting with 'big egos' the way you put it. On the other hand the answer is probably not only intellectual and coming from the intellectual thinking about it but the way one feels about it. The way I feel hasn't changed here in years is the amount of learning. I literally could not believe I could learn so much as I am learning right now. There is something that is open to learning if the weather is not too....

Participant C: Too bad.

Participant D: You see, yes.

Participant C: Absolutely. This is the game.

Participant D: There is no question that this is the game there is no question about that and the virtue I see in it is that there is some kind of dialectic relationship somewhere in there, I'm sure of that. Yet there is a virtue also in letting things go by themselves in the way that it seems it has kind of you know like of (evolved) put a little bit further away some attitudes.

Participant C: I totally agree I suppose what I am saying is that if we open the door slightly and the wind comes howling in will we still be able to function? Because we do need fresh air. It's a real problem... If you open the door you get fresh air and you get turbulence.

Participant D: So you have to charge somebody to open the door who can function responsibly. (laughter)

Participant C: I think we have, together we have more or less achieved what is my perspective on this. We have to keep the door ajar to let the fresh air come in and yet not be...

Participant M: This is the balance between the static and dynamic, the being and the becoming.

Where Do We Go From Here?

Participant C: Yes, that's where we're at.

Participant B: I would have thought that the concept of persuading members of the foundation to join us is totally irrelevant because they have their own situation.

Participant C: That's it.

Participant B: So they don't need to join us.

Participant C: And they won't!

Participant B: No, and we don't want them to! (laughter)

Participant S: These kinds of questions we are raising and the decisions that will need to be taken cannot be taken just as far as I know in a group of this size. They haven't been in the past they have been taken by a Planning Committee sort of on the overall advice of who is here. I mentioned this before and I will mention it again and that is it is my feeling that that we need some new experienced people on this Planning Committee in order to do anything more or different than what we have been doing. It may be very well just doing the same site, the same sort of format can have a tendency to run down. In fact somebody said to me at this conference 'We had a good run getting to this octave', not (that) perhaps there is something significant about that, but we have to have … (tape inaudible). So that is a question and I hope some of you who are interested in this and have some experience with it would consider perhaps participating so that the thing doesn't run down.

Facilitator: I should say that we haven't quite finished the round and after that there is supposed to be an open forum where perhaps these kinds of things could be discussed. So if we could just drop the subject for a moment, continue and then open it up again. J. would you like to speak?

Participant J: Well this is my first time here and I didn't have any expectations when I came and I am certainly not leaving disappointed. The image I have developed of the conference is that here is 'Bognor Regis', Bognor Regis I don't know why it always wants to make me smile when I say the word, and I see people coming from Greece and Switzerland and Norway and Scotland and North America, East Coast, West Coast, Brazil. There is sort of like this commitment, this effort and this hunger and I think I am very pleased at what I have personally got out of this. I liked the seminars very much I also think the presenting papers is an extremely good idea. I don't enjoy friction but I welcome it and since I have only been here for the first time it has been very interesting to hear people say 'This is really different, you should have been here two years ago when there was this, that and the next thing' (laughter) That's going to sound like 'Mm, I'm sorry I missed that but I'm glad that I wasn't here!' I am going to keep it really short because I think it is really important to look at the dynamics of continuation. So I just want to thank you very much. I want to thank the people who organised this and everybody and I actually feel a sense of family. It is very interesting to me because this is my home country and I do not have any organic family here and it is so curious to feel connections which are, feel both old and new but that's a very personal feeling and I really have enjoyed my conversations. I just want to say one more thing and then I'll stop. We have plenty opportunity nowadays for digital communications and it is absolutely to me invaluable to be in a room with people. I have always envied the cafe system where people would sit and talk. So I would certainly contribute my energy to keep communication on the personal level where people are in the same room and not rely too much on current technology for ideas because ideas completely change when I hear the person who has got the ideas talk to me. I am totally involved with that. So thank you all very much.

Participant J: I came in contact with this Gurdjieff work about eleven years ago and shortly after that I read *Beelzebub's Tales*. I found it a very interesting book with a lot of ideas and then I put it away because there are so very many interesting things to read in the world about Gurdjieff and other interesting things. I often heard people talk about that there was, there might even be more in it and found books about Gurdjieff and books about books about Beelzebub and I somehow got the idea that it was all chewed out. Every sentence had been looked over ten times and that there were people who knew it all, so that it was, well what is the use of reading it and trying to figure out what was in there. And being here and talking, hearing different opinions and I like people with strong opinions and especially if they are different, because that makes me realise that no one really knows and there is something to bring in for everyone. So it has motivated me very much to really read it and to really try to find out what I think of it so that the next time or the time after I will be able to contribute something which I just never thought I was able because there were all these specialists who already knew it and they just had to tell me and that was it! That was the fastest way, but you have to do it yourself and that was a good realisation.

Participant D: Forgive me if I am totally wrong. I think it is not that nobody knows; it is that we all know! (laughter)

Participant J: I didn't have that realisation yet! And apart from that it was very nice. The atmosphere was very nice over here and in the bar, the surroundings, the environment, although parts of the hotel are almost falling apart it has a very pleasant atmosphere. It was extremely nice and thank you all for that especially those who organised it.

Participant O: Well there are two things that I have to say about this gathering or about this conference, it was way better than the conference in 1997. That is because through certain experience in the last five years I have developed a deeper emotional relationship the book *Beelzebub's Tales to His Grandson*. The conference matured emotionally very much because there were no big egos sucking energy and doing their things and hiding behind their over-educatedness so I was very pleased with that and I hope that that will continue because last night in that movie I personally … (tape inaudible) … that I am allergic to people that make low-scale careers in this thing or eating the crumbs of; in this case Mr Gurdjieff's table and I don't like that. Its not, it has never been my intention in doing what I was trying to do and am trying to do, hard. So I was very pleased to meet people here again that I met in 1997 also and I felt very welcome and that was a very nice feeling. About the hotel this also, I noticed this also. I have an album of the pop-group

Where Do We Go From Here?

The Kinks that I like very much. I think Ray Davies was one of the biggest song-writers, he is one of the biggest song-writers of the last century and he has an album that is called The Decline and Fall of The British Empire. (laughter) I felt that on the train ride and also here in the hotel.

Participant D: C. (tape inaudible) ... put it in a positive way - he said 'Dorothy, didn't you notice, this hotel is shabby-chic.'

Facilitator: OK, I think we have an open forum now and I'd like to leave five or seven minutes, O. wants to read something from *All & Everything* which might be a fitting closure to this conference. For fifteen minutes let's have an open forum and let's discuss perhaps should we want another meeting? Should it be in Bognor? Maybe we should address those questions. Some of the questions that C. brought up I think require much more discussion and exchange and personally I don't think we have time to arrive at a conclusion about that but it is something to think about for the future. So why don't we just open it up and see what happens and remember we are going to finish off with a little reading.

Participant S: May I give just some nuts and bolts information in terms of thinking about next year if we have a conference. Easter is considerably later. It is April 20th next year. Historically we have had the conference always before Easter, the last few years in the two weeks before Easter mainly because the travel costs seem to go up considerably after Easter. Bearing that in mind I made some dates here with this hotel only so we have the dates. It doesn't mean we have to keep them or anything like that. I also enquired about pricing here, as you know we are paying about £43 per person. They think it will go up a little bit because they are doing some re-modelling, spending some money, but they don't think it will go up a lot but I wasn't able to get any firm commitment on price. So if we had it two weeks before Easter and for the same length of time it would be from Wednesday April 2d through Sunday April 6th. This is just by way of information.

Participant D: We have always had folks couldn't attend because of the cost. So if anybody has an idea that they have researched or something about how to do this conference and keep the cost lower... S. and I did go to this hotel down the street and I think they will negotiate. It is not that we would prefer that hotel down the street, that is not the case at all. These folks here have been wonderful to us but as an alternative in case this one becomes too pricey.

Participant J: I think there is the matter of cost but there is a certain atmosphere in this hotel and this room, the bar and the sitting area are what enable us to have all these personal conversations and meetings and rests in between and maybe we can take for granted what enables the things to work well. It may be shabby-chic and it may well be in the decline of the British Empire but it is not bad for the purposes we have and I wonder if the same atmosphere would be available to us in another place. It is just a reservation that I have about that. I think this is quite good it has always worked for us.

All & Everything Conference 2002

Participant D: Down the street they do have good meeting facilities. They have a negative of being so close to the road that we will be competing with the traffic noise on a 24 hour basis. I mean you are right on the road.

Facilitator: J. you wanted to speak?

Participant J: I was just thinking about when we said whether we are willing to have another conference or not because my impression is that everyone in the room wants the conference to continue. That was my impression.

Facilitator: What about what C. brought up about the next conference being in Bognor or is there any thoughts or a desire to for it to move to North America for a year?

Participant S: Just by way of information for those of you who don't know. We tried it once in North America it was three years ago, 2000 in Maine. One of the issues is that we need people on the ground to find a hotel, organise equipment and that sort of thing. We also need to have the conference not too far from a major airport if we expect people to come from different countries.

Participant M: There is one additional motivation, if I may, to the state of Maine and that is we now have a train M-track comes up from Boston to Portland and that does afford people who are flying into Boston transportation to Portland.

Participant S: The other thing I think was true is that we didn't get a whole lot of people from the UK, nor from European countries when we had it in Maine. We did get a lot more Americans. It was about the same size with just under thirty people, but it was almost all Americans and by way of being different you could see that as a pro or a con. It seems like the Americans have been willing to come here more than the other way.

Participant D: The air fare, for some reason that I don't understand, is much cheaper for us to come over here than for you folks to come to our country in the exact same week.

Participant A: For me it is easier to come here than there for people from South America.

Participant C: I don't have strong feelings about this. I'm not attached to either place but it is said that America is the country of raw energy and relatively open essences. That is also a big...

Participant B: That's not true any more! (laughter)

Participant C: I'm way behind the times. It is just that the number of emails I get on my website. There are more people enquiring from the States than anywhere else.

Participant S: Can I ask a question of those of you who live this side of the pond? How many of you would come to America? No commitment just a show of hands...

Where Do We Go From Here?

Participant O: If it was combined I would consider it?

Participant S: Combined with what?

Participant O: Combined with another gathering.

Participant A: Like the Rolling Stones?

Participant O: No, not like the Rolling Stones, we can invite them though. No because we have been doing gatherings for five or six years too every year and I am partly here because there is another gathering in Amsterdam next week and if our sort of gatherings like we had at Salt Lake City and we had in Portland or at the farm I would consider it.

Participant A: How do people feel about coming here next year? Can we have a show of hands?

Facilitator: You can't show two hands.

(Discussion about Scotland as location)

Participant C: If we are coming to the UK then we are going to have it here. I don't think we need go into that one.

Participant A: Shall we take a vote on how many people would rather have it in the United States?

Participant M: So it looks like here!

(general agreement)

Participant S: Here being this side of the pond, not necessarily here at this hotel

Participant J: I think Bognor Regis is great. I think it is ridiculous, this is great.

Participant D: Bring your own light-bulbs!

Participant S: What about C.'s idea that if you keep having it in the same place, same hotel, (to paraphrase C.'s arguments) isn't it going to run down?

Facilitator: Its once a year, it is hardly a habit.

Participant T: I do think it is insidious how the form takes over. So I think it is a point we should strive to remember because it is very easy in twenty years to say...

Participant C: (feigning old-age) "Is that T.?" T. replies, "You haven't changed!" (laughter)

All & Everything Conference 2002

Participant D: This year in particular from my point of view the new people that are here for the first year are wonderful. First of all we need youth because we are falling off. The young folks are so prepared, enlightened; it is just a great group. Usually our new folks are kind of spiritual shoppers in other years this year has proved wonderful. We need you next year.

Participant B: Yes, M., S. we need you.

Facilitator: Ladies and gentlemen I have to close it down. I know you would like to continue but we are going to have a small reading so that we can stop the conference on time and allow people to get away.

Participant S: I feel this is an important question and I have mentioned it twice. I have been on this Planning Committee for seven years. I don't feel it is appropriate, unless there is some new blood, that the same old, same old people which have been reduced in number now keep having, keep doing it. This has always been an unorganised thing, it has always been a bit ad hoc, you don't have to declare yourself here, but there are only three official people here on the Planning Committee right now, B., myself and M. with K.'s able assistance. Let us know please anybody who wants to pitch in and help make some of these decisions and do some of this work. Otherwise maybe we shouldn't have it any more.

Participant B: Particularly in the UK. It is unfair of the people who expect it to happen without making it happen.

Participant A: I offer myself that to help with those graphical things and this is a kind of meditation for me among other things.

Facilitator: Well perhaps if people could give some thought to that and might get in touch with S. by if they would like to join the Planning Committee and I'm sure he'll give you some advice. O. is going to read you something.

Participant O: I would never have come here in 1997 if it would not have been for, if M. S. and T. had not been here in 1997. One of the reasons I am here now is that I might have been here if M. had been here too but one of the reasons I am here now is because he is not here and I get the chance to be here. And when I came here it was planned to pick up B. and T. and to come with J. was nice but there was something more here and I really got something from it. Last year when I went to the United States to go to Michael and he was going to leave us here he gave me some thing very special. He gave me a small hawk which is from Egyptian mythology and he said, "It is about consciousness, remember that, it is all about consciousness, Horus stands for Consciousness." That went very deep for me because this for me it is about consciousness. Rodney Collin writes about it in *The Theory of Eternal Life* and he compares it with electric current, consciousness. This piece in Beelzebub for me is about that, about consciousness:

Where Do We Go From Here?

"And so, my boy as I have already told you, after these cosmic arisings had perfected their Reason to the necessary gradation of the sacred scale of Reason, they were in the beginning taken onto the Sun Absolute for the fulfilment of roles predestined for them by our CREATOR ENDLESSNESS." (*Beelzebub's Tales*, p.768)

"The first highest kind of being-Reason is the 'pure' or objective Reason which is proper only to the presence of a higher being-body or to the common presences of the bodies themselves of those three-brained beings in whom this higher part has already arisen and perfected itself, and then only when it is the, what is called, 'center-of-gravity-initiator-of-the-individual-functioning' of the whole presence of the being." (*Beelzebub's Tales*, p.770)

End of Session

Appendix 1 - Report on an Experiment

I was asked to give attention exercises at this year's All & Everything Conference in Bognor Regis, UK. By attention excercises, I understood this to be the simple exercises traditionally given in the beginning of a Movements class to, among other things, galvanize a class in preparation for the intense demand of the Gurdjieff Movements.

Without thinking much about it, I agreed. During the preparation to give these exercises, I had some doubts as its usefulness, but in the spirit of an experiment, I decided to proceed with one session while being very watchful of the results and only after the one session, decide whether or not to continue.

As planned, for one short period, some exercises were given on the first full day of the Conference (with the help of a very nice drum resourcefully created out of materials at hand by Mr Bert Sharp).

After the class, I reflected. There were two aspects I felt uneasy about. Firstly, these exercises were conceived as a preparation for work on a Movement and had never been separated from the Movements. To work solely on the excercises, subtracting the purpose for which they had been designed and with no intent to lead to the practice of the Movements in the future seemed, while doing no harm, is another unnoticeable yet insidious way to bring the Gurdjieff teaching down to our level by substituting an exercise, something made up by someone or other, for the real thing i.e. the Sacred Movements as composed by Gurdjieff.

The second disturbing aspect came directly from the first. What if there were individuals participating in this who had never worked in a Movements class? Even though I stated clearly at the beginning of the class that these exercises were not Movements, the association with Movements was very close. Was this a responsible way to introduce this kind of work to those who may sometime have the opportunity to work in a Movements class in the future? No one can give the experience of the sacred in the Movements to another but for beginning students, the first work on Movements, the others in the class, the person working in front and the musician and music have a deep and lasting impression which must be respected and served as well as possible by those who presume to be responsible.

As a result of these ponderings, I decided the best course was not to continue with the exercises.

I must end this with the report that later, during the Conference, I was approached by an individual who had never had the opportunity to work in a Movements class and who was very touched by working on the exercises. She felt the experience of great value. Although this doesn't change the

Appendix 1 - Review of Beelzebub's Tales to His Grandson in Russian

principles I understand at present, it is clear that this is a 'principle in process' and still needs much pondering. In that light, I would be most interested to hear of any impressions, etc. related to this question.

Toddy Smyth
May 13 2002

Appendix 2 - List of Attendees

Martin Brown - UK
Nikolas Bryce - Canada
Keith & Marlena Buzzell - USA
Jean Cavendish - USA
Anne M. Clark - USA
Jan Van Dam - Holland
Ana Fragomeni - Brasilia
Seymour Ginsburg - USA
Jon Jerstad - Norway
Simon Knox - UK
Conti Canseco Meehan - USA
Edgar Clark - UK
Stefamos Elmazis - Greece
Gin O'Meara - USA
Dimitri Peretzi - Greece
Bonnie Phillips - USA
June Poulton - USA
Wouter Rikmans - Holland
John Scullion - UK
Bert Sharp - UK
Toddy Smyth - USA
Sondre Solberg - Norway
Elin Star - UK
Paul Beekman Taylor - Switzerland
Chris Thompson - UK
Dorothy Usiskin - USA
Sophia Wellbeloved - UK

Index

A

Abrustdonis, 57
Absolute, 65, 71, 104
active, 4, 26, 29, 52, 73, 74, 82, 83, 84, 94, 101, 115, 117, 119, 120, 123, 126, 179, 180, 191
Advaita, 162
affirm, 75, 146
affirmation, 43, 49
affirming, 52, 75, 85, 115, 126, 171, 177, 178
Africa, 95
Aim, 4, 41, 113, 172, 182, 190
air, 23, 25, 30, 81, 97, 158, 194, 198
aka bodies, 97
Salzmann, de, Jean; Michel, 12, 14, 30, 31, 32, 35, 138
allegorical, 153
allegory, 161, 165
America, 10, 17, 20, 21, 23, 25, 28, 30, 32, 35, 36, 64, 80, 88, 101, 109, 111, 149, 180, 195, 198
Anderson, Margaret, 24, 25, 26, 30, 34
Angel, 123, 126, 147, 148, 150, 151, 154, 155, 156, 157, 158, 160, 161, 162, 166, 171, 172, 178, 185
Antkooano, 117
Anulios, 55, 61, 64, 66, 69, 70, 71, 144
ape, 106
Archangel, 123, 126, 147, 148, 149, 154, 171, 172
Aristotle, 191
Armenia, 142
Armenian, 121, 142
ascend, 117, 171
ascending, 116, 186
Ashiata Shiemash, 117, 118
Ashish, Sri Madhava, 13

Askokin, 55, 57, 60, 61
Atlantis, 70
atma, 162
Atom, 44, 78, 105, 157
Atomic, 80, 82, 85, 104
Attention, 4, 16, 18, 23, 29, 59, 80, 83, 103, 107, 111, 119, 130, 131, 132, 137, 146, 164, 169, 172, 178, 181, 202
awareness, 17, 62, 65, 79, 81, 82, 84, 89, 100, 163, 164, 166
axis, 42, 44

B

Beekman Taylor, Paul, 1, 13, 20, 34, 138, 140, 141, 142, 143, 204
Beelzebub, 3, 4, 10, 14, 15, 16, 28, 38, 42, 43, 54, 55, 56, 57, 58, 63, 68, 69, 93, 113, 114, 115, 116, 117, 118, 119, 120, 123, 124, 125, 130, 131, 132, 133, 134, 135, 136, 146, 147, 148, 149, 150, 151, 152, 154, 158, 160, 161, 163, 165, 171, 172, 173, 175, 176, 178, 179, 187, 189, 190, 196, 200, 201
Beelzebub's Tales
  The Tales, 19, 60, 61, 63, 65, 68, 115, 122, 123, 125, 128, 129, 135, 147, 149, 150, 153, 161, 185, 190, 191, 192, 193
Being, 14, 17, 18, 19, 22, 30, 50, 54, 55, 56, 57, 58, 60, 61, 62, 63, 64, 68, 69, 70, 72, 73, 74, 75, 80, 82, 84, 85, 89, 91, 92, 93, 94, 95, 97, 98, 99, 103, 106, 113, 114, 115, 116, 117, 118, 119, 122, 123, 125, 127, 128, 129, 130, 131, 135, 136, 140, 144, 147, 150, 151, 153, 156, 157, 158, 159, 160, 163, 164, 165, 166, 170, 171, 173, 176, 177, 178, 179, 180, 181, 182, 183, 184, 185, 186, 187, 188, 190, 191, 194, 196, 198, 199, 201, 202

being-bodies, 128, 129, 165
being-instinct, 69
Bennett, John G., 10, 18, 24, 25, 26, 34, 38, 44, 46, 47, 48, 51, 52, 60, 66, 155, 158, 193
Big Bang, 62, 63
Blake, Anthony, 66
Blavatsky, Helena P., 26, 167
Bodhisattva, 125
Brain, 3, 19, 54, 57, 74, 77, 78, 79, 81, 82, 87, 88, 91, 92, 95, 97, 100, 102, 180, 185
breath, 81, 139
breathe, 139, 158
breathing, 139
brother, 11, 13, 30, 35, 97, 138, 141, 145, 191
Buddha, 75
Buzzell, Keith, 1, 2, 4, 12, 15, 16, 54, 87, 88, 89, 90, 91, 92, 93, 94, 113, 120, 121, 122, 123, 124, 125, 126, 127, 128, 129, 144, 169, 204

C

Campbell, Joseph, 111
Canada, 4, 32, 185, 204
Castanios-Flores, John, 11, 13
Causal, 84
center, 10, 12, 24, 64, 70, 71, 73, 74, 78, 91, 111, 133, 137, 139, 166, 170, 186, 190, 201
Chakra, 85
child, 21, 47, 52, 80, 106, 138, 139
children, 12, 14, 49, 59, 102, 103, 106, 138, 139, 140, 141, 151, 158
China, 101, 103
Chinese, 80, 173
Christ, 46, 52, 123, 127, 128, 152, 154, 179
Christian, 85, 107, 127, 128, 161
Christianity, 108, 109, 111, 127, 128
coat
   coated, 113, 129
   coating, 55
Colombo, John Robert, 26

comet, 61, 62, 64, 67, 74, 147, 148, 149
Commission, 3, 14, 16, 69, 144, 146, 147, 148, 149, 154, 159, 160, 161, 170
compassion, 106, 107, 125
concentrate, 60, 139
concentration, 60, 139
Conscience, 69, 70, 74, 115, 125, 155, 158, 179
conscious, 69, 76, 81, 82, 85, 97, 98, 100, 106, 107, 116, 117, 125, 129, 139, 157, 162, 165, 172, 182
Conscious Labor, 116, 117
consciousness, 18, 49, 54, 63, 78, 79, 82, 83, 84, 107, 134, 137, 145, 163, 164, 165, 166, 172, 179, 182, 200
contemplate, 172
   contemplation, 96
Cortex, 92
cosmic, 18, 38, 57, 60, 61, 62, 68, 114, 116, 117, 118, 121, 123, 173, 183, 201
cosmology, 63, 64
Creation, 42, 43, 44, 45, 47, 48, 52, 60, 61, 62, 63, 65, 68, 104, 118, 148, 170, 180, 182, 193
creative, 65, 96, 98, 100, 134, 189
Creator, 115, 147, 148, 149, 160, 162
Creed, Lewis, 11, 13, 127
crystallize, 72
   crystallization, 72, 75, 163
   crystallized, 84, 151, 163, 164, 165, 176

D

daughter, 11, 13, 21, 31, 32, 35, 95, 101, 102, 103, 138
Daumal, Rene, 30, 31, 32, 34
death, 10, 12, 14, 19, 22, 23, 24, 25, 26, 33, 84, 86, 95, 135, 151, 158
Denying, 41, 43, 52, 75, 76, 85, 87, 115, 171, 177, 178
Dervish, 36, 164
Descartes, Rene, 78
descend, 189
descending, 104, 116, 171, 189

descent, 28, 69
Descent, 118
devil, 43, 123, 155, 179
Dicker, The, 11, 13
die, 19, 23, 100, 158, 159
dimension, 4, 71, 154, 157
disharmonized, 128
DNA, 101, 103
   genes, 78
dog, 156, 157
Dramatic Universe, 38, 48, 52, 66, 155
dream, 131, 166, 170
dying, 23, 25

E

Earth, 18, 19, 28, 40, 55, 61, 64, 66, 78, 81, 97, 104, 107, 109, 113, 114, 115, 117, 125, 128, 131, 132, 135, 137, 147, 148, 149, 151, 159, 160, 162, 175, 191
Ego, 67, 184, 190, 191, 194
   egoism, 184
Egypt, 28, 52, 95, 99, 101
Egyptian, 200
Einstein, 41
electricity, 36, 83, 118
electron, 41
element, 26, 34, 42, 47, 62, 79, 82, 83, 95, 104, 105, 119, 193
emotion, 49, 60, 73, 91, 93, 97, 158, 186
emotional, 60, 64, 73, 79, 81, 82, 84, 85, 91, 92, 99, 100, 154, 186, 188, 196
Endlessness, 44, 56, 60, 63, 115, 116, 118, 123, 125, 127, 147, 149, 154, 157, 160, 161, 162, 163, 164, 165, 166, 174, 176, 201
England, 4, 14, 17, 20, 25, 35
Enneagram, 13, 87
entropy, 43, 53
esoteric, 12, 14, 17, 20, 29, 102, 108, 111, 131, 146, 162, 164, 172
Essence, 40, 51, 79, 82, 162, 165, 166, 178, 191
Essene, 29, 85

Eternal-Retribution, 128
Eternity, 127
Etievan, Alfred, 140, 141
Evil, 75, 104, 115, 116, 117, 118, 120, 121, 123, 124, 125, 146, 148, 150, 175, 176, 177, 178, 179, 180, 181, 182, 183, 184, 185
Evolution, 19, 47, 52, 69, 71, 105, 115, 116, 118, 123, 130, 175, 180, 182
   evolutional, 115, 117, 118, 119, 120, 171
   evolutionary, 97, 117, 118
Evolve, 81, 97, 104, 117, 126
Exercise, 4, 72, 103, 111, 155, 164, 165, 173, 190, 202
exoteric, 108, 123

F

Faith, 78
father, 14, 25, 52, 56, 98, 99, 106, 118, 141, 151, 155, 158
Feeling, 54, 64, 67, 77, 79, 89, 90, 92, 93, 103, 105, 133, 135, 136, 187, 195, 196
Fire, 41, 49, 83, 85, 182
first liberation, 60
flatland, 155
flood, 96
Food, 12, 44, 51, 61, 68, 97, 101, 134, 138, 140, 156, 183
force, 29, 41, 42, 43, 49, 52, 70, 71, 74, 76, 81, 97, 99, 116, 118, 119, 120, 121, 133, 139, 153, 165, 177, 179, 182, 191
Formatory, 136, 137
Foundation, 10, 12, 186, 194
Fourth Way, 10, 11, 12, 14, 145, 159
France, 14, 20, 22, 31, 32, 36, 138, 142, 143, 149
friction, 175, 195
Fundamentalism, 132

G

Galileo, 79, 82, 84, 85
Geometry, 77, 82, 83

Germany, 25, 35
Gilgamesh, 13, 71, 96
Ginsburg, Seymour, 1, 2, 11, 13, 15, 18, 144, 145, 151, 153, 160, 163, 167, 168, 169, 204
GNOSIS, 17
Gnostic, 145
Gobi, 27, 28
God, 41, 43, 46, 47, 51, 52, 62, 63, 65, 81, 83, 88, 97, 98, 100, 105, 106, 108, 119, 127, 128, 147, 148, 151, 154, 161, 162, 163, 175, 176, 179, 180, 185
Good, 15, 17, 115, 116, 117, 118, 120, 124, 150, 175, 176, 177, 178, 179, 180, 182, 183, 193
Gornahoor Harharkh, 152, 153, 157
Gospel, 85, 133, 134
gravity, 74, 137, 186, 201
Greece, 4, 132, 188, 189, 195, 204
Greek, 126, 131, 148, 152, 191
Gurdjieff, G. I., 3, 10, 11, 12, 13, 14, 15, 17, 18, 20, 21, 22, 23, 24, 25, 26, 27, 28, 29, 30, 31, 32, 33, 34, 35, 36, 38, 41, 43, 46, 51, 52, 54, 55, 56, 59, 60, 62, 63, 66, 67, 68, 69, 70, 71, 72, 74, 75, 77, 78, 79, 80, 83, 85, 86, 87, 88, 89, 90, 91, 93, 95, 97, 102, 103, 108, 110, 111, 113, 114, 115, 117, 121, 122, 123, 124, 125, 127, 128, 131, 132, 133, 134, 138, 139, 140, 141, 142, 143, 144, 147, 153, 154, 158, 159, 160, 161, 162, 163, 164, 165, 166, 170, 171, 172, 173, 175, 179, 182, 183, 185, 186, 188, 189, 192, 193, 196, 202
Gurdjieff, Luba, 25, 138, 140, 143
Guru, 28

H

harmonium, 139
Harnelmiatznel, 38
Hartmann, Thomas and Olga de, 10, 26, 35
Hasnamuss, 128, 129
Heap, Jane, 30
heart, 67, 72, 133, 187

heaven, 11, 13, 96, 104, 107, 128
Heaven, 27, 98, 99, 126, 127
Hebrew, 114, 149, 152
Helkdonis, 57
Hell, 41, 127, 128
Help, 156
Heptaparaparshinokh, 60
Hermetic, 18, 19, 112
Heropass, 56, 62, 65
hierarchical, 163
hierarchy, 41, 98, 161, 162, 172, 173, 192
higher being-body, 115, 163, 201
highest being-body, 129
Hindu, 13
Hitler, 35, 48, 52
holistic, 12, 86
Holy Affirming, 75, 117, 124, 126
Holy Denying, 75
Holy Reconciling, 76, 116, 118
Hope, 71, 84, 116, 125, 127, 179, 186, 187, 188, 192, 193, 195, 196
Horus, 200
Howarth, Dushka, 36, 138, 141
Howarth, Jessmin, 36
Hulme, Kathryn, 25, 30
Huna, 85, 95, 96, 101

I

I Am, 18, 162
Identification, 47, 51, 72, 155, 166
Idiot, 139
imagination, 47, 51, 96, 100, 165
impartial, 54, 56, 120, 132, 147, 160, 161, 183
impressions, 4, 73, 98, 114, 121, 122, 126, 185, 187, 189, 203
In Search of the Miraculous, 10, 14, 86, 132, 151, 163, 164, 183
 Fragments, 69, 182
India, 14, 26, 28, 36, 96, 99, 101
Individual, 18, 19, 46, 49, 56, 64, 65, 67, 68, 81, 87, 90, 95, 107, 112, 117, 119, 121,

133, 148, 154, 156, 158, 163, 166, 181, 182, 191, 201, 202
initiation, 18
insight, 67, 117, 190
Instinctive, 69, 80, 157
Institute, 12, 13, 20, 21, 22, 23, 24, 25, 30, 85, 89
Institute for the Harmonious Development of Man, 20
Intellectual, 19, 22, 72, 73, 90, 93, 99, 100, 154, 163, 166, 186, 190, 192, 194
intention, 146, 157, 196
interconnected, 61, 91
Introvigne, Massimo, 190
Involution, 47, 115, 116, 117, 118, 123, 125, 175, 180
   involutional, 75, 115, 116, 117, 118, 119, 120, 121, 124, 137, 171, 183
   involutionary, 133

J

Jesus, 96, 98, 99, 123, 179
Jew, 31, 33, 102
Jewish, 31, 33, 102
Jung, Carl G., 17, 110, 166
Justice, 113, 114, 115, 116, 117, 118, 119, 120, 121, 122, 124, 125, 126, 129, 130, 136, 173, 175, 178, 179, 180, 183

K

Kahuna, 3, 95, 96, 97, 98, 99, 100, 101, 102, 105, 107, 108, 161
Karatas, 93, 123
Kepler, Johannes, 158
Kondoor, 61, 64, 65, 67, 74, 149
Konuzion, 161
Kunda, 74, 75
Kundabuffer, 55, 56, 57, 60, 61, 66, 69, 70, 71, 72, 73, 74, 75, 113, 124, 135, 137, 156, 160, 171, 176

L

ladder, 78, 79, 87, 88, 90, 91, 189
laughter, 68, 93, 194, 195, 196, 197, 198, 199
Law, 3, 38, 40, 41, 44, 46, 47, 48, 51, 53, 60, 61, 62, 66, 81, 86, 116, 117, 118, 121, 137, 163, 171, 172, 184
Law of Seven, 38
Law of Three, 38, 39, 75, 116
Law-conformable, 60
lawful, 60, 117, 118, 120, 121, 124
Legominism, 146
Lenin, 35, 48, 52
Lentrohamsanin, 128, 129
Life is Real, 10, 162, 193
light, 50, 52, 55, 60, 61, 62, 63, 72, 81, 83, 85, 86, 87, 98, 99, 146, 156, 159, 166, 199, 203
Limbic, 92
Littlehampton, 11, 13, 18
Long, Max Freedom, 95, 96, 107
Looisos, 160
Love, 17, 28, 44, 49, 58, 73, 80, 82, 85, 93, 107, 135, 147, 159, 180
Lubovedsky, 29
Lucifer, 184

M

magic, 29, 43, 47, 95
magnet
   magnetic, 64, 70, 71
maintenance, 23, 61, 62, 65, 148, 156, 193
March, Louise, 25, 34
Mars, 54, 117
Masonic, 27, 36
material, 10, 18, 29, 51, 53, 71, 75, 96, 104, 105, 107, 122, 131, 135, 158, 173
matter, 16, 19, 31, 33, 43, 47, 52, 54, 55, 62, 67, 77, 81, 84, 85, 87, 106, 135, 142, 157, 158, 160, 161, 172, 188, 189, 190, 197
mechanical, 69, 73, 84, 86, 125, 134, 136, 137, 171, 182
meditate, 94, 190

meditation, 81, 165, 166, 200
Meetings with Remarkable Men, 3, 20, 27, 28, 29, 35, 122, 150, 193
Megalocosmos, 113, 118, 147
mentation, 112, 147
Mercurov, 27
Merston, Miss, 36
mesoteric, 172
metanoia, 162, 165, 166
Mevlevi, 97
Mexico, 11, 13, 21, 23, 24, 26, 30, 34
migrations, 96, 101, 103
mind, 4, 18, 19, 20, 22, 67, 68, 79, 81, 82, 85, 90, 92, 93, 98, 99, 100, 101, 106, 131, 142, 147, 161, 166, 180, 189, 197
Mitochondria, 101
monastery, 29
monk, 13, 91
Moon, 40, 55, 61, 62, 64, 66, 69, 70, 71, 144, 156
Moore, James, 10, 24, 26, 27, 29, 32, 33, 34
Moral, 20, 22, 23, 33, 51, 118, 121, 127
   Morality, 179
Moscow, 27
mother, 11, 13, 17, 24, 25, 31, 32, 35, 52, 80, 138, 142, 147, 158
Mouravieff, Boris, 12
Movements, 10, 190, 202
Moving, 44, 56, 72, 73, 74, 84, 124, 125, 181
music, 13, 22, 26, 29, 46, 103, 139, 153, 170, 190, 193, 202
myth, 65, 66, 114
mythology, 200

N

Nature, 2, 12, 15, 43, 45, 48, 52, 55, 71, 77, 78, 79, 80, 81, 82, 83, 84, 86, 92, 96, 97, 103, 106, 123, 133, 134, 150, 156, 157, 160, 163, 166, 172, 178, 180, 190, 193
Navaho, 110, 111
Negative emotion, 164
nervous system, 92
neural, 74

Neutral, 83
   Neutralizing, 119
New Age, 10
Newton, Issac, 81, 87
Nicoll, Maurice, 17, 111
nine, 23
Nisargadatta, 162
nothing, 19, 25, 31, 43, 46, 49, 62, 64, 67, 71, 74, 91, 96, 100, 107, 109, 117, 127, 128, 134, 135, 139, 141, 149, 153, 155, 159, 163, 172, 179
Nothingness, 117
Nott, Stanley and Rosemary, 35, 138
Nyland, W, 10, 12, 88, 89, 138

O

Objective, 19, 56, 64, 66, 84, 89, 113, 114, 116, 117, 119, 120, 121, 125, 129, 130, 146, 159, 163, 164, 165, 166, 171, 172, 179, 183, 184, 201
octave, 61, 158, 195
Oldham, Ronald and Muriel, 10, 13
Omnipresent, 147
one-brained, 57
Opium, 32
Orage, Alfred, 10, 11, 13, 20, 21, 22, 23, 24, 25, 26, 27, 28, 30, 33, 35, 36, 91, 121, 131, 138
organic, 28, 58, 60, 69, 83, 195
organon, 191
Ors, 149
Orthodox, 123, 128
Oskiano, 58, 135, 161, 163
Ostrowska, Julia, 142
Ouspensky, P. D., 12, 14, 21, 26, 27, 33, 34, 35, 86, 91, 93, 132, 138, 163, 164, 165, 181, 184

P

Parable, 112
Paris, 11, 12, 13, 14, 24, 30, 31, 32, 34, 36, 138, 140, 141, 142, 143

Partkdolg-duty, 73, 130, 136, 178
passive, 42, 52, 73, 82, 84, 106, 115, 117, 119, 120, 123, 124, 126, 180
Pentland, John, 138
Peretzi, Dimitri, 204
personality, 70, 74, 140, 178
Peters, Fritz, 32, 142, 175, 179
Philadelphia, 12, 24
physical, 22, 55, 69, 79, 81, 82, 83, 84, 85, 97, 104, 134, 136, 154, 158, 166
physics, 80, 82
planet, 51, 54, 55, 56, 59, 60, 61, 66, 80, 93, 109, 113, 115, 116, 121, 122, 123, 125, 128, 129, 136, 147, 148, 150, 154, 158, 159, 161, 162, 175, 178, 183
planetary, 54, 113, 164, 180
Podkoolad, 118
Pogson, Beryl, 18, 19
politics, 23
Polynesia, 101
ponder, 15, 16, 120, 187
pondering, 15, 145, 146, 203
Pope, 158
Popoff, Irmis, 12, 193
Pray, 98, 99, 100, 103, 105, 107
Prayer, 17, 43, 96, 98, 99, 100, 106, 173, 174, 179
presence, 21, 30, 33, 79, 102, 119, 120, 124, 157, 162, 182, 201
Priest, 135, 185
Prieuré, 10, 11, 13, 20, 21, 22, 24, 35, 36, 59, 138, 140, 141, 142
prism, 85, 87
psyche, 152, 177, 178, 179
psychological, 10, 13, 69, 134, 178
psychologist, 93
psychology, 20, 37, 69, 95
Purgatory, 56, 66, 114, 115, 116, 117, 121, 125, 126, 127, 128, 129, 154, 165
Putnam, Nick, 25, 32
Pyramid, 28
Pythagorean, 19

Q

Quanta, 81
Quantum, 41, 81

R

radiation, 84, 98
Ray of Creation, 40, 44, 52, 98, 117, 157, 171, 172
Reason, 4, 18, 20, 24, 29, 56, 60, 73, 75, 84, 86, 104, 114, 115, 118, 121, 123, 134, 158, 159, 171, 198, 201
Reciprocal, 56, 57, 61, 62, 156, 180
Reconcile, 90
   Reconciliation, 65, 117, 120, 182
   Reconciling, 42, 76, 85, 118, 120, 171
Relativity, 180
religion, 10, 12, 95, 162, 175, 178
Remember, 38, 43, 44, 54, 58, 70, 89, 93, 98, 118, 125, 131, 132, 135, 137, 138, 139, 140, 142, 143, 150, 155, 156, 158, 160, 165, 166, 171, 180, 182, 185, 186, 197, 199, 200
   Remembering, 3, 53, 138, 141, 181
Remorse, 115, 125, 126, 127, 128, 129
Remorse-of-Conscience, 115, 125, 126, 127, 129
Repentance, 129
repetition, 72, 73, 134, 165
resonance, 66, 114, 153
Resurrection, 107
Retribution, 98, 128, 129, 134
Roerich, Nikolai, 26, 27, 28, 29, 30, 34, 36
Rosicrucian, 145, 153, 159
Russia, 14, 26, 27, 29, 30, 34, 36, 64, 69, 114, 121, 122, 126, 142, 146, 148, 149, 150, 176

S

Sacred, 3, 13, 16, 29, 60, 61, 65, 67, 69, 95, 117, 118, 123, 144, 146, 147, 148, 149, 154, 155, 156, 157, 158, 159, 160, 161, 164, 166, 170, 171, 201, 202

Sacred Individual, 3, 16, 61, 65, 123, 144, 146, 147, 148, 149, 154, 155, 156, 157, 158, 159, 160, 161, 166, 170
sacrifice
   sacrificial, 117, 149
Sarmoung (also Surmang), 29, 52
Saturn, 150, 152, 170
Science, 10, 12, 13, 63, 77, 78, 80, 95, 154
Scientific, 121, 143, 178
Second Conscious Shock, 73, 76, 136
seeing, 12, 31, 56, 57, 66, 67, 69, 72, 82, 83, 91, 116, 161, 171, 175, 177, 180, 192
Self, 97, 98, 99, 100, 129, 162, 163, 164, 167, 176
Self Observation, 79, 89, 164, 175
Self Remembering, 145, 164, 165
Self-consciousness, 163, 164
Self-Reproach, 129
sensation, 42, 54, 59, 64, 72, 73, 89, 134
senses, 78, 84, 98
Sensing, 164, 165
Sensory, 73, 78
serpent, 74
seven, 18, 64, 65, 85, 118, 164, 190, 197, 200
seventh, 15
Sex, 134
   sexual, 118
Sharp, H. J. (Bert), 1, 17, 102, 103, 104, 105, 106, 107, 108, 109, 110, 111, 112, 152, 153, 169, 202, 204
Shiva, 164
shock, 36, 61, 66, 76, 84, 90, 179, 180, 191
sin, 49, 98, 109, 184
sing, 17, 141, 150, 157
singer, 31
singing, 150
sister, 25, 31, 138, 140, 141, 157, 191
Sitting, 107, 143, 170, 191, 192, 197
Sleep, 63, 70, 74, 94, 137, 139, 157, 182
Smith, Russell A., 18
Solano, Solita, 25, 30
solar plexus, 74, 165

son, 25, 27, 28, 95, 115, 117, 125, 138, 142, 151, 158
Sophia, 92, 193, 204
sound, 54, 114, 152, 153, 157, 180, 195
sounding, 17, 78, 148, 150, 153
spine, 74, 75, 124
Spirit, 26, 55, 82, 90, 97, 98, 106, 150, 163, 166, 202
   spiritual, 17, 25, 70, 93, 95, 96, 103, 108, 146, 163, 166, 192, 200
   spirituality, 123
St. Petersburg (also Petersburg), 26, 35
Stalin, 26, 35
Staveley, A.L., 4, 12, 133, 179
Stopinder, 56, 186
subconscious, 54, 64, 73, 81, 153
subjective, 67, 90, 118, 124, 171, 177, 179, 181, 182
substance, 60, 98
Suffer, 52, 73, 86, 133, 171, 181
   Intentional Suffering, 117, 165
   suffered, 24, 25, 52
   suffering, 52, 72, 73, 75, 106, 126, 129, 149, 181, 187
Sufis, 85
Sufism, 164
Sun, 23, 40, 51, 52, 61, 62, 70, 109, 111, 115, 117, 124, 125, 128, 129, 135, 147, 157, 170, 201
Sun Absolute, 115, 117, 124, 125, 128, 129, 147, 201
Swedenborg, 104
Symbol, 42, 52, 71, 77, 81, 82, 86, 97, 99, 114, 119, 145, 176, 178, 180
   symbolic, 79, 82, 87, 107, 145, 170, 173
   symbolism, 28, 52
   symbology, 12, 128

T

Tail, 55
Taliesin, 22
Tao
   Dao, 85

Tarot, 14, 114
telepathic, 98, 99, 100
telepathically, 99, 100
telepathy, 98, 100
Tereshchenko, Nicolas, 1, 11, 13, 14, 16, 18, 48, 64, 114, 121, 126, 145, 146, 151, 153, 168
Tetartocosmos, 56, 66, 148, 162
The Fourth Way, 184
Theosophical, 13, 114, 164
Theosophy, 26
Third Force, 70, 71, 75, 115, 116, 117, 120, 121, 177, 178, 179, 182
3rd Force, 118
Thompson, Chris, 204
three-brained, 54, 55, 56, 57, 59, 68, 69, 73, 93, 116, 123, 129, 135, 136, 137, 148, 160, 161, 162, 176, 178, 201
Tibet, 27
Tikliamish, 178
time, 4, 12, 21, 24, 25, 26, 27, 28, 29, 30, 31, 32, 38, 51, 53, 55, 57, 58, 59, 62, 63, 65, 66, 69, 70, 75, 76, 77, 78, 86, 87, 88, 91, 92, 94, 96, 100, 102, 104, 106, 108, 109, 113, 114, 117, 120, 122, 125, 127, 128, 129, 132, 135, 136, 138, 139, 141, 142, 143, 144, 145, 147, 148, 152, 154, 158, 159, 161, 164, 168, 169, 171, 172, 175, 178, 180, 182, 183, 186, 187, 191, 192, 193, 195, 196, 197, 200
Tooilan, 117
Toomer, Jean, 11, 13, 21, 22, 23, 24, 33, 35, 91
Tracol, Henri, 30, 31, 140
transform, 52
transformation, 10, 13, 106, 120, 170, 173
Triad, 41, 43, 45, 46, 47, 48, 49, 52, 120
Triamazikamno, 60, 149
Triangle Editions, 162
Trinity, 39, 52, 98
Trogoautoegocrat, 67
    Trogoautoegocratic, 60, 183

U

uncertainty principle, 41
unconscious, 69, 100, 103, 107, 110
unconsciousness, 84
understanding, 57, 73, 77, 81, 83, 84, 113, 114, 118, 119, 122, 125, 166, 170, 182, 187, 191
Union, 25, 28, 29, 36, 138
universe, 41, 46, 48, 51, 52, 56, 61, 62, 63, 67, 69, 76, 78, 86, 104, 118, 129, 133, 148, 159, 162, 175
USA, 204

V

Vacuum, 78, 191
vein, 18, 160
vibration, 75, 157, 165

W

Walker, Kenneth, 109
Washington, 11, 24, 25, 26, 29
Water, 41, 49, 53, 85, 97, 99, 155, 182, 191
Webb, James, 24, 27, 34, 36, 142
Welch, William and Louise, 138, 139
Wellbeloved, Sophia, 204
Will, 42, 51, 52, 123
Wisdom, 18, 29, 34, 68, 80, 98
wiseacre
    wiseacring, 75, 149
Word, 100, 127, 145, 147
Work, 10, 11, 12, 13, 14, 25, 34, 64, 68, 87, 88, 90, 95, 117, 125, 163, 175, 179, 183
world, 19, 21, 22, 24, 25, 26, 31, 33, 34, 35, 39, 40, 44, 51, 52, 56, 61, 63, 65, 67, 68, 70, 71, 73, 78, 80, 81, 82, 83, 90, 91, 92, 93, 94, 96, 104, 106, 110, 116, 117, 118, 120, 123, 124, 128, 131, 134, 135, 141, 147, 148, 151, 158, 159, 162, 163, 166, 170,☐171, 172, 175, 176, 178, 179, 181, 182, 183, 184, 185, 186, 187, 190, 193, 196

Y

Yoga, 81, 85, 152
   Karma, 161
   Kundalini, 74, 75, 124

Z

Zirlikner, 117, 126
Zodiac
   Cancer, 80
Zuber, Rene, 31

www.ingramcontent.com/pod-product-compliance
Lightning Source LLC
Chambersburg PA
CBHW081917170426
43200CB00014B/2754